Life is Just a Bowl of Cherries

And Other Delicious Sayings

Anne Bertram

NTC

NTC Publishing Group

NTC/Contemporary Publishing Company

Library of Congress Cataloging-in-Publication Data

Bertram, Anne.
    [NTC's dictionary of proverbs and clichés]
    Life is just a bowl of cherries : and other delicious sayings/
Anne Bertram.
        p. cm. -- (The artful Wordsmith series)
    Originally published: NTC's dictionary of proverbs and clichés.
Lincolnwood, Ill. : National Textbook Co., c1993
    Includes index.
    ISBN 0-8442-0900-7 (pbk. : alk. paper)
    1. Proverbs. 2. Clichés. 3. Figures of speech I. Title.
II. Series.
PN6405.B57   1997   96-51179
398.9'21--dc21   CIP

Published by NTC Publishing Group
An imprint of NTC/Contemporary Publishing Company
4255 West Touhy Avenue, Lincolnwood (Chicago), Illinois 60646-1975 U.S.A.
Copyright © 1997 by NTC/Contemporary Publishing Company
Printed in the United States of America
International Standard Book Number: 0-8442-0900-7
 3 4 5 6 7 VRS/VRS 0 5 4 3 2

Contents

Introduction

Proverbs turn up everywhere. They serve as the punch lines of jokes and the refrains of songs. Proverbs sum up situations and give advice in short, terse phrases. They are thought to express long-standing cultural values. Clichés are also in constant use—and because of that, many people object to their use in writing. Clichés are condemned because they reflect poorly on the user's ability to create original, interesting, and effective English sentences. Indeed, proverbs and other common sayings *become* clichés through overuse. This book focuses on common proverbs and the clichés that have been derived from them.

In some instances it is difficult to understand what these sayings really mean. For instance, *A good husband makes a good wife* needs to be explained or at least thought about for awhile before it makes sense. Some sayings preserve older forms of English words as well as older style and syntax. It can also be difficult to understand some sayings because people tend to use them metaphorically. For instance, have you ever heard *A stitch in time saves nine* used in reference to sewing?

While many of these sayings are supposed to embody the values of the culture that uses them, the reader will find many sayings in this book expressing ideas that do not reflect past or present values and which may in fact be offensive. Some expressions such as *The only good Indian is a dead Indian* are simply proverbial in form and do not express a notable value in Western culture. It is hard to separate the sayings expressing values from those that have survived solely because they are proverbial in form and are also clichés. Contradictory sayings such as *Too many cooks spoil the broth* and *Many hands make light work* also suggest caution in interpreting sayings too broadly as cultural values.

This dictionary is a selection of familiar expressions, many of which were brought to America by the English settlers. Some of the expressions are also found in other major European languages. Each expression is explained or defined and a literary source is provided if one is known. Also, a brief dialog accompanies each expression, showing the typical way that the expression is used. In most cases knowing what a saying means is not as important as knowing when it can be used and the significance of its use. These dialogs make this collection of proverbs and clichés unique.

Proverbs and clichés often have a lot of variants. Usually only one or two of the possible variants are listed in this dictionary. A Phrase-Finder Index is provided at the back of the book to permit the reader to find the form of an entry head simply by looking up any major word in the saying. Many of the older sayings preserve older forms of the English language. Although virtually all of the sayings refer to males, most of them can be used to refer to either sex. Some people alter these expressions by changing the male reference, e.g., *To each her own; To each his or her own; To each their own*—all from *To each his own.* However, these forms are not the historical forms that are the subject of this book. The definition or explanation will indicate whether or not a saying is meant to be exclusively male.

This dictionary is designed for browsing. The reader will get an idea of the types of cultural messages available in these expressions and will see in the example dialogs the ways that these expressions are used.

Guide to the Use of the Dictionary

1. Entry heads are alphabetized according to an alphabetical order that ignores punctuation and hyphens.

2. Entry heads appear in **boldface type**. When words or expressions that are not entries in this dictionary are cited, they appear in *italics*.

3. An entry head may have one or more alternative forms. The alternatives are printed in **boldface type** and are preceded by "AND."

4. Definitions and paraphrases are in roman type. Alternative or closely related definitions and paraphrases are separated by semicolons.

5. A definition or paraphrase may be followed by comments in parentheses. These comments give additional information about the expression, and list the common clichés derived from the entry heads.

6. If you cannot find the expression you want, or if you cannot decide on the exact form of the expression, look up any major word in the expression in the Phrase-Finder Index, which begins on page 241. Pick out the expression you want—or the closest one to it—and look it up in the dictionary.

A

A bad excuse is better than none.   If you offer a bad excuse, there is a slight chance that it will be accepted and you will therefore not be in trouble, but if you have no excuse at all, you do not even have that slight chance. □ FRED: *I can't believe we played cards till midnight! What will I tell my wife when she asks why I'm so late getting home?* BILL: *Tell her something came up at the office.* FRED: *But that's a lousy excuse. She'll never believe it.* BILL: *A bad excuse is better than none.* □ JILL: *How come you missed our lunch date?* JANE: *I got so absorbed in a TV movie that I forgot about it.* JILL: *That's a pretty feeble excuse.* JANE: *I know, but a bad excuse is better than none.*

A bad penny always turns up.   A worthless person always comes back to the place he or she started out. (Also the cliché: **a bad penny,** a worthless person.) □ JILL: *I just found out that Tom left town after we fought last Saturday. What if I never see him again?* JANE: *Don't worry. A bad penny always turns up.* □ *My little brother is a real bad penny. Every time he shows up, he wants to borrow money.*

A barking dog never bites.   Someone who makes threats all the time seldom carries out the threats. □ *Old Mrs. Smith keeps saying she'll call the police if we walk on her lawn, but don't worry. A barking dog never bites.* □

My boss threatens to fire me at least once a week, but a barking dog never bites.

A bird in the hand is worth two in the bush. Having something for certain is better than possibly getting something better. □ *I might get a better offer, but a bird in the hand is worth two in the bush.* □ *Bill has offered to buy my car for $3,000. Someone else might pay more, but a bird in the hand is worth two in the bush.*

A blessing in disguise Something that at first seems bad, but later turns out to be beneficial. □ *Tony's motorcycle accident was a blessing in disguise, because he got enough insurance money from the other driver to make a down payment on a house.* □ *Dad's illness was a blessing in disguise; it brought the family together for the first time in years.*

A bolt from the blue A sudden surprise. □ *Joe's return to Springfield was a bolt from the blue.* □ *The news that Mr. and Mrs. King were getting a divorce struck all their friends as a bolt from the blue.*

A bully is always a coward. Bullies will only intimidate people who are weaker than they are, because they are afraid of having to fight their equals. □ CHILD: *Dad, Joey keeps picking on me. How can I make him stop?* FATHER: *Try fighting back. A bully is always a coward.* □ *Artie ceaselessly victimized the younger children, but he was quiet and docile around the older ones. A bully is always a coward.*

A burnt child dreads the fire. If something has hurt you once, you avoid it after that. □ JILL: *Let's go ride the roller coaster!* JANE: *No, thanks. I got sick on one of those once, and a burnt child dreads the fire.* □ *Ever since Cynthia rebuffed me so rudely, I've avoided asking her for anything; a burnt child dreads the fire.*

A castle in Spain   A daydream. (Also the cliché: **building castles in Spain,** daydreaming.) □ *The children spent the whole evening discussing what they would be when they grew up, building all kinds of castles in Spain.* □ *Someday I'd like to take a year off work and travel all around the world. But that's just a castle in Spain, really; I'll never have the money to do it.*

A cat can look at a king.   No one is so important that an ordinary person cannot look at him or her; everyone has the right to be curious about important people. □ JANE: *I get so angry at those people who read tabloid magazines. The private lives of television stars are none of their business.* ALAN: *Don't be so hard on them. A cat can look at a king.* □ FRED: *You shouldn't stare at me like that. I'm your boss.* JILL: *A cat can look at a king.*

A cat has nine lives.   Cats can survive things that are severe enough to kill them. (You can also refer to a particular cat's *nine lives.*) □ JILL: *My cat fell off a third-floor balcony and just walked away. How can he do that?* JANE: *A cat has nine lives.* □ *I think my cat used up one of her nine lives when she survived being hit by that car.*

A cat in gloves catches no mice.   Sometimes you cannot get what you want by being careful and polite. □ JILL: *I've hinted to Mary several times that I need her to pay me the money she owes, but she just ignores me.* JANE: *A cat in gloves catches no mice, Jill. Tell her bluntly that you need the money.* □ *Every night for a month, I've gone downstairs to ask the neighbors to turn their stereo down, but they've turned it up loud again tonight. I'm going to call the police on them. A cat in gloves catches no mice.*

A chain is no stronger than its weakest link.   If one member of a group fails, the whole group fails. (Also the cliché: **someone or something is the weak link,** meaning that someone or something is the part of the group most likely to fail.) □ *George is completely out of shape. I don't want him on our ball team; a chain is only as strong as its weakest link.* □ *Joan's hasty generalizations about the economy were definitely the weak link in her argument.*

A chip off the old block   A child who is very much like one of his or her parents. (Usually a son who is like his father.) □ *Dennis's father is a musician, and even before he learned to walk, Dennis loved to pick out tunes on the piano; he's definitely a chip off the old block.* □ JILL: *Is that a picture of your son? He looks so much like you!* ALAN: *Yes, he's a chip off the old block, all right.*

A contented mind is a perpetual feast.   If you are contented by nature, you will always feel that you have enough of everything, and will not have to strive to get more. □ *I'm glad you're making so much money, son, but I think you ought to concentrate on being happy with what you have, rather than always trying to get more. A contented mind is a perpetual feast.* □ JILL: *Lillian doesn't make very much money, but she seems to be happy all the time. I wonder how she manages that?* JANE: *A contented mind is a perpetual feast.*

A creaking door hangs longest. AND **A creaking gate hangs longest.**   Sickly people often live longer than healthy ones. □ JILL: *I'm worried that my grandmother may not live much longer. She's been sick for so many years.* JANE: *Well, if it's any comfort, I've heard that a creaking door hangs longest.* □ *Aunt Edna always likes to make it sound as if she could die any minute, but I'm betting she'll outlive us all; a creaking gate hangs longest.*

A creaking gate hangs longest.   See the previous entry.

A door must be either shut or open.   If you have only two alternatives, you must choose one or the other; you cannot have both. □ JILL: *Are you going to quit your job?* JANE: *I think I might sort of quit.* JILL: *There's no such thing as "sort-of quitting." A door must be either shut or open.* □ *Either you're going to marry that girl, or you're not. A door must be either shut or open.*

A drop in the bucket AND **A drop in the ocean** An insignificant contribution toward solving a large problem. □ SANDRA: *We need to stop spending so much.* ALAN: *OK. I'll buy a cheaper brand of toothpaste.* SANDRA: *But that's just a drop in the bucket.* □ *Many companies donated food and medicine to help the survivors of the earthquake, but it was just a drop in the ocean of what was needed.*

A drop in the ocean See the previous entry.

A drowning man will clutch at a straw. When you are desperate, you will look for anything that might help you, even if it cannot help you very much. (Also the cliché: **to clutch at straws,** to draw hope from things that probably will not help.) □ *Scott thinks this faith healer will cure his baldness. A drowning man will clutch at a straw.* □ *I think John might like me. He smiled at me when he said hello. Or am I just clutching at straws?*

A fine kettle of fish A troublesome situation; a vexing problem. (Casual. Usually appears in the expression, *This is a fine kettle of fish!*) □ *This is a fine kettle of fish. My husband is not here to meet me at the train station, and there's no phone here for me to call him.* □ ALAN: *Oh, no! I've burned the roast. We don't have anything to serve our guests as a main dish.* SANDRA: *But they'll be here any minute! This is a fine kettle of fish.*

A fish out of water Someone who does not belong in a particular situation; someone out of place. □ *Louise is a very casual person, so she felt like a fish out of water at the formal dinner.* □ *Joe started college at the age of* *forty-three, and at first he felt like a fish out of water among all the young students.*

A fool and his money are soon parted. Foolish people spend money easily, without thinking. (Perceived as a rebuke if you say it about the person you are addressing.) □ *Go ahead and buy a diamond collar for your dog if you really want to. A fool and his money are soon parted.* □ *Bill sends a check to every organization that asks him for money. A fool and his money are soon parted.*

A fool's paradise Being happy for foolish or unfounded reasons. □ *I'm afraid that Cecilia's marital happiness is a fool's paradise; there are rumors that her husband is unfaithful.* □ *Fred is confident that he'll get a big raise this year, but I think he's living in a fool's paradise.*

A friend in need is a friend indeed. Someone who helps you when you need it is a true friend. (Also the cliché: **a friend in need,** someone who helps you when you need it.) □ *Ernest posted bail for Oscar. A friend in need is a friend indeed.* □ *Jane is a real friend in need; she will take care of the kids while I stay with Dad in the hospital.*

A golden key can open any door. Sufficient money can accomplish anything. □ JILL: *I'm amazed that Sally got into a good university; her grades were so poor.* JANE: *Well, she comes from a wealthy family, and a golden key can open any door.* □ SANDRA: *How did Fred manage to get invited to the party at the country club? It's so exclusive there.* ALAN: *Yes, but a golden key can open any door.*

A good husband makes a good wife. If a husband wants his wife to be respectful and loving to him, he should be respectful and loving to her. □ BILL: *My wife spent the whole party flirting with other men. I ought to divorce her.* ALAN: *But, Bill, you flirt with other women all the time.* BILL: *What does that have to do with it?* ALAN: *A* *good husband makes a good wife.* □ *Don't blame your wife for being short-tempered with you; you've been so unpleasant to her lately. A good husband makes a good wife.*

A good Jack makes a good Jill. If a man treats his girlfriend or wife well, she will treat him well in return. (Figuratively, you must treat your subordinates well if you want them to treat you well in return.) □ *Eric's mother told him, "You may be partly to blame for your wife's bad temper. A good Jack makes a good Jill."* □ FRED: *Every secretary I've ever had is lazy and insolent. How can I get them to change?* SANDRA: *Keep in mind that a good Jack makes a good Jill.*

A good man is hard to find. See *Good men are scarce.*

A good time was had by all. Everyone had a good time. (You can use this to describe a social event that was pleasant.) □ JILL: *How was the party?* JANE: *A good time was had by all.* □ *After seeing the movie, the ten of us went out for ice cream, and a good time was had by all.*

A growing youth has a wolf in his belly. Young people who are growing fast are hungry all the time. □ *If you doubt that a growing youth has a wolf in his belly, you should see how much my fourteen-year-old cousin eats.* □ *Jimmy isn't being greedy; it's just that a growing youth has a wolf in his belly.*

A guilty conscience needs no accuser. If you have done something wrong and feel guilty about it, you will be uncomfortable and want to confess even if no one accuses you of wrongdoing. □ *Even though no one noticed him eating most of the cookies, Peter felt so bad about it that he told us what he had done. A guilty conscience needs no accuser.* □ JILL: *Why do you suppose Roberts confessed to the crime? No one even suspected him.* JANE: *A guilty conscience needs no accuser.*

A heavy purse makes a light heart. If you have plenty of money, you will feel happy and secure. □ *Everyone in the office is especially cheerful on payday, since a heavy purse makes a light heart.* □ JILL: *Bill is usually so gloomy; why do you suppose he's so gleeful today?* JANE: *He won the lottery, and a heavy purse makes a light heart, you know.*

A hedge between keeps friendship green. Your friendship will flourish if you and your friend respect each other's privacy. □ PENELOPE: *Mimi avoided me all day. I think I'll go over to her house and ask her what's wrong.* SANDRA: *Maybe you ought to leave her alone for a while. A hedge between keeps friendship green.* □ *Lynne and I are the best of friends, but we often like to spend time apart. A hedge between keeps friendship green.*

A house divided against itself cannot stand. If the members of a group fight each other, the group will disintegrate. (Often the group under discussion is a family.) □ *The leader of the newly formed union tried hard to reconcile the different factions within his organization, because he knew that a house divided against itself cannot stand.* □ *We have to get Aunt Eleanor and Aunt Lena to make up with each other. A house divided against itself cannot stand.*

A jack of all trades is a master of none. If you are able to do a lot of things fairly well, you will not have time to learn to do one thing extremely well. (Also the cliché: **a jack of all trades,** someone who can do a great many things fairly well.) □ JILL: *I envy Vincent; he can do so many things. He writes novels, paints pictures, makes sculptures, and even plays the dulcimer.* JANE: *It's true he does a lot of things, but he probably doesn't do them all terribly well. A jack of all trades is a master of none, you know.* □ *My landlord is a jack of all trades; he can re-*

pair almost anything that breaks in the building, from the plumbing to the electrical system.

A leopard cannot change his spots.   One cannot change the basic way one is. □ *Bill may say he'll stop being so jealous after Cindy marries him, but I doubt he will. A leopard can't change his spots.* □ JILL: *Joe shouldn't be so depressed all the time now that he's seeing a psychiatrist.* JANE: *Don't get your hopes up. A leopard can't change his spots.*

A liar is not believed (even) when he tells the truth.   If people think that you are a liar, they will not believe anything you say. □ *As it turned out, Fred was right when he warned his friends that the police were planning to raid their party; but they paid no attention to him, since they knew him to be a liar, and a liar is not believed even when he tells the truth.* □ *Rick had the reputation of being a liar, so he couldn't get anyone to believe he was dying of cancer, no matter how desperately he tried. A liar is not believed when he tells the truth.*

A light purse makes a heavy heart.   If you do not have enough money, you will worry and be unhappy. □ *Nathan is a cheerful person by nature, but since he lost his job, worry has made him glum. A light purse makes a heavy heart.* □ *When Danny lost all his money in the stock market crash, he learned that a light purse makes a heavy heart.*

A little bird told me.   A way of indicating that you do not want to reveal who told you something. (Sometimes used playfully, when you think that the person you are addressing knows or can guess who was the source of your information.) □ JILL: *Thank you for the beautiful present! How did you know I wanted a green silk scarf?* JANE: *A little bird told me.* □ BILL: *How did you find out it was my birthday?* SANDRA: *A little bird told me.*

A little knowledge is a dangerous thing. AND **A little learning is a dangerous thing.** If you do not know anything about a subject, you will refrain from making judgments about it, and if you know a lot about a subject, your judgments will be well informed, but if you only know a little about something, you may feel you are qualified to make judgments when, in fact, you are not. □ *When Marcia broke her leg, Robert said he could get her to the hospital safely because he had had a first-aid course. In fact, he didn't know how to deal with broken bones and wound up hurting her badly. A little knowledge is a dangerous thing.* □ *After Bill read a book on the history of Venezuela, he felt he was an authority on the subject, but he wound up looking like a fool in discussions with people who knew a lot more about it than he did. A little learning is a dangerous thing.*

A little learning is a dangerous thing. See the previous entry.

A man is known by the company he keeps. A person tends to associate with people who are like him or her. □ *Son, when you go away to school, spend your time with serious people; don't hang around with people who go to parties all the time. A man is known by the company he keeps.* □ *If you want to know what kind of person George is, look at his friends. A man is known by the company he keeps.*

A man's home is his castle. A man can do whatever he wants to in his own home. □ *Don't tell me not to go around the house in my underwear. A man's home is his castle.* □ *I'll play my radio loud if I want to. A man's home is his castle.*

A miss is as good as a mile. Almost having done something is the same as not having done it at all, since in both cases the thing does not get done. □ *We only* *missed the train by one minute? Well, a miss is as good as a mile.* □ *I made it to the semifinals in the contest, but I still did not win the prize. A miss is as good as a mile.*

A new broom sweeps clean. See *New brooms sweep clean.*

A nod's as good as a wink to a blind horse. You cannot get someone to take a hint if he or she is determined not to. □ JILL: *I keep hinting to the boss that I deserve a raise, but he doesn't seem to get the point.* JANE: *I'm not surprised. A nod's as good as a wink to a blind horse.* □ SANDRA: *Let's drop a hint to Ellen that her son has been beating up the other kids on the playground.* ALAN: *It won't do any good; you know she dotes on that boy. A nod's as good as a wink to a blind horse.*

A penny for your thoughts! What are you thinking about? (Playful.) □ *Noticing that Janet looked pensive, Bill said, "A penny for your thoughts!"* □ *You seem very pleased with yourself today. A penny for your thoughts!*

A penny saved is a penny earned. Money that you save is more valuable than money that you spend right away; it is good to save money. □ *Now that you have your first job, you ought to open a savings account. A penny saved is a penny earned.* □ *Dora worked hard to save money; she knew that a penny saved is a penny earned.*

A picture is worth a thousand words. Pictures convey information more efficiently and effectively than words do. □ *It's much easier to learn how machines work by looking at pictures, rather than by hearing someone describe them. A picture is worth a thousand words.* □ *The newspaper editor decided to devote more space to photographs of the disaster than to text, since a picture is worth a thousand words.*

A place for everything, and everything in its place. Everything in order and put away where it belongs.

(Used to describe a very orderly thing or place.) □ *I like to put my books in alphabetical order by author. A place for everything, and everything in its place.* □ *Barbara's room is so tidy. A place for everything, and everything in its place.*

A prophet is not without honor save in his own country. Everyone recognizes that a wise person is wise, except for the people close to him or her. (Biblical.) □ *No one in the novelist's country would publish her books, but last year she won the Nobel Prize. A prophet is not without honor save in his own country.* □ FRED: *My calculations clearly show that the economy is going to improve this quarter.* JANE: *You and your stupid calculations, Fred.* FRED: *A prophet is not without honor save in his own country, I see.*

A reed before the wind lives on, while mighty oaks do fall. An insignificant, flexible person is more likely not to get hurt in a crisis than a prominent or rigid person. □ *Our office has new managers now; I plan to be as inconspicuous as possible while they reorganize everyone. A reed before the wind lives on, while mighty oaks do fall.* □ *When I went off to teach school, Grandmother advised me, "Try not to stand out; just do what the others do. Then you won't get in trouble. A reed before the wind lives on, while mighty oaks do fall."*

A rich man's joke is always funny. Everyone wants to curry favor with rich people and so will always laugh at their jokes. (From a poem by Thomas Edward Brown.) □ *We all thought that Mr. Lisle was a narrow-minded, unpleasant old man, but we were careful to act otherwise, because he was wealthy. A rich man's joke is always funny.* □ JILL: *Why do people always flatter Christopher? Is it just because he's rich?* JANE: *Exactly. A rich man's joke is always funny.*

A rolling stone gathers no moss.   A person who does not settle down is not attached to anything or anyone. (Can be said in admiration or in censure, depending on whether or not the speaker feels it is good to be attached to something or someone.) □ *I worry about Tom. He's never lived in the same place for two years in a row, and he keeps changing jobs. A rolling stone gathers no moss.* □ *I'm so jealous of Tom. He's lived in so many different places, and he isn't tied down to a single job. A rolling stone gathers no moss.*

A rose by any other name would smell as sweet.   The nature of a thing is more important than what it is called. (From Shakespeare's play, *Romeo and Juliet*.) □ *The famous novelist secretly published a book under another name, and the public loved it just as much as all his other novels. It just goes to show you, a rose by any other name would smell as sweet.* □ *Bob was upset when his job title was changed from "administrative assistant" to "secretary." We tried to convince him that a rose by any other name would smell as sweet.*

A soft answer turneth away wrath.   If you speak softly and meekly to someone who is angry with you, that person will calm down. (Biblical.) □ *It won't do any good for you to yell at John because he yelled at you. Remember that a soft answer turneth away wrath.* □ *Don't get defensive when you go to talk to your boss. A soft answer turneth away wrath.*

A square peg in a round hole   Someone who is uncomfortable or who does not belong in a particular situation. (Also the cliché: **trying to fit a square peg into a round hole,** trying to combine two things that do not belong together.) □ *I feel like a square peg in a round hole at my office. Everyone else there seems so ambitious, competitive, and dedicated to the work, but I just want to make a living.* □ *Trying to teach me math is like trying to fit a* *square peg into a round hole. I'm convinced my brain is not built right to understand algebra.*

A still tongue makes a wise head. If you are wise, you do not talk very much; you only speak when you have judged that it is appropriate to do so. □ *Don't chatter about whatever comes to your mind. A still tongue makes a wise head.* □ *Kathy really offended Mr. Parker by talking so much about his ex-wife. She needs to learn that a still tongue makes a wise head.*

A stitch in time saves nine. If you fix a small problem right away, it will not become a bigger problem later. □ *Let's patch the roof before that hole gets bigger. A stitch in time saves nine.* □ *If you don't apologize to Linda now, she'll only get more angry at you. A stitch in time saves nine.*

A tale never loses in the telling. When people tell stories, they tend to exaggerate. □ *Johnny's bicycle accident tale did not lose in the telling; he convinced his friends that four semi trucks had been involved, when in fact he only ran into one parked car.* □ JILL: *I wasn't as hysterical as Maria described me when she told everyone about my finding the spider in the washroom.* JANE: *A tale never loses in the telling.*

A thing of beauty is a joy forever. Beautiful things give pleasure that lasts even longer than the beautiful things themselves. (This is a line from John Keats' poem "Endymion." Also **a thing of beauty and a joy forever,** used to describe something beautiful in lofty terms, often ironically.) □ JILL: *I don't understand why someone would pay millions of dollars to have some old painting.* JANE: *Because a thing of beauty is a joy forever, and joy forever is worth a pretty good price, don't you think?* □ ALAN: *What do you think of my new tie?* SANDRA: *It is a thing of beauty and a joy forever.*

A thing you don't want is dear at any price.   You should not buy something just because it is cheap. □ JILL: *There's a sale on black-and-white film; we should get some.* JANE: *We never use black-and-white film.* JILL: *But it's so cheap.* JANE: *A thing you don't want is dear at any price.* □ ALAN: *This catalog has a good price on sofa pillows.* SANDRA: *A thing you don't want is dear at any price.*

A trouble shared is a trouble halved.   If you tell someone about a problem you are having, or request someone's help with a problem, the problem will not seem so daunting. (Can be used to encourage someone to confide in you or ask for your help.) □ JILL: *Is something wrong? You've seemed so depressed lately.* JANE: *Oh, I wouldn't want to bother you with it.* JILL: *Don't be silly. A trouble shared is a trouble halved, remember.* □ *Don't try to solve all your problems alone. A trouble shared is a trouble halved.*

A watched pot never boils.   Something you are waiting for will not happen while you are concentrating on it. □ *Don't just sit there staring at the phone while you wait for Lucy to call. A watched pot never boils.* □ *I'd better do something besides look out the window waiting for Emily to drive up. A watched pot never boils.*

A wolf in sheep's clothing   A dangerous person pretending to be harmless. □ *Carla thought the handsome stranger was gentle and kind, but Susan suspected he was a wolf in sheep's clothing.* □ MIMI: *Why shouldn't I go out with David? He's the nicest man I've ever met.* ALAN: *He's a wolf in sheep's clothing, Mimi. Can't you tell?*

A woman's place is in the home.   Women should remain in the home, cooking, cleaning, and raising children. (This notion is generally regarded as old-fashioned or even offensive.) □ WIFE: *The manager at the grocery* *store offered me a job there, and I want to take it.* FRIEND: *There are things to do around your house. A woman's place is in the home.* □ *As soon as our child is old enough to go to school, I'm going to go back to my job at the newspaper. And don't give me any of that nonsense about a woman's place being in the home.*

A woman's work is never done. Cooking, cleaning, sewing, and raising children are jobs that must be done constantly. (Typically said by a woman to indicate how busy she is. Some people object to characterizing such activities as *woman's work*.) □ *"As soon as I finish washing the breakfast dishes, it's time to start fixing lunch," Elizabeth observed. "A woman's work is never done."* □ *After a difficult day at the office, Greta came home and began cooking dinner. "A woman's work is never done," she sighed.*

A word (once) spoken is past recalling. Once you have said something, you cannot undo the result of having said it. (Also the cliché: **past recalling,** not reclaimable.) □ *Hilary apologized for having called Mark's suit cheap, but Mark was still offended. A word once spoken is past recalling.* □ *I tried to fix the oven, but I'm afraid it's past recalling.*

A word to the wise (is enough). AND **A word to the wise is sufficient.** You only have to hint something to wise people in order to get them to understand it; wise people do not need long explanations. (Often used to signal that you are hinting something.) □ *John's a pleasant man, but I wouldn't trust him with money. A word to the wise, eh?* □ *Donna hinted about Lisa's drinking problem to Lisa's fiancé, hoping that a word to the wise would be enough.*

A word to the wise is sufficient. See the previous entry.

Abandon hope, all ye who enter here. If you come in, be prepared for the worst. (Describes a hopeless situation or one somehow similar to Hell. Often used humorously. This is the English translation of the words on the gate of Hell in Dante's *Inferno*.) □ *Mark has a sign on his office door that says, "Abandon hope, all ye who enter here."* □ *This is our cafeteria. Abandon hope, all ye who enter here.*

Absence makes the heart grow fonder. You like someone or something better if that person or thing is far away. □ *Ever since Carla's boyfriend moved away, she can't stop thinking about him. Absence makes the heart grow fonder.* □ *I won't forget about you because I'm going home over the summer. Absence makes the heart grow fonder, you know.*

Absolute power corrupts absolutely. The more power someone has, the worse he or she will eventually abuse it. □ *We thought that Johnson would be a responsible mayor, but within a year of taking office, he was as corrupt as his predecessors. Absolute power corrupts absolutely.* □ JILL: *Fred has become such a tyrant since he got promoted to division head.* JANE: *Absolute power corrupts absolutely.*

Accidents will happen. It is impossible to completely prevent things from going wrong. (Often used to console someone who has made a mistake or caused an accident.) □ CHILD: *Mommy, I spilled grape juice all over the carpet!* MOTHER: *Don't cry, honey. Accidents will happen.* □ JILL: *I'm so embarrassed. I was just tapping on your window to wake you up; I didn't mean to break it.* JANE: *Accidents will happen.*

According to Hoyle Strictly according to the rules. (Edmond Hoyle wrote a book on the rules for various games.) □ *We thought that the candidates might cheat at* *the election, but both of them seem to have behaved according to Hoyle.* □ *The manager frowned on dishonest business practices. He insisted that everything be according to Hoyle.*

According to someone's lights From someone's point of view; in someone's opinion. □ *I went bike riding with Mike, the professional cyclist. He told me the big hill wouldn't be too difficult. It may not have been difficult according to his lights, but it was pretty near impossible according to mine.* □ *According to my father's lights, nobody should get married before the age of thirty.*

Actions speak louder than words. What you do is more significant than what you say. □ *Lily talks a lot about how much she loves her family, but she never goes to visit them. Actions speak louder than words.* □ *You keep saying that you'll do your fair share of the housework; need I remind you that actions speak louder than words?*

Add insult to injury To hurt someone's pride after having hurt him or her in some other, more concrete way. □ *The burglars took my television, my bicycle, and my jewelry, and then, to add insult to injury, they wrote things all over the walls with my lipstick.* □ *Norma added insult to injury by first breaking up with George and then telling all their mutual friends that she never really loved him.*

After a storm comes a calm. Things are often calm after an upheaval. □ *After their violent quarrel, Bea and George were mild and polite to one another for almost a month. After a storm comes a calm.* □ JILL: *I can't believe how peaceful the office is today, when yesterday everyone was either being fired or threatening to quit.* JANE: *After a storm comes a calm.*

All cats are gray in the dark. It is hard to distinguish things in the dark; in the dark, appearances are meaningless. (A rude sexual interpretation means that, in the dark, all women are suitable to copulate with.) □ POLICE OFFICER: *Can you describe the man who robbed you? Or can you at least tell me what kind of car he drove away in?* VICTIM: *How am I supposed to know that? It was the middle of the night; all cats are gray in the dark!* □ *I don't care if my date is ugly. All cats are gray in the dark.*

All good things must (come to an) end.   All experiences, even pleasant ones, eventually end. □ *It's time to get out of the swimming pool, honey. All good things must end.* □ *We've had a lovely visit, but all good things must come to an end.*

(All) other things being equal   If everything else about the alternatives is the same. □ *Other things being equal, cats are healthier if they get one large meal once a day, instead of several small meals throughout the day.* □ JILL: *If I have a choice between leather shoes and synthetic ones, should I always buy the leather?* JANE: *All other things being equal, yes. But if the leather shoes are poorly made and the synthetic ones look sturdy, opt for quality rather than materials.*

All that glitters is not gold.   Just because something looks attractive does not mean it is genuine or valuable. (Often said as a warning.) □ *Hollywood may look like an exciting place to live, but I don't think you should move there. All that glitters is not gold.* □ *I know Susie is popular and pretty, but you shouldn't make friends with her. All that glitters is not gold.*

All work and no play makes Jack a dull boy.   It is not healthy for someone to work all the time and never play. (Often used to exhort someone to stop working, or to justify why you have stopped working. You can substitute the name of the person you are addressing for *Jack.*) □

Don't come to the office this weekend. All work and no play makes Jack a dull boy. □ *I'd like to take a week's vacation next month. All work and no play makes Jack a dull boy.*

All's fair in love and war. In some situations, such as when you are in love or waging war, you are allowed to be deceitful in order to get what you want. (Often said as an excuse for deception.) □ *I cheated on the entrance exam, but I really want to get into that school, and all's fair in love and war.* □ *To get Judy to go out with him, Arnold lied and told her that her boyfriend was seeing another woman. All's fair in love and war.*

All's for the best in the best of all possible worlds. Everything is fortunate and satisfying. (This is the English translation of a phrase in Voltaire's novel, *Candide*. Also **It's all for the best,** an unfortunate event will probably lead to fortunate consequences.) □ *I've been in love with Billy for ages, and today I just happened to meet him in the hall and he asked me out. All's for the best in the best of all possible worlds.* □ *I'm sorry to hear that your wife has left you, but I think it's all for the best. The two of you were never happy together.*

Am I my brother's keeper? See *I am not my brother's keeper.*

An apple a day keeps the doctor away. Apples are so nutritious that if you eat an apple every day, you will be so healthy you will not ever need to go to the doctor. □ *Remember to take an apple in your lunch today. An apple a day keeps the doctor away.* □ *Grandma always fed us lots of apples when we visited her. She believed that an apple a day keeps the doctor away.*

An army marches on its stomach. An army needs to have food in order to advance or to fight. □ *The invading army will soon have to retire. An army marches on* *its stomach, and they cannot find food in the barren countryside.* □ *The general emphasized that his men needed plentiful provisions, since an army marches on its stomach.*

An empty sack cannot stand upright.   A poor or hungry person cannot function properly. □ *Sit down and have something to eat before you go back to work. An empty sack can't stand upright.* □ *You can't blame poor people for feeling hopeless. You'd feel the same way in their situation. An empty sack cannot stand upright.*

An eye for an eye (and a tooth for a tooth).   If someone hurts you, you should be able to punish the offender by hurting him or her in the same way. (Biblical. Not everyone agrees with this idea of justice.) □ *Louisa was extremely bitter in the first months after the accident. "That drunk driver maimed me for life," she would say. "So he should be maimed, too. An eye for an eye and a tooth for a tooth."* □ *When they were children, the two brothers operated on the principle of an eye for an eye, so that if the older one hit the younger one, the younger one was entitled to hit him back just as hard.*

An idle brain is the devil's workshop.   People who have nothing worthwhile to think about will usually think of something bad to do. □ *We need to figure out something constructive for Ricky to do in the afternoons after school. An idle brain is the devil's workshop.* □ *The second-grade teacher, believing that an idle brain is the devil's workshop, always assigned her students enough homework to ensure that their brains were never idle.*

An old poacher makes the best gamekeeper.   The best person to guard something is someone who knows all about how to steal it, so he or she can anticipate what thieves might do. □ FRED: *How could they hire Bill as a night watchman? He spent time in jail for robbing a* *bank!* ALAN: *They must think an old poacher makes the best gamekeeper.* □ *We should hire the computer criminal to design computer security systems. An old poacher makes the best gamekeeper.*

An ounce of common sense is worth a pound of theory. Common sense will help you solve problems more than theory will. □ *The psychologist had many elaborate theories about how to raise her child, but often forgot that an ounce of common sense is worth a pound of theory.* □ ALAN: *In theory, pressing this button ought to make the tape machine record.* SANDRA: *An ounce of common sense is worth a pound of theory, Alan. Let's look at the manual for the tape machine before we try pressing the button.*

An ounce of discretion is worth a pound of wit. Knowing when to refrain from making jokes is better than being able to make jokes all the time. □ *Mabel makes fun of everybody, regardless of whether or not she hurts their feelings. Someone should tell her that an ounce of discretion is worth a pound of wit.* □ *Amy may be a peculiar woman, but don't mock her; she's a powerful person and could be of help to you. Remember, an ounce of discretion is worth a pound of wit.*

An ounce of prevention is worth a pound of cure. If you put in a little effort to prevent a problem, you will not have to put in a lot of effort to solve the problem. □ *Brush your teeth every day; that way you won't have to go to the dentist to have cavities filled. An ounce of prevention is worth a pound of cure.* □ *If you get in the habit of being careful with your new stereo, chances are you won't break it and have to have it fixed later. An ounce of prevention is worth a pound of cure.*

Another colony heard from See the following entry.

Another country heard from AND **Another colony heard from** Yet another person adds to the conversation.

(Used when someone joins a discussion other people are having. Somewhat sarcastic; implies that the person about whom you are saying it is not welcome in the discussion.) □ ALAN: *You ought to take a vacation tomorrow. You really look tired.* FRED: *I am not tired and I don't need a vacation.* JANE: *But you do seem awfully short-tempered.* FRED: *Well, well, another country heard from!* □ BROTHER: *Let's go to the movies.* FATHER: *I'm too busy to take you to the movies.* SISTER: *I want to go to the movies, too. Let's go to the movies!* FATHER: *Oh, splendid. Another colony heard from.*

Any port in a storm When you are in a lot of trouble, you will accept help from anyone, even someone you would not usually deal with. □ *After Jenny got evicted, she went to live with her sister, whom she's been fighting with for ten years. Any port in a storm.* □ *I swore I'd never speak to George again, but he's offered to loan me money, and I really need it. Any port in a storm.*

Appearances can be deceiving. Things can look different from the way they really are. □ *Edward seems like a very nice boy, but appearances can be deceiving.* □ *June may look like she doesn't understand you when you talk to her, but she's really extremely bright. Appearances can be deceiving.*

April showers bring May flowers. Although rain in April is not very pleasant, it helps flowers, which are pleasant, to grow later. (Figuratively, this can mean that something you do not enjoy may lead to something you do enjoy.) □ CHILD: *I hate all this rain. Why does it have to rain?* MOTHER: *April showers bring May flowers.* □ *Although it was a dreary, rainy day, we felt cheerful, since April showers bring May flowers.*

Art is long and life is short. Works of art last much longer than human lives; or, life is too short to learn everything you need to know about a particular discipline. □ ALAN: *You ought to do something besides paint pictures in your spare time. Come out with us, have some fun.* VINCENT: *Having fun will not win me immortality. Only my paintings can do that. Art is long and life is short.* □ *I always feel a sense of awe when I look at the Babylonian statues in the art museum and realize that they were made thousands of years ago. Art is long and life is short.*

As a man sows, so shall he reap. See *As you sow, so shall you reap.*

(As) bald as a baby's backside See the following entry.

(As) bald as a coot AND **(As) bald as a baby's backside** Completely bald. (The *baby's backside* version is extremely casual; both are disrespectful of the person you are describing.) □ *If Tom's hair keeps receding like that, he'll be bald as a coot by the time he's thirty.* □ FRED: *Now, I'll admit my hair is thinning a little on the top, but—* JANE: *Thinning? You're not thinning, you're as bald as a baby's backside!*

(As) black as a sweep Extremely dirty. (*Sweep* refers to a chimney sweep.) □ *After playing in the mud all morning, the children were as black as sweeps.* □ *When Sandra came in from working on her car, Alan told her, "Wash before you come to the dinner table. You're black as a sweep!"*

(As) black as coal AND **(As) black as pitch** Completely black. (Also the cliché: **pitch dark, pitch black,** used to describe a completely dark night or room.) □ *Mark's eyes were as black as coal.* □ *The stranger's clothes were all black as pitch.* □ *It was pitch dark in the closet, so I couldn't find anything in there.*

(As) black as pitch See the previous entry.

(As) blind as a bat Completely blind. (*Blind* can mean either literally blind, or ignorant, unwilling to see.) □ *I'm as blind as a bat without my glasses.* □ *Connie is blind as a bat when it comes to her daughter's disgraceful behavior.*

(As) bold as brass Very bold; bold to the point of rudeness. □ *Lisa marched into the manager's office, bold as brass, and demanded her money back.* □ *The tiny kitten, as bold as brass, began eating the dog's food right in front of the dog's nose.*

(As) bright as a button Intelligent; quick-minded. (Usually used to describe children.) □ *Why, Mrs. Green, your little girl is as bright as a button.* □ *You can't fool Mandy. She may be only six years old, but she's bright as a button.*

(As) bright as a new pin Bright and clean; shiny. □ *After Nora cleaned the house, it was as bright as a new pin.* □ *My kitchen floor is bright as a new pin since I started using this new floor wax.*

(As) busy as a beaver Busy; industrious. □ *Sue is as busy as a beaver arranging things in her new apartment.* □ *Joe has been busy as a beaver with his photography. Last weekend he was hired to take pictures at six different weddings.*

(As) busy as a bee Industrious. (Cute. Used only to describe people. Also **a busy bee,** an industrious person.) □ *When I went to visit my daughter's kindergarten class, all the students were just as busy as bees, either working on their art projects or cleaning up after themselves.* □ *What a busy bee Aunt Mabel has been, preparing all the food for our party!*

(As) busy as a cat on a hot tin roof Full of lively activity; very busy. □ *I'm afraid I can't go to lunch with you on Saturday; I'll be busy as a cat on a hot tin roof, be-*

tween working overtime and the two parties I have to go to. □ *Jerry's three part-time jobs kept him as busy as a cat on a hot tin roof.*

(As) clean as a hound's tooth Very clean. (Casual. *Clean* can mean innocent, as in the first example.) □ *John had faith that he would not be convicted for the robbery, since he had been clean as a hound's tooth since getting out of prison.* □ *After his mother scrubbed him thoroughly, James was as clean as a hound's tooth.*

(As) clean as a whistle Completely clean. □ *The car was as clean as a whistle after the Girl Scouts washed it.* □ *Andrea's record was clean as a whistle; she had never committed even the smallest infraction.*

(As) cold as a witch's tit Very cold indeed. (Describes bitterly cold weather. Vulgar.) □ BILL: *How's the weather today?* FRED: *Cold as a witch's tit.* □ *Make sure to put on your long underwear today. It's as cold as a witch's tit.*

(As) cold as marble Very cold indeed. (Used to describe a person who is either physically or emotionally cold.) □ *Raymond took Joanna's hand. It was cold as marble.* □ *No one ever got a smile out of Caroline, who was as cold as marble.*

(As) common as dirt Vulgar; ill-mannered. □ FRED: *Did you notice Mr. Cartland blowing his nose into the linen napkin at dinner?* ELLEN: *I'm not surprised. Everyone knows that the Cartlands are as common as dirt.* □ *Despite Mamie's efforts to imitate the manners of the upper class, the town's leading families still considered her common as dirt.*

(As) cool as a cucumber Extremely calm; imperturbable. (Casual.) □ *Joan felt nervous, but she acted as cool as a cucumber.* □ *The politician kept cool as a cucumber throughout the interview with the aggressive journalist.*

(As) crazy as a loon   Crazy. (Casual.) □ *Don't pay atten-tion to anything Natasha tells you; she's as crazy as a loon.* □ JILL: *David's a little eccentric, isn't he?* JANE: *Crazy as a loon, I'd say.*

(As) dead as a doornail AND **Deader than a doornail** Dead. (Often used figuratively, to describe an electric de-vice that is not working, as in the first example.) □ *When I tried to start my car this morning, I discovered that the battery was deader than a doornail.* □ JILL: *I see a wasp on the windowsill. Is it dead?* JANE: *As dead as a door-nail.*

(As) dead as the dodo   Obsolete; out of fashion. □ *When I was a kid, everyone had an 8-track tape player, but now 8-track tapes are dead as the dodo.* □ *The salesman assured me that typewriters will soon be as dead as the dodo, and everyone will use word processors instead.*

(As) deaf as a post   Deaf. □ *When my cousin was a teen-ager, she played her drum set without ear protection, and she was as deaf as a post by the age of twenty-five.* □ *Mark can't hear you even if you shout; he's deaf as a post.*

(As) drunk as a lord   Very drunk. □ *After his fifth cock-tail, Michael was as drunk as a lord.* □ *Don't try reason-ing with Adam; he's drunk as a lord.*

(As) drunk as a skunk   Disgustingly drunk; sodden. □ *You're drunk as a skunk again!* □ *Judy bought herself a case of beer and proceeded to get as drunk as a skunk.*

(As) dry as a bone AND **Bone-dry**   Completely dry. □ *Dur-ing the drought, the soil was as dry as a bone.* □ *The dog's water dish was bone-dry.*

(As) dull as dishwater   See the following entry.

(As) dull as ditchwater AND **(As) dull as dishwater** Dull; boring. □ *Gwendolyn's parties are always as dull as ditchwater.* □ *Life in our town is dull as dishwater.*

(As) easy as A, B, C Very easy. □ *If you use a cake mix, baking a cake is easy as A, B, C.* □ ALAN: *I've never danced the fox-trot before.* SANDRA: *Don't worry. It's as easy as A, B, C.*

(As) fat as a pig Exceptionally fat; grotesquely fat. □ *If I don't stop eating this cake, I'll be fat as a pig!* □ *You really ought to go on a diet; you're as fat as a pig.*

(As) fit as a fiddle In very good health. □ *You may feel sick now, but after a few days of rest and plenty of liquids, you'll be fit as a fiddle.* □ GRANDSON: *Are you sure you'll be able to climb all these stairs?* GRANDMOTHER: *Of course! I feel as fit as a fiddle today.*

(As) flat as a board Very flat. (Also used to describe someone's chest or abdomen, referring to well-developed abdominal muscles or small or absent breasts or pectoral development—in either sex.) □ *Andrea was flat as a board until she was sixteen, when she suddenly blossomed.* □ *The terrain in that part of the country is as flat as a board.*

(As) flat as a pancake Very flat. (Usually used to describe something that is not normally flat but has been flattened.) □ *After the garbage truck ran over my hat, the hat was as flat as a pancake.* □ *Lucy can mash an aluminum can flat as a pancake with one blow from her heel.*

(As) free as (the) air Completely free; without obligations or responsibilities. □ *The day I got out of the army, I felt as free as air.* □ *No, I'm not married. I don't even have a girlfriend. I'm free as the air.*

(As) gaudy as a butterfly Gaudy; colorful. □ *Marie looked as gaudy as a butterfly in her new dress.* □ *Michael's scarf is gaudy as a butterfly.*

(As) gentle as a lamb Very gentle. (Used to describe people.) □ *Don't be afraid of Mr. Schaeffer. He may look fierce, but he's as gentle as a lamb.* □ *Lisa was gentle as a lamb when dealing with children.*

(As) good as gold Very good; usually used to describe children. □ MOTHER: *Thank you for taking care of Gretchen; I hope she hasn't been too much trouble.* GRANDMOTHER: *Not at all; she's been as good as gold.* □ *We knew that Daddy would not read us a bedtime story unless we behaved, so we tried to be good as gold.*

(As) graceful as a swan Very graceful. □ *The boat glided out onto the lake as graceful as a swan.* □ *Anna is graceful as a swan.*

(As) grave as a judge See *(As) sober as a judge.*

(As) gruff as a bear Gruff; curt and unsociable. □ *I hate to ask Erica questions; she's always gruff as a bear.* □ *I'm always as gruff as a bear before I've had my first cup of coffee.*

(As) happy as a clam Contented; very happy. □ *I've been as happy as a clam since I moved to the country.* □ *I don't need much. Just somewhere to live, some work to do, and a TV to watch, and I'm happy as a clam.*

(As) happy as a lark Happy; carefree. □ *As long as Joanne has some music to listen to, she's as happy as a lark.* □ *Matthew was happy as a lark throughout his whole vacation.*

(As) hard as nails Stern; unyielding. (Used to describe people.) □ *Don't try to bargain with Liz. She's as hard as nails.* □ *Virgil may seem sweet and easily swayed, but in fact he's hard as nails.*

(As) hoarse as a crow Hoarse. □ *After shouting at the team all afternoon, the coach was as hoarse as a crow.* □ JILL: *Has Arthur got a cold?* JANE: *No, he's always hoarse as a crow.*

(As) hot as fire Very hot; burning hot. □ *I'm afraid Betsy has a high fever. Her forehead is hot as fire.* □ *In the summertime, the concrete sidewalks feel as hot as fire.*

(As) hungry as a hunter Very hungry. □ *Is there anything to eat? I've been out hoeing my garden all morning, and I'm as hungry as a hunter!* □ *We'd better have a big meal ready by the time Tommy gets home; he's always hungry as a hunter after soccer practice.*

(As) keen as mustard Very eager or enthusiastic. (British.) □ *Jane is as keen as mustard on learning to ski.* □ SANDRA: *Does your little boy dread having to start school in the fall?* NIGEL: *Quite the opposite; he's keen as mustard to go.*

(As) light as a feather AND **(As) light as air** Light in weight; or, said of cakes and pastries, delicate and airy. □ *Carrying Esther from the car to the house was no problem; she was as light as a feather.* □ *What a delicious cake, Arthur! And light as air, too.*

(As) light as air See the previous entry.

As luck would have it As it happened, either fortunately or unfortunately. □ *The minute I stepped out of the train, the rain started pouring down, but as luck would have it, I had brought an umbrella with me.* □ *I drove fifteen miles just to shop at the antique store, but it was closed when I got there, as luck would have it.*

(As) mad as a hatter Crazy; or, angry. □ *James' grandfather wanted to leave his entire fortune to his pet goldfish, which made James think that the old man must be as mad as a hatter.* □ *When the cleaners ruined my new suit, I was mad as a hatter.*

(As) mad as a March hare Crazy. (British.) □ *Every time Roger falls in love, he acts as mad as a March hare.* □ *We don't like to let Uncle Bertie out in public; he's mad as a March hare.*

(As) meek as a lamb Meek; quiet and docile. □ *Only an hour after their argument, Joe went to Elizabeth and, meek as a lamb, asked her to forgive him.* □ *Betsy terrorizes the other children, but she's as meek as a lamb around her elders.*

(As) merry as a cricket Cheerful. (Old-fashioned.) □ *Bertha is as merry as a cricket whenever she has company come to call.* □ *George is such a pleasant companion; he's usually merry as a cricket.*

(As) naked as a jaybird Naked; bare. □ *Two-year-old Matilda escaped from her nurse, who was bathing her, and ran out naked as a jaybird into the dining room, where her parents were having a dinner party.* □ *Uncle Lenny sometimes spends a whole day walking around his house as naked as a jaybird.*

(As) neat as a pin Neat and orderly. □ *Brad is such a good housekeeper; his apartment is always as neat as a pin.* □ *Joanne certainly is well-organized. Her desk is neat as a pin.*

(As) nutty as a fruitcake AND **Nuttier than a fruitcake** Crazy. (Casual.) □ *Don't pay any attention to John; he's nutty as a fruitcake.* □ *Mary's schemes for making money are nuttier than a fruitcake.*

(As) obstinate as a mule See *(As) stubborn as a mule.*

(As) old as the hills Very old; ancient. □ *That's not a new joke; it's as old as the hills!* □ *Our family custom of eating black-eyed peas on New Year's Day is old as the hills.*

(As) pale as a ghost   Very pale. □ *Laura came into the room, as pale as a ghost. "What happened?" her friends gasped.* □ *Did something frighten you? You're pale as a ghost!*

(As) pale as death   Extremely pale. (The reference to death gives this phrase ominous connotations.) □ *Rita was as pale as death when she came out of the doctor's office.* □ *What's the matter? You're pale as death!*

(As) patient as Job   Very patient. (Also the cliché: **to have the patience of (a) Job,** to be extremely patient.) □ *If you want to teach young children, you must be as patient as Job.* □ *The director who is working with that temperamental actor must have the patience of Job.*

(As) plain as a pikestaff   Obvious; very clear. □ JILL: *Why does the Senator always vote for measures that would help the tobacco industry?* JANE: *It's as plain as a pikestaff—because there are a lot of tobacco growers in his district, and he wants them to vote for him.* □ FRED: *I have a suspicion that Marcia is upset with me.* ALAN: *A suspicion? Come on, Fred, that's been plain as a pikestaff for quite some time!*

(As) plain as the nose on one's face   Very obvious. (Usually used in the expression *It's as plain as the nose on your face!* meaning It's obvious!) □ BILL: *Is Lucy in a bad mood?* JANE: *Can't you tell from the way she snaps at everyone? It's as plain as the nose on your face!* □ SANDRA: *I don't understand why Professor Potter has been so friendly this week.* ALAN: *It's plain as the nose on your face; he wants to be nominated for Professor of the Year.*

(As) pleased as Punch   Delighted; very pleased. □ CHILD: *Do you think Grandma will like the picture I'm making for her?* FATHER: *I think she'll be as pleased as Punch.* □ *Fred was pleased as Punch to discover that Ellen was making lemon pie, his favorite, for dessert.*

(As) poor as a churchmouse Penniless; very poor. (Old-fashioned.) □ *Geoffrey and Enid were poor as church-mice when they were first married.* □ *During my years at school, I was as poor as a churchmouse.*

(As) proud as a peacock AND **(As) vain as a peacock** Overly proud; vain. □ *Chester's been strutting around proud as a peacock since he won that award.* □ *I some-times think Elizabeth must spend all day admiring her-self in a mirror. She's as vain as a peacock.*

(As) pure as the driven snow Pure and virginal. (Often used ironically.) □ JILL: *Dora must have gone to bed with every man in town.* JANE: *And I always thought she was as pure as the driven snow.* □ *Robert was notoriously promiscuous, but tried to convince all his girlfriends that he was pure as the driven snow.*

(As) queer as a three-dollar bill Very strange; or, homo-sexual. (The latter usage is derogatory.) □ *Today I saw a woman pushing a lawn mower down the street and sing-ing to it as she went. I thought she was queer as a three-dollar bill.* □ JILL: *In all the years I've known him, Mike has never had a girlfriend.* FRED: *That's because he's as queer as a three-dollar bill.*

(As) quick as lightning AND **(As) swift as lightning** Ex-tremely fast. □ *The police were on the scene of the acci-dent as quick as lightning.* □ *The Olympic track star was as swift as lightning.*

(As) quiet as a mouse Very quiet. □ *You'd better be as quiet as a mouse while Grandma takes her nap so you won't wake her up.* □ *Nancy told her little son to be quiet as a mouse during the church service.*

(As) red as a cherry Bright red. (Somewhat old-fashioned.) □ *When the children came in from ice-skating, Clara's nose was as red as a cherry.* □ *When*

Lester proposed marriage, Nancy blushed as red as a cherry.

(As) red as a poppy Bright red. (Usually used to describe someone blushing.) □ *You must be embarrassed—you're as red as a poppy!* □ *When her boss praised her in front of the whole office, Emily turned red as a poppy.*

(As) red as a rose AND **Rose-red** Intense red. □ *Bill blushed as red as a rose when we teased him.* □ *I would like to make a dress out of that beautiful rose-red velvet.*

(As) red as a ruby AND **Ruby-red** Deep red. (Often used to describe a person's lips.) □ *Linda has a beautiful face, with big blue eyes and lips as red as rubies.* □ *Anna painted her fingernails with ruby-red polish.*

(As) red as blood AND **Blood-red** Completely red; deep red. (The reference to blood gives this expression sinister connotations.) □ *The magician's cape was lined with satin as red as blood.* □ *I want to have my car painted red as blood.* □ *Andrea's boyfriend sent her a dozen blood-red roses.*

(As) regular as clockwork Very regular; completely predictable. □ *George goes down to the bus stop at 7:45 every morning, as regular as clockwork.* □ *You can always depend on Nancy to complain about the office for fifteen minutes every afternoon, regular as clockwork.*

(As) right as a trivet Fine; all right. (British.) □ *Give Colin a few minutes to calm down, and he'll be right as a trivet.* □ *I was sick earlier in the week, but now I'm as right as a trivet.*

(As) right as rain Perfectly fine; all right. □ *Lily has sprained her ankle, but after a few weeks of rest she should be as right as rain.* □ *All we need to do is tidy the house up; then it will be right as rain.*

(As) scarce as hen's teeth AND **Scarcer than hen's teeth** Scarce; seldom found. (Casual.) □ *I do declare, decent people are as scarce as hen's teeth in these chaotic times.* □ *Handmade lace is scarcer than hen's teeth; most lace is made by machine.*

(As) sharp as a razor AND **Razor-sharp** Extremely sharp. (Usually used to describe cutting edges, but can be used to describe someone who is mentally sharp.) □ *Alan keeps all his kitchen knives as sharp as a razor.* □ *Be careful with those scissors; they're razor-sharp.*

(As) sharp as a tack Intellectually bright. □ *Melissa doesn't say very much, but she's sharp as a tack.* □ *Adele can figure things out from even the slightest hint. She's as sharp as a tack.*

(As) silent as the dead AND **(As) silent as the grave** Completely silent. (Has ominous connotations because of the reference to death. Usually used to promise someone that you will be silent and therefore not betray a secret.) □ *I knew something was wrong as soon as I entered the classroom; everyone was silent as the dead.* □ *Jessica is as silent as the grave on the subject of her first marriage.* □ *If you tell me what Katy said about me, I promise to be as silent as the grave.*

(As) silent as the grave See the previous entry.

(As) silly as a goose Very foolish. (Also **a goose,** a foolish person.) □ *Edith is as silly as a goose. She thinks that reading aloud to her houseplants will help them grow.* □ JILL: *The ad in the newspaper said this lotion would make my hair grow faster, but I've been using it for a whole month and my hair is still the same length.* JANE: *You goose! Do you believe everything you read in newspaper ads?*

(As) slippery as an eel Devious and untrustworthy, but impossible to catch. □ *Don't sign a lease with that land-*

lord; I think he's as slippery as an eel. □ *The con artist was slippery as an eel. Although he defrauded many people, he never went to prison.*

(As) slow as molasses in January AND **Slower than molasses in January** Slow. (Casual; somewhat countrified.) □ *Can't you get dressed any faster? I declare, you're as slow as molasses in January.* □ *The traffic on the way to the concert was slower than molasses in January.*

(As) smooth as glass Smooth and shiny. (Often used to describe calm bodies of water.) □ *The bay is as smooth as glass, so we should have a pleasant boat trip.* □ *Eugene polished the floor until it was smooth as glass.*

(As) snug as a bug in a rug Wrapped up tight, warm, and comfortable. (Playful; often used when addressing a child.) □ *The bedroom in Aunt Lydia's house was cold, but after she wrapped me up in four or five quilts and put a stocking cap on my head, I was snug as a bug in a rug and ready to go to sleep.* □ ALAN: *Are you warm enough?* SANDRA: *Yes, I'm as snug as a bug in a rug.*

(As) sober as a judge AND **(As) grave as a judge** Very serious. □ *Charlie's face was as sober as a judge, though inwardly he wanted to laugh out loud.* □ *I knew I was going to get a severe punishment when I saw that my father looked grave as a judge.*

(As) soft as down Soft to the touch. □ *The kitten's fur was as soft as down.* □ *The baby's skin was soft as down.*

(As) soft as velvet AND **Velvety-soft** Very soft to the touch. □ *The horse's nose felt as soft as velvet.* □ *This lotion will make your skin velvety-soft.*

(As) solid as a rock AND **Rock-solid** Very solid; dependable. □ *Jean has been lifting weights every day, and her arm muscles are solid as a rock.* □ *This company has always built rock-solid typewriters.*

(As) sound as a dollar Dependable; trustworthy. □ *George may be ninety years old, but his heart is as sound as a dollar.* □ *That investment is sound as a dollar; you can't possibly lose money by it.*

(As) sour as vinegar Sour and disagreeable. □ *The old man greeted us ill-naturedly, his face as sour as vinegar.* □ JILL: *Is Andrea in a bad mood today?* JANE: *Yes, sour as vinegar.*

(As) steady as a rock AND **Rock-steady** Steady; stable. □ *Linda held the ladder as steady as a rock while Michael climbed up it.* □ *Maria was steady as a rock throughout the harrowing business of arranging her mother's funeral.* □ *We set the fence-post in concrete so that it would be rock-steady.*

(As) stiff as a poker Rigid and inflexible; or, stiff and awkward. (Usually used to describe people.) □ *You'll never get Miranda to change her mind. She's as stiff as a poker.* □ *John is not a very good dancer; he's stiff as a poker.*

(As) still as death Immobile; completely still. (The reference to death gives this expression ominous connotations.) □ *George sat as still as death all afternoon.* □ *When the storm was over, everything was suddenly still as death.*

(As) straight as an arrow Very straight [with things]; honest or forthright [with people]. □ *The road to my house is as straight as an arrow, so it should be very easy to follow.* □ *Tom is straight as an arrow. I'd trust him with anything.*

(As) strong as a horse AND **(As) strong as an ox** Very strong. (Used to describe people.) □ JILL: *My car broke down; it's sitting out on the street.* JANE: *Get Linda to help you push it; she's as strong as a horse.* □ *The athlete* *was strong as an ox; he could lift his own weight with just one hand.*

(As) strong as a lion Very strong. □ *See if you can get Melissa to help us move our furniture. She's as strong as a lion.* □ *The football player was strong as a lion.*

(As) strong as an ox See *(As) strong as a horse.*

(As) stubborn as a mule AND **(As) obstinate as a mule** Very stubborn. □ *I tried to convince Jake to go to the doctor, but he's as stubborn as a mule.* □ *For four years, Henry pestered his parents to let him learn the trumpet. They tried to talk him into some other, quieter instrument, but he was stubborn as a mule.*

(As) sure as death Sure; very certain. □ *As political tension increased, it became more and more apparent that war was coming, as sure as death.* □ JILL: *Is the company definitely going to lay people off?* JANE: *Sure as death.*

(As) sweet as honey AND **Sweeter than honey** Very sweet; charming. □ *Larry's words were sweeter than honey as he tried to convince Alice to forgive him.* □ JILL: *Is Mary Ann nice?* JANE: *Yes, indeed, she's as sweet as honey.*

(As) sweet as sugar Sweet; delightful or charming. □ *Your little girl is darling! Just as sweet as sugar.* □ *Joanne was always sweet as sugar for her grandmother.*

(As) swift as an arrow Very fast. □ *The new intercity train is swift as an arrow.* □ *My week of vacation sped by as swift as an arrow.*

(As) swift as lightning See *(As) quick as lightning.*

(As) swift as the wind AND **Like the wind** Very fast. □ *This new car is as swift as the wind.* □ *Joe ran like the wind, trying to get home in time.*

(As) swift as thought Extremely fast. □ *Thanks to modern communication devices, news can now travel almost as swift as thought.* □ *You won't have to wait for me long; I'll be there, swift as thought.*

As the twig is bent, so is the tree inclined. A grown person will act the way he or she was taught to act as a child. □ *Alice's parents thought it was cute when she threw tantrums, and you'll notice that she still throws tantrums now that she's grown up. As the twig is bent, so is the tree inclined.* □ *Don't encourage your son to be so greedy. As the twig is bent, so is the tree inclined.*

(As) thick as thieves Conspiratorial; scheming together. □ *What are you two planning? You've been as thick as thieves all week!* □ *Bill and Fred must be plotting something. They're thick as thieves.*

(As) tight as a drum Sealed tight; or, stretched tight. □ *Now that I've caulked all the windows, the house should be tight as a drum.* □ *Julia stretched the upholstery fabric over the seat of the chair until it was as tight as a drum.*

(As) tight as a tick Extremely stingy; or, drunk. □ *You'll never convince Harry to give you a loan. He's tight as a tick.* □ *You'd better not drive; you're as tight as a tick!*

(As) tough as (shoe) leather Tough; or, able to endure a lot of hardship. □ *The meat they serve at the corner restaurant is as tough as shoe leather.* □ *When Brian was lost in the mountains, his friends did not fear for him; they knew he was tough as leather.*

(As) true as steel Very loyal and dependable. □ *Through all my troubles, my husband has been as true as steel.* □ *Pedro was a staunch friend, true as steel.*

(As) ugly as a toad Very ugly. □ *Maria may be a beautiful woman, but when she was a child she was as ugly as* a toad. □ *The shopkeeper was ugly as a toad, but he was kind and generous, and everyone loved him.*

(As) ugly as sin Extremely ugly. □ *Why would anyone want to buy that dress? It's as ugly as sin!* □ *Harold is ugly as sin, but his personality is very charming.*

(As) vain as a peacock See *(As) proud as a peacock.*

(As) warm as toast Warm and cozy. □ *It was cold outside today, but I was as warm as toast with my new wool muffler.* □ *Come in out of the snow and have a cup of cocoa; it will make you warm as toast.*

(As) weak as a baby Physically very weak. (Only used to describe people.) □ *Six weeks of illness left the athlete as weak as a baby.* □ *Hot, humid weather like this always makes me feel weak as a baby.*

(As) white as a sheet Extremely pale. (Used to describe people who have suddenly become pale.) □ *Marilyn turned as white as a sheet when the policeman told her that her son had been in a car crash.* □ *Did something scare you? You're white as a sheet!*

(As) white as snow AND **Snow-white** Pure white. □ *Evidently Georgia never goes outside in the sun. Her skin is as white as snow.* □ *Lydia made up the bed with her best snow-white linen sheets.*

(As) wise as Solomon Very wise. (Also the cliché: **the wisdom of Solomon,** great wisdom.) □ *If you are in trouble, get Chris to advise you. He's as wise as Solomon.* □ *This is a difficult problem. You'd need the wisdom of Solomon to be able to solve it.*

As you make your bed, so you must lie upon it. You have to suffer the consequences of what you do. (Often used as a rebuke.) □ *Rick insisted on taking a trip to Florida in August, after we all told him how hot it was. Now that he's there, all he does is complain about the*

heat. As you make your bed, so you must lie upon it. □
You were the one who chose these housepainters because
they were cheap. I told you they'd do a terrible job. You
made your bed; now you have to lie in it.

As you sow, so shall you reap. AND **As a man sows, so**
shall he reap. If you behave well, good things will happen to you; if you behave badly, bad things will happen
to you. (Biblical.) □ *You should stop being so cruel to*
other people. As you sow, so shall you reap. □ *Fred built*
an immense fortune by swindling others, but lost it all
when someone swindled him. As a man sows, so shall he
reap.

Ask me no questions, I'll tell you no lies. See the following entry.

Ask no questions and hear no lies. AND **Ask me no ques-**
tions, I'll tell you no lies. A reply to a question you do
not want to answer, or a way of warning someone not to
ask you a question. Implies that if you answer, you will
tell a lie, because you do not want to tell the truth. □
What am I going to give you for your birthday? Ask no
questions and hear no lies. □ *Maybe I like Greg, and*
maybe I don't. Ask me no questions, I'll tell you no lies.

At sixes and sevens Chaotic; disordered. □ *I have to fig-*
ure out some way to organize my collection of books.
Right now it's at sixes and sevens. □ *Everything in the*
office has been at sixes and sevens since the manager
went on vacation.

At the drop of a hat At any opportunity; whenever possible. □ *When Lou comes to visit, don't mention music,*
singing, or songs of any kind. He is an amateur singer
and will break into song at the drop of a hat. □ *Nobody*
takes Mary's tears seriously. It's well known that Mary
will cry at the drop of a hat.

At this point in time   Right now. (Bureaucrats often use this expression.) □ *The politician asked the reporters, "Is there anything else I can clarify for you at this point in time?"* □ *The bank is unable to approve your request for a loan at this point in time.*

B

Babe in the woods   A helpless person; someone who cannot take care of him- or herself in a particular situation. □ *I like to think I'm a fairly knowledgeable person, but when it comes to investment planning, I'm a real babe in the woods.* □ *When Charles first moved to New York City, he felt like a babe in the woods.*

Back to the salt mine.   It is time to go back to work. (Often said as a way of ending a conversation.) □ *It's been nice talking to you. Back to the salt mine.* □ ALAN: *See you later, Fred.* FRED: *Back to the salt mine, eh?*

Bad money drives out good.   If there is counterfeit or inflated currency in circulation, people will hoard their genuine currency; worthless things will drive valuable things out of circulation. (This principle is also known as *Gresham's Law.*) □ *When the government reduced the amount of copper in the pennies it produced, we saw that bad money drives out good; everyone saved copper pennies and only spent the less pure ones.* □ *Ever since cheap, flimsy furniture began to be manufactured in large quantities, it has been very difficult to find solid, well-made furniture. Bad craftsmanship, like bad money, drives out good.*

Bad news travels fast.   Information about trouble or misfortune disseminates quickly (more quickly than good news). □ MELVIN: *Hi, Andy. I'm sorry to hear you got fired.* ANDY: *How did you know about that already? It only happened this morning.* MELVIN: *Bad news travels fast.* □ *I called my mother to tell her about my car accident, but my aunt had already told her. Bad news travels fast.*

Bark up the wrong tree Pursue an erroneous course of action; do something that will not lead to what you want. □ *Debra's barking up the wrong tree, picketing the TV station to get them to take that program off the air. She ought to write to the companies who sponsor the show and threaten to boycott their products; then the companies will put pressure on the station to cancel the program.* □ DETECTIVE: *Where were you on the night of the murder?* SUSPECT: *You're barking up the wrong tree— I don't know anything about it!*

Batten down the hatches Prepare for calamity. □ *Batten down the hatches! Lucy's on her way here, and she's boiling mad.* □ *When we heard the tornado warning on the radio, we battened down the hatches and awaited the storm.*

Be just before you're generous. You should do what you are obliged to do before you do things that you want to do; you should pay your debts before you give money away. □ JILL: *It's payday! I can't wait to go out and buy my niece that nice toy train set for her birthday.* JANE: *But, Jill, we have bills to pay. Be just before you're generous.* □ *Be just before you're generous; pay your taxes before you make donations to charity.*

Be one's own man AND **Be one's own master** Not be controlled by other people; be independent. □ *Bert longed to be his own master, but at the same time feared losing the security he had as the employee of a large company.*

☐ *When I go away to college, I'll be my own man. My parents won't be able to tell me what to do anymore.*

Be one's own master   See the previous entry.

Be one's own worst enemy   Consistently cause oneself to fail; be more dangerous to oneself than other people are. ☐ *Alicia's addiction to drugs made her her own worst enemy.* ☐ ELLEN: *My boss is my enemy. She never says anything good about me.* SANDRA: *Ellen, you're your own worst enemy. If you did your job responsibly, your boss would be nicer.*

Beard someone in his den   See the following entry.

Beard the lion in his den AND **Beard someone in his den**   To confront someone on his or her own territory. ☐ *I spent a week trying to reach Mr. Toynbee by phone, but his secretary always told me he was too busy to talk to me. Today I walked straight into his office and bearded the lion in his den.* ☐ *If the landlord doesn't contact us soon, we'll have to beard him in his den.*

Beat a dead horse   See *Flog a dead horse.*

Beauty is in the eye of the beholder.   Different people have different ideas about what is beautiful. ☐ BOB: *I can't believe Ted bought that ugly old car.* FRED: *Beauty is in the eye of the beholder.* ☐ JILL: *Have you seen Bonnie's pictures of her new baby? I'm afraid it's not a very good-looking kid.* JANE: *Beauty is in the eye of the beholder.*

Beauty is only skin-deep.   A person who looks beautiful may not have a pleasing personality; a person's good looks may not last. ☐ FRED: *I hope Nancy will go out with me. She's so beautiful!* SANDRA: *I hate to disillusion you, but in Nancy's case, beauty is definitely only skin-deep.* ☐ *Don't be so proud of your pretty face. Beauty is only skin-deep.*

Before you can say Jack Robinson Very quickly. □ *When the little girl broke her toy truck, her father said, "Don't cry, honey. Just give it to me, and I'll get it fixed before you can say Jack Robinson." □ Come on inside, sit down by the fire, and have a cup of cocoa. We'll have you nice and warm before you can say Jack Robinson.*

Beggars can't be choosers. If someone gives you something you asked for, you should not complain about what you get. □ *I asked Joe to lend me his bicycle, and he sent me this old, rusty one. Beggars can't be choosers.* □ JILL: *Let me wear your green dress; I don't like the blue one you lent me.* JANE: *Beggars can't be choosers.*

Believe nothing of what you hear, and only half of what you see. Rumors are usually false, and sometimes the things you see can be misleading as well. □ JILL: *I heard the football team is losing its best player.* JANE: *Believe nothing of what you hear, and only half of what you see.* □ *There's a rumor that the city government is going bankrupt, but I believe nothing of what I hear, and only half of what I see.*

Better be an old man's darling than a young man's slave. A young woman should prefer to marry an old man who dotes on her rather than a young man who may treat her badly. □ *When Mr. Nash proposed to me, I thought he was too old, but my mother advised me, "Better be an old man's darling than a young man's slave." □ When Marion's friends objected that her fiancé was much too old for her, she said, "Better be an old man's darling than a young man's slave."*

Better (be) safe than sorry. You should be cautious; if you are not, you may regret it. □ *It may be time-consuming to check the oil in your car every time you buy gasoline, but better safe than sorry.* □ BOB: *I don't need a tetanus shot just because I stepped on a nail.*

MARY: *I still think you should get one. Better be safe than sorry.*

Better be the head of a dog than the tail of a lion. It is better to be the leader of a less prestigious group than to be a subordinate in a more prestigious one. □ JOE: *I can be the headmaster of a small secondary school, or I can be a teacher at a famous university. Which job offer do you think I should take?* NANCY: *Better be the head of a dog than the tail of a lion.* □ *Vincent was by far the best writer in the amateur writing workshop he belonged to. A professional writing workshop had asked him to join, but he elected to stay with the amateurs, since he thought it better to be the head of a dog than the tail of a lion.*

Better late than never. Doing something late is better than not doing it. □ *I'm sorry I'm late to the party. Better late than never, right?* □ JILL: *Lisa's birthday was two months ago. Should I send her a card now?* JANE: *Better late than never.*

Better left unsaid Not wise or polite to say. □ *Andrea's motivations for marrying Nigel were better left unsaid.* □ *Mother, I think that the details of my recent bout of dysentery are perhaps better left unsaid.*

Better the devil you know than the devil you don't know. If you have to choose between a familiar but unpleasant situation and an unfamiliar situation, choose the familiar one because the unfamiliar situation may be worse. □ JILL: *I hate my job so much that I'm thinking of asking for a transfer.* JANE: *I'd advise against it. Better the devil you know than the devil you don't know.* □ *Although she was unhappy in her marriage, Donna never considered pursuing romances with other men. "Better the devil you know than the devil you don't know," was her philosophy.*

Between a rock and a hard place   See the following entry.

Between the devil and the deep blue sea AND **Between a rock and a hard place**   Having to choose one of two unpleasant alternatives. □ *I'm between the devil and the deep blue sea; if I go to the party, my ex-husband will be there and it will be very awkward for everyone, but if I don't go, the hostess will never forgive me.* □ *If Maria confessed to stealing the money, she would have to go to jail; but if she didn't confess, her best friend would go to jail for her crime. Maria was, in other words, between a rock and a hard place.*

Between you and me and the bedpost AND **Between you and me and these four walls**   A somewhat affected way of signaling that you are about to tell a secret. □ ALAN: *What's wrong with Ellen these days? She seems so touchy.* SANDRA: *Between you and me and the bedpost, I've heard that her boyfriend is seeing someone else.* □ JILL: *How much did you get for your electric typewriter?* JANE: *Well—between you and me and these four walls— five hundred dollars.*

Between you and me and these four walls   See the previous entry.

Beware of Greeks bearing gifts.   Do not trust an opponent who offers to do something nice for you. □ JILL: *I can't believe Melanie brought me cookies today, when we've been fighting for weeks.* JANE: *Beware of Greeks bearing gifts. She probably has ulterior motives.* □ *When the rival company invited all his employees to a Christmas party, Tom's first impulse was to beware of Greeks bearing gifts, but then he upbraided himself for being paranoid.*

Beyond a shadow of a doubt   Without doubt; definitely. □ *This experiment proves, beyond a shadow of a doubt,* *that my prediction was correct.* □ Jill: *Was Henry really guilty of the crime he was arrested for?* Jane: *Beyond a shadow of a doubt.*

Birds in their little nests agree. People who live together should try hard to get along peacefully. (Usually used to admonish children not to fight with each other.) □ Brother: *She called me a name!* Sister: *I did not! He's a liar!* Father: *Now, now, kids—birds in their little nests agree.* □ *Let's not argue about this, guys. Birds in their little nests agree.*

Birds of a feather flock together. Similar people tend to associate with each other. □ *I always thought Amy was pretentious, and now she's going out with that snobbish boy, Louis. Birds of a feather flock together.* □ George: *Why do you think Donald is dishonest?* Ned: *All his friends are dishonest. Birds of a feather flock together.*

Bite the hand that feeds you Behave ungratefully; hurt someone who has helped you. □ *Vincent got grant money from the government to write his book, which turned out to be a harsh satire on government policies. That's what I call biting the hand that feeds you.* □ Jill: *A newspaper reporter called me today and asked me to tell him the details of the corrupt dealings my boss has been involved in. Do you think I should?* Jane: *No. Don't bite the hand that feeds you.*

Bless one's lucky star AND **Bless one's stars** Be thankful for a lucky thing that happened. (Also **Bless my stars!**, a mild interjection of surprise.) □ *I bless my lucky star that I met you, dear.* □ *I was in a car crash yesterday, and I bless my stars that no one was hurt.* □ Alan: *Look, honey! I gave the house a thorough cleaning while you were away.* Sandra: *Bless my stars!*

Bless one's stars See the previous entry.

Blessed is he who expects nothing, for he shall never be disappointed. If you do not expect good things to happen, you will not be disappointed when they fail to happen. □ ELLEN: *This is going to be the best vacation we've ever had; we're going to have fun every minute of every day.* FRED: *Blessed is he who expects nothing, for he shall never be disappointed.* □ JILL: *Do you think you'll win the contest?* JANE: *I like to keep in mind that blessed is he who expects nothing, for he shall never be disappointed.*

Blood is thicker than water. People who are related have stronger obligations to each other than to people outside the family. □ *My friends invited me to go camping on Saturday, but I have to go to my cousin's wedding instead. Blood is thicker than water, after all.* □ *If you ever need help, don't ask your friends. Come home and ask us, your family. Blood is thicker than water.*

Blood-red See *(As) red as blood.*

Blood will have blood. People will use violence to get revenge for violent acts; murderers will be murdered. □ *Although no one suspected him of the murder he had committed, Parker lived in fear. He had heard that blood will have blood.* □ *I am afraid that the two gangs will never stop killing each other. Blood will have blood.*

Blood will tell. A person whose ancestors were bad in some way will eventually turn out to be bad in the same way. □ *Lisa's father was a gambler, and now Lisa has started to gamble, too. Blood will tell.* □ *William went to all the best schools, but he's just as vulgar as the rest of his family. Blood will tell.*

Bone-dry See *(As) dry as a bone.*

Born on the wrong side of the blanket Illegitimate. □ *All his life, Edward felt that people looked down on him because he was born on the wrong side of the blanket.* □

Just between you and me, I suspect Mrs. Potter's oldest child was born on the wrong side of the blanket.

Born with a silver spoon in one's mouth Born into wealth and privilege. □ *James doesn't know anything about working for a living; he was born with a silver spoon in his mouth.* □ *Most of the students at the exclusive private college were born with silver spoons in their mouths.*

Boys will be boys. Boys are expected to be irresponsible or boisterous. (Also said ironically about men.) □ *You can't blame David for breaking the window with his baseball. Boys will be boys.* □ *My husband can't resist driving eighty miles an hour in his new sports car. Boys will be boys.*

Bread is the staff of life. Food is necessary for people to survive. □ *Miranda likes to give money to charities that feed people. "Other services are important," she reasons, "but bread is the staff of life."* □ JILL: *Want to go to lunch with us, Vincent?* VINCENT: *No. I must work on my novel while inspiration lasts.* JILL: *Don't forget to eat. Bread is the staff of life, you know.*

Brevity is the soul of wit. Jokes and humorous stories are funnier if they are short. □ *Dale took ten minutes to tell that joke; he obviously doesn't know that brevity is the soul of wit.* □ *The comedian was in the middle of a long, tedious story when someone in the audience shouted, "Brevity is the soul of wit!"*

Bright-eyed and bushy-tailed Awake and alert. (Often used ironically, as in the first example.) □ JILL: *Hi, Jane! How are you on this beautiful morning?* JANE: *Bright-eyed and bushy-tailed, just as you might expect, since I've only had three hours of sleep.* □ *Despite the early hour, Dennis was bright-eyed and bushy-tailed.*

Bring home the bacon To bring back money, a prize, or anything good. (Casual.) □ *George may not be the politest guy in the world, but he brings home the bacon and he's good to the kids.* □ *Frankly, I doubted Mary would win the contest, but I have to admit that she brought home the bacon.*

Build castles in the air To daydream about accomplishing something that you want; to imagine a future that you hope will come to pass. (Also the cliché: **castles in the air**, daydreams about a desired future.) □ *When Kay and I were kids, we'd build castles in the air about how she would be a famous musician and I would discover the cure for cancer.* □ FRED: *Have you made any progress with the novel you were writing?* SANDRA: *What novel?* FRED: *The novel you used to talk about all the time.* SANDRA: *Maybe I used to talk about a novel I wanted to write, but that was just a castle in the air.*

Burn not your house to fright the mouse away. Do not do something drastic when it is not necessary. □ ELLEN: *I don't like the shape of my nose; I think I'll have surgery to make it look better.* JANE: *But you can make your nose look better just by using different makeup. Don't burn your house to fright the mouse away.* □ *When someone pointed out a small flaw in Vincent's latest painting, Vincent wanted to tear the whole painting to shreds. "Now, now, Vincent," his friends said, "burn not your house to fright the mouse away."*

Burn one's bridges (behind one) To destroy all possible ways of retreating; to commit yourself to going forward. □ *When Jenny decided to stay in Chicago, she burned her bridges behind her, selling her plane ticket home.* □ VINCENT: *I've decided to quit my job and write the Great American Novel.* ALAN: *Don't burn your bridges. Keep in touch with your old employers in case you ever want your job back.*

Burn the candle at both ends To use your energy extravagantly; to work much too hard. □ *When I was in college, I burned the candle at both ends, often going without sleep for two or three nights every week in order to get my homework done.* □ *Unless you stop burning the candle at both ends, you're going to have some kind of breakdown.*

Burn the midnight oil To stay up late working. □ *Laurel is really burning the midnight oil; when I called her at one in the morning, she was still awake, writing her term paper.* □ *We'll need to burn the midnight oil to get this project finished on time.*

Bury the hatchet To make peace; to end a quarrel. (Casual.) □ *You and Emily have been fighting for over a month now; I think it's time for you guys to bury the hatchet.* □ *The two brothers had been rivals in everything for most of their lives, but when their father died, they buried the hatchet.*

Busiest men find the most time. See *The busiest men have the most leisure.*

Business before pleasure You should finish your work before starting to relax and enjoy yourself. □ ALAN: *Hi, Ted. Shall we get something to drink?* TED: *Business before pleasure, Alan. Do you have the statistics I asked you to bring?* □ *I'd love to go waterskiing with you today, but I have a few things to do in the office. Business before pleasure, I'm afraid.*

Butter wouldn't melt (in someone's mouth). Someone is acting innocent. □ *By the time her parents came home, Emily had cleaned up all evidence of having broken the valuable figurine, and she looked as though butter wouldn't melt in her mouth.* □ JANE: *How can you suspect George of playing that practical joke on you? He* *looks so innocent.* JILL: *Yes, butter wouldn't melt, I'm sure.*

Buy a pig in a poke To buy something without examining it beforehand. □ JILL: *When I bought the piano, I didn't realize that this key didn't work, and that the varnish was peeling off.* JANE: *In other words, you bought a pig in a poke.* □ *Before you buy a used record album, hold it up to the light and look for scratches. If the sales staff won't let you, don't buy it. Never buy a pig in a poke.*

By the sweat of one's brow By hard work. (Often used in the phrase *to earn by the sweat of one's brow.*) □ *After Johnson lost all his money in the stock market crash, he had to earn his living by the sweat of his brow.* □ *You really don't understand what money is worth until you've earned it by the sweat of your brow.*

By word of mouth By people talking to each other; without writing something down. (Usually in the phrase *spread by word of mouth,* disseminate information through people talking to one another.) □ *Praise of the new restaurant spread by word of mouth, and soon it was packed with diners every night.* □ JILL: *Will you advertise your boutique in the newspaper?* ELLEN: *I can't afford it right now; I'm depending on advertising by word of mouth.*

C

Caesar's wife must be above suspicion. The associates of public figures must not even be suspected of wrongdoing. (Julius Caesar is supposed to have said this when asked why he divorced his wife, Pompeia. Because she was suspected of wrongdoing, he could not associate with her anymore.) □ JILL: *I don't think the mayor is trustworthy; his brother was charged with embezzlement.* JANE: *But the charges were never proved.* JILL: *That doesn't matter. Caesar's wife must be above suspicion.* □ *When the newspapers reported the rumor that the lieutenant governor had failed to pay his taxes, the governor forced him to resign, saying, "Caesar's wife must be above suspicion."*

Call a spade a spade To speak directly to the point; to say exactly what you mean. □ JILL: *Do you know Helen? The rather heavyset girl who—* JANE: *Heavyset? Just call a spade a spade and say that she's fat!* □ *Elsie, who always insisted on calling a spade a spade, refused to refer to herself as a senior citizen. "I'm no senior citizen; I'm an old woman," she said.*

Call no man happy till he dies. You cannot tell if a person's life has been happy on the whole until that person's life is over; no matter how happy someone is now, something bad may happen to destroy his or her happiness. □

ALAN: *You must be very happy with your new wife.* BILL: *Call no man happy till he dies.* □ JILL: *That movie star must be the happiest person in the world. He's rich, people love him, and he likes his work.* JANE: *Call no man happy till he dies.*

Cannot call one's soul one's own   To be in someone else's power completely. □ *Alicia's husband dominates her so much, she can't call her soul her own.* □ *I've got to put in so many hours at work that I can't call my soul my own.*

Cannot hit the broad side of a barn   Cannot aim a projectile accurately enough to hit even a large target. □ *Even after several months of training at the rifle range, Phillip still couldn't hit the broad side of a barn.* □ *No one wanted Billy on his side of a snowball fight, because everyone knew he couldn't hit the broad side of a barn.*

Cannot see the wood for the trees   Cannot perceive the important things because there are too many confusing details. □ *The information presented in this textbook is so disorganized that I can't see the wood for the trees.* □ *The politician's opponents claimed that she couldn't see the wood for the trees, because she spent so much time trying to solve minor problems.*

Can't hold a candle to someone   Cannot be compared to someone; is nowhere near as good as someone. □ *Lillian was an excellent piano player, but she couldn't hold a candle to her mother.* □ *Grandmother told me she'll never remarry; she has never met a man who could hold a candle to her late husband.*

Carry coals to Newcastle   To take something to a person or place that already has plenty of it. □ ALAN: *What shall we take to dinner at the Hamiltons' tonight?* SANDRA: *How about a bottle of wine?* ALAN: *That would be carrying coals to Newcastle; they have their own wine cellar.*

☐ *Whenever I give Ellen a gift, I feel as if I'm carrying coals to Newcastle; she already seems to have everything.*

Cast one's bread upon the waters   To be foolishly generous; or, to be generous because you feel it is right and not because you expect a reward. (Biblical.) ☐ *Joseph is casting his bread upon the waters, supporting Vincent while he works on his novel.* ☐ *Cast your bread upon the waters; make a generous contribution to our cause.*

Cast pearls before swine   To give something to someone who cannot appreciate it. (Biblical.) ☐ *Professor Irons felt that delivering her brilliant lectures to freshmen was casting pearls before swine.* ☐ *Feeding caviar to your cats is casting pearls before swine.*

Cast the first stone   To be too eager to punish or blame someone; to want to punish someone when you are guilty as well. (Biblical.) ☐ *Many of the jurors at Lisa's trial seemed disconcertingly ready to cast the first stone.* ☐ JILL: *I hope Fred gets fired. He comes in late all the time, and he's always rude to other people.* JANE: *Don't cast the first stone; you have your faults, too.*

Catch-as-catch-can   By any possible means. ☐ *Joe was out of work for a year and a half, and earned his money catch-as-catch-can.* ☐ *He conducts his business catch-as-catch-can, without much regard for ethics.*

Charity begins at home.   You should take care of people close to you before you worry about more distant people. ☐ *I don't think our church should send money to starving people in Africa when there are people starving right here in our city. Charity begins at home.* ☐ *If you really want to make the world a better place, start by being polite to your sister. Charity begins at home.*

Cheats never prosper.   If you cheat people, they will not continue to do business with you, and so your business will fail. ☐ CUSTOMER: *You charged me for ten artichokes,* *but you only gave me nine.* GROCER: *Too bad. You should have counted them before you paid for them.* CUSTOMER: *Cheats never prosper, you know.* □ ELLEN: *The guy who sold me this ring said it was diamond, but when I stepped on it, it broke.* JANE: *Well, you'll have your revenge on him sooner or later. Cheats never prosper.*

Children and fools tell the truth. Children have not yet learned, and fools never did learn, that it is often advantageous to tell a lie; no knowledgeable person tells the truth. □ FRED: *What will I tell Ellen when she asks why I'm so late getting home?* ALAN: *Tell her the truth—we were out having a few drinks.* FRED: *Children and fools tell the truth, Alan.* □ *The police officer decided to ask questions of the suspect's young son, since he had heard that children and fools tell the truth.*

Children should be seen and not heard. Children should not speak in the presence of adults. (Often used as a way to rebuke a child who has spoken when he or she should not.) □ *You may come out and meet the party guests if you'll remember that children should be seen and not heard.* □ FATHER: *As I was saying, the important thing—* CHILD: *Daddy, Daddy, what are you talking about? Are you talking about work again? Do you want to see what I made in school?* FATHER: *Children should be seen and not heard.*

Christmas comes but once a year. Since Christmas only happens once a year, we should treat it as a special time by being good to others or by indulging children. □ MOTHER: *Don't let Sally have so much Christmas candy, Mother. You'll spoil her appetite.* GRANDMOTHER: *Oh, let me indulge her. Christmas comes but once a year.* □ *Christmas comes but once a year and is the perfect time to remember those less fortunate than ourselves, so we urge you to give to this Christmas charity campaign.*

Circumstances alter cases. In unusual situations, people are allowed to do unusual things. □ JILL: *They should sentence that woman to death for killing her husband.* JANE: *I think you're being too harsh. He had abused her for five years. After all, circumstances alter cases.* □ CASHIER: *I'm sorry, this store does not accept personal checks.* CUSTOMER: *But I need this medicine, and I don't have any cash. I've shopped at this store for fifteen years. Surely you can trust me this once.* CASHIER: *Well, all right. Circumstances alter cases.*

Civility costs nothing. AND **Courtesy costs nothing.** It never hurts you to be polite. □ *Always greet people politely, no matter what you think of them. Civility costs nothing.* □ *Why not write Mildred a thank-you note? Courtesy costs nothing.*

Cleanliness is next to godliness. It is very important to keep yourself clean. □ CHILD: *How come I have to take a bath?* MOTHER: *Cleanliness is next to godliness.* □ *The woman sitting next to me on the bus had obviously never heard that cleanliness is next to godliness.*

Close, but no cigar. Something came close to succeeding, but did not succeed. (Casual and playful. Often used as a reply to someone who has come close to guessing the right answer, as in the second example.) □ JILL: *How did you do in the contest?* JANE: *Close, but no cigar. I got second place.* □ ELLEN: *Guess who I saw today.* FRED: *Sandra.* ELLEN: *Close, but no cigar. I saw her husband.*

Close enough for government work Sufficiently close; done just well enough. □ *I didn't do the best job of mending your shirt, but it's close enough for government work.* □ SANDRA: *Did you finish putting up the shelves?* ALAN: *Close enough for government work.*

Clothes make the man. People will judge you according to the way you dress. □ *Father told me, "Don't be hesi-*

tant to pay a good price for a fine suit. Clothes make the man." □ *Jim was always careful about how he dressed. He believed that clothes make the man.*

Cold hands, warm heart People whose hands are usually cold have kind and loving personalities. □ JILL: *Why are you rubbing your hands? It's so warm out.* JANE: *My hands are always cold.* JILL: *Cold hands, warm heart.* □ NANCY: *I don't like holding hands with Joe. His hands are so cold.* SANDRA: *Cold hands, warm heart.*

Come easy, go easy. See *Easy come, easy go.*

Come on like gangbusters To act aggressively and loudly. □ *The band conductor said, "At this point in the piece, the trombones should come on like gangbusters."* □ ALAN: *Is Ted always so effusive when he meets people?* SANDRA: *Yes, he always comes on like gangbusters.*

Come out smelling like a rose To succeed; to do better than anyone else in some situation. (Also the cliché: **smelling like a rose,** doing extremely well.) □ *Everyone else in the firm lost money in the real estate deal, but Bob came out smelling like a rose.* □ *If I can just finish my research paper on time, I'll be smelling like a rose by the end of the school year.*

Come up roses To succeed extremely well. (Often used in the phrase "Everything's coming up roses," everything is going very well.) □ *Much to Edith's surprise, the bake sale came up roses, even though she hadn't contributed any of her cakes.* □ SANDRA: *How are things at work lately?* ALAN: *Everything's coming up roses, believe it or not.*

Come within a hair's breadth of something. See the following entry.

Come within an inch of something. AND **Come within a hair's breadth of something.** Almost do something; narrowly avoid doing something. (Usually implies that the thing you narrowly avoided doing was dangerous.) □ *I came within an inch of telling that vulgar Mrs. Wallace what I really think of her.* □ *He came within a hair's breadth of falling off the balcony.*

Coming events cast their shadows before. Significant events are often preceded by signs that they are about to happen. (From Thomas Campbell's poem, "Lochiel's Warning.") □ JILL: *I think Fred and Ellen will be divorced soon.* JANE: *How do you know?* JILL: *Coming events cast their shadows before. They've both spent an awful lot of time talking to lawyers lately.* □ *If you pay attention to the news, you can generally tell when something momentous is about to happen. Coming events cast their shadows before.*

Conscience does make cowards of us all. People sometimes fear to do what they want or what they believe is necessary because they think it is wrong. (From Shakespeare's play, *Hamlet.*) □ ALAN: *I really want to go to the ball game with you guys this afternoon, but it just doesn't seem right to skip work to do it.* FRED: *Conscience does make cowards of us all, eh, Alan?* □ *The police believed that the only way to prevent the murderer from killing more people was to kill him, but they also believed that it was wrong for them to kill anyone. Conscience does make cowards of us all.*

Conspicuous by one's absence Absent when expected to be present; drawing attention to oneself by not appearing when one should. □ *Julie was conspicuous by her absence at her daughter's wedding.* □ *All the other salesmen came to work on Thursday, which made Edward all the more conspicuous by his absence.*

Constant dripping wears away a stone. See the following entry.

Constant dropping wears away a stone. AND **Constant dripping wears away a stone.** Persistence accomplishes things. □ JILL: *How did you get Fred to give you a raise?* JANE: *I just kept asking him for it, every month for two years. Constant dropping wears away a stone.* □ VINCENT: *The magazine will never publish my poetry.* PENELOPE: *Don't give up; keep sending them your poems. Constant dropping wears away a stone.*

Cool, calm, and collected A playful way of describing a calm person. (Often used ironically, as in the first example.) □ *James wasn't at all upset to hear that the phone is broken again. He's cool, calm, and collected, as you can tell from the screams emerging from his office.* □ *The bad news didn't seem to distress Lydia at all. She remained cool, calm, and collected.*

Cost a pretty penny To be expensive. □ JILL: *Those are gorgeous shoes.* JANE: *They ought to be. They cost a pretty penny.* □ *Furnishing the apartment is going to cost us a pretty penny.*

Councils of war never fight. A group of people cannot act decisively. □ *I asked my family to help me decide which college I should attend, but it was soon apparent that they wouldn't finish arguing about it until well after the time when I needed to decide. Councils of war never fight.* □ *We tried to convince the boss not to form a committee to discuss the problem. We knew that councils of war never fight.*

Courtesy costs nothing. See *Civility costs nothing.*

Cowards die many times before their death(s). Cowards are often afraid that they are going to die, so that they often feel what it is like to die, while brave people only feel the fear of death when they are really about to die. (From Shakespeare's play, *Julius Caesar.*) □ *After the bombardment, Julian was discovered in the farm-*

house cellar, practically incoherent with terror, demonstrating once more that cowards die many times before their death. □ *Every time Nina walked down the alley to my house, she was as scared as if she were being followed by thugs. Cowards die many times before their deaths.*

Crazy like a fox   Clever; crafty. □ *I don't trust that landlord. He's crazy like a fox.* □ *I never worry about Belinda. She's crazy like a fox and can trick her way out of any dangerous situation.*

Cross that bridge when one comes to it   To delay worrying about something that might happen until it actually does happen. (Usually used in the phrase, "Let's cross that bridge when we come to it," a way of telling someone not to worry about something that has not happened yet.) □ ALAN: *Where will we stop tonight?* SANDRA: *At the next town.* ALAN: *What if all the hotels are full?* SANDRA: *Let's cross that bridge when we come to it.* □ *Edward decided not to worry about what would happen if his partner discovered that he had been embezzling funds; he'd cross that bridge when he came to it.*

Cross the stream where it is shallowest.   To do things in the easiest possible way. □ *Don't drive yourself crazy trying to knit a sweater in time for Leo's birthday. Cross the stream where it is shallowest; call Leo and tell him his birthday present will be late, and then take all the time you need to finish it.* □ JILL: *How can I get Fred to give me permission to start this project?* JANE: *Cross the stream where it is shallowest. First ask Fred's boss for permission; I'm sure she'll give it to you. Then Fred will have to agree.*

Crosses are ladders that lead to heaven.   Having to endure trouble can help you to be virtuous. (Also the cliché: **to have a cross to bear,** to have trouble one must endure.) □ *When Tina was diagnosed with cancer, her* *mother consoled her by saying that crosses are ladders that lead to heaven, and that though she might have to suffer in this world, she would surely be rewarded in the next.* □ *Everyone has a cross to bear; Jeffrey's was his family's poverty.*

Cry all the way to the bank   To pretend to be sorry for something you did that made a lot of money. (Usually said only of a third person.) □ SANDRA: *Have you read the new book by that romance novelist? They say it sold a million copies, but it's so badly written that the author ought to be ashamed of herself.* ALAN: *I'm sure she's crying all the way to the bank.* □ *That dreadful movie had no artistic merit. I suppose the people who produced it are crying all the way to the bank.*

Curiosity killed the cat.   Being curious can get you into trouble. (Often used to warn someone against prying into your affairs.) □ JILL: *Where did you get all that money?* JANE: *Curiosity killed the cat.* □ *You shouldn't follow your classmates home to see where they live. Curiosity killed the cat.*

Cut off one's nose to spite one's face   To hurt yourself in an attempt to hurt someone else. (Often in the form, "Don't cut off your nose to spite your face.") □ JILL: *Why are you selling all your records?* JANE: *Because it will really upset my boyfriend.* JILL: *But you love your music! Don't cut off your nose to spite your face.* □ *Isaac dropped out of school because he wanted to make his father angry; years later, he realized that he had cut off his nose to spite his face.*

D

Damn someone with faint praise   To praise someone un-
enthusiastically or for trivial reasons, thus implying that
the person is not very commendable. □ JILL: *Is Leon a
nice guy?* JANE: *His personal hygiene is impeccable.* JILL:
That's certainly damning with faint praise. □ *Fred's letter of recommendation damned me with faint praise,
saying only that I was punctual and dressed well.*

Damned if you do, damned if you don't.   No matter
what you do, it will cause trouble. (Casual.) □ *If I use
this money to pay the rent, I won't have enough left over
for food. But if I don't use the money to pay the rent, my
landlord will evict me. Damned if I do, damned if I
don't.* □ HELEN: *If I invite Shirley to the party, I'm sure
she'll get drunk and make an unpleasant scene. But if I
don't invite her, she'll never forgive me.* JANE: *Damned if
you do, damned if you don't, huh?*

Dead men don't bite.   Dead people cannot hurt you. (Implies that it would be good if a threatening person were
dead.) □ *At his opponent's funeral, the dictator gave a
eulogy filled with praise, but everyone was aware that
his real sentiment was relief that dead men don't bite.* □
GANGSTER: *What am I going to do about that police detective? He's got almost enough evidence to put us in jail for
life.* HENCHMAN: *Dead men don't bite.*

Dead men tell no tales.   Dead people will not betray any secrets. □ *The club members liked to hold their secret meetings in a graveyard, since dead men tell no tales.* □ GANGSTER: *Mugsy is going to tell the police that we robbed the bank. How can we stop him?* HENCHMAN: *Dead men tell no tales.*

Deader than a doornail   See *(As) dead as a doornail.*

Death is the great leveler.   Death makes everyone equal, because it does not spare anyone, not even the wealthy, famous, or talented. (Also the cliché: **the great leveler, death.**) □ *The wealthy tycoon lived as though he were exempt from every law, but death is the great leveler and came to him the same as to everyone else.* □ *We hoped that the brilliant pianist would entertain us with her music for many decades, but death, the great leveler, did not spare her.*

Desert and reward seldom keep company.   If you deserve a reward, you are not necessarily going to get it. □ JILL: *I worked so hard on that project, and Fred is taking all the credit for it.* JANE: *You know how it goes; desert and reward seldom keep company.* □ *Julie was the best violinist in the school, but the orchestra director picked someone else to be first chair. Desert and reward seldom keep company.*

Desires are nourished by delays.   The longer you have to wait for something you want, the more eager you will be to get it. □ *We all thought that Maria's enthusiasm for getting a car would abate during the many months it took for her to save enough money, but we forgot that desires are nourished by delays.* □ *The longer I had to postpone my trip to San Francisco, the more vehemently I wanted to go. Desires are nourished by delays.*

Desperate diseases must have desperate remedies.   If you have a seemingly insurmountable problem, you must do things you ordinarily would not do in order to solve it. □ *Georgia had tried everything she could think of to lose weight, but nothing worked. Finally, figuring that desperate diseases must have desperate remedies, she confined herself to eating nothing but celery.* □ FRED: *All my employees have been surly and morose for months. How can I improve their morale?* ALAN: *Why not give everyone a raise?* FRED: *That's a pretty extreme suggestion.* ALAN: *Yes, but desperate diseases must have desperate remedies.*

Devil take the hindmost   See *Every man for himself (and the devil take the hindmost).*

Different strokes for different folks   Different people like different things; different people live in different ways. □ JILL: *I don't understand why Mary wears high heels every day. They're so uncomfortable, and besides I don't think they look that good.* JANE: *Different strokes for different folks.* □ *My neighbor spends all his free time working in his garden. I would never want to do that, but different strokes for different folks.*

Diligence is the mother of good luck.   If you work carefully and constantly, you will very likely have a chance to get what you want. □ MIMI: *I'll never get work as an actress; I always have such bad luck at auditions.* SANDRA: *Keep working at it. Diligence is the mother of good luck.* □ *The encyclopedia salesman went to every house in the neighborhood before he made a sale, but the sale he made was a big one. The family bought a set of encyclopedias for each of their six children. For the salesman, diligence was the mother of good luck.*

Discretion is the better part of valor.   It is good to be brave, but it is also good to be careful; if you are careful, you will not get into situations that require you to be brave. □ *In the middle of the night, Elsie heard a noise* *in her living room. She peeked out from behind her bedroom door and saw a man taking her TV set. At first she thought she should go out and confront him, but then she decided that discretion was the better part of valor and sneaked over to her neighbor's house to call the police.* □ SON: *Can I go hang gliding with my friends?* FATHER: *No.* SON: *But they'll say I'm chicken if I don't go!* FATHER: *Discretion is the better part of valor, and I think you'd rather have them call you chicken than spend several months recuperating from broken bones.*

Distance lends enchantment (to the view). Things that are far away from you appear better than they really are. □ JILL: *High school was the happiest time of my life.* JANE: *But that was fifteen years ago. I think distance lends enchantment to the view.* □ ELLEN: *When we're as wealthy as the McCutcheons, we'll have the happiest life.* FRED: *Distance lends enchantment. Rich people have problems, too.*

Divide and conquer. In order to achieve a victory, you should make your enemies fight against each other, so that they do not join together to fight against you. □ *George won the election for club president by instigating a fight between the other two candidates. Divide and conquer.* □ *The children always manage to get what they want by setting their parents against each other. Divide and conquer.*

Do as I say, not as I do. Take my advice, even though I am acting contrary to it. (Sometimes used as an apology for behaving hypocritically.) □ JILL: *Why are you walking on the grass when I told you not to?* JANE: *But you're walking on the grass.* JILL: *Do as I say, not as I do.* □ *No, you may not borrow one of my cigarettes. You shouldn't smoke at all. Do as I say, not as I do.*

Do as you would be done by.   See *Do unto others as you would have them do unto you.*

Do not let the sun go down on your anger.   See the following entry.

Do not let the sun go down on your wrath. AND **Do not let the sun go down on your anger.**   Do not stay angry with anybody; calm your anger by the end of the day. □ Son: *Billy broke my bicycle, and I'm never going to speak to him again.* Mother: *Now, now, don't let the sun go down on your wrath.* □ *I was very upset by what you did, but I don't want to let the sun go down on my anger. Let's make up.*

Do not wash your dirty linen in public.   Do not talk about your private family problems in public. □ Grandson: *How are we going to make Dad stop drinking?* Grandmother: *Hush! Don't wash your dirty linen in public.* □ *Everyone knew that Jessica's mother was in a mental hospital, since Jessica could never restrain herself from washing her dirty linen in public.*

Do unto others as you would have them do unto you. AND **Do as you would be done by.**   You should treat other people the way you want them to treat you. (Jesus Christ says this in Luke 6:31; it is also known as "The Golden Rule.") □ Mother: *Don't call your playmates names.* Child: *Why not?* Mother: *Because you should follow the Golden Rule: do unto others as you would have them do unto you.* □ *It's hard to be kind to people sometimes, but I try to remember to do as I'd be done by.*

Doesn't have the sense God gave geese   Is very foolish. □ *Mary's going out in this incredibly cold weather without a hat or gloves. She doesn't have the sense God gave geese.* □ *It was obvious that the man was a swindler, but George gave him all his money anyway. I swear, George doesn't have the sense God gave geese.*

Dog does not eat dog. One disreputable person will not harm other disreputable people. (Also *dog-eat-dog,* viciously competitive.) □ ELLEN: *My lawyer did such a bad job that I want to hire another lawyer to sue him.* JANE: *You'll never find a lawyer to take on that job. Dog does not eat dog.* □ *Advertising is a dog-eat-dog business.*

Don't bite off more than you can chew. Do not commit yourself to doing more than you can actually do. (Also the cliché: **to bite off more than one can chew,** to take on too much responsibility.) □ *I don't think you ought to take dance lessons three times a week; you're already working two jobs. Don't bite off more than you can chew.* □ *Bill's really bitten off more than he can chew with his new job.*

Don't change horses in midstream. Do not make changes when you are in the middle of doing something. □ JANE: *I've written a rough draft of my research paper, but the topic doesn't interest me as much as I thought. Maybe I ought to pick a different one.* JILL: *Don't change horses in midstream.* □ *Leo wanted to get a new secretary while our old one was in the middle of typing an important paper for us, but I convinced him not to change horses in midstream.*

Don't count your chickens before they are hatched. Do not act as though something has turned out favorably for you until it has really turned out that way. (Also **to count one's chickens before they are hatched,** to prematurely assume that something will turn out in your favor.) □ JILL: *When I get my raise, I'll use the extra money to go on vacation.* JANE: *But you don't know for sure that you're going to get a raise. Don't count your chickens before they are hatched.* □ *Elizabeth went shopping for a wedding gown today, but her boyfriend hasn't even proposed to her yet. She's really counting her chickens before they're hatched.*

Don't cry before you are hurt. Do not be upset about a bad thing that might happen; only be upset when something bad really does happen. □ FRED: *What am I going to do? There's a possibility that my job will be eliminated!* JANE: *Don't cry before you are hurt. They haven't eliminated you yet.* □ CHILD: *Mommy! Mommy! Johnny's going to hit me!* MOTHER: *If Johnny hasn't hit you yet, why are you screaming like that? Don't cry before you are hurt.*

Don't cry over spilled milk. See *It's no use crying over spilled milk.*

Don't judge a book by its cover. Do not draw a conclusion about something just from the way it looks. □ *Just because Sam dresses sloppy doesn't mean he's a bad person. Don't judge a book by its cover.* □ JILL: *How can you be so sure this will be a boring movie?* JANE: *The poster for it is so boring.* JILL: *Don't judge a book by its cover!*

Don't look a gift horse in the mouth. Do not look for defects in a gift. □ JILL: *I wonder why Grandma gave me this table. Maybe it has one leg shorter than the others.* JANE: *Don't look a gift horse in the mouth.* □ MIKE: *This letter says I just won a trip to Hawaii. I bet there's some kind of catch.* KEITH: *Don't look a gift horse in the mouth.*

Don't put all your eggs in one basket. Do not risk everything on one undertaking. □ *Keep your day job while you pursue your acting career at night, just in case the acting doesn't go so well. You know—don't put all your eggs in one basket.* □ *Bet $25 on four different horses instead of $100 on one horse. Don't put all your eggs in one basket.*

Don't put off for tomorrow what you can do today. Do not procrastinate. □ FATHER: *Take out the garbage.* CHILD: *I'll do it later.* FATHER: *Don't put off for tomorrow what you can do today.* □ *I'd rather sunbathe today than*

*work on my term paper, but I suppose I shouldn't put off
for tomorrow what I can do today.*

Don't put the cart before the horse.   Do not do things in
the wrong order. (Can imply that the person you are addressing is impatient. Also **to put the cart before the
horse,** to do things in the wrong order.) □ *Tune the guitar first, then play it. Don't put the cart before the horse.*
□ *Sheila is putting the cart before the horse. She bought
two tickets for the concert, but she hasn't yet asked her
husband if he would like to go.*

Don't teach your grandmother to suck eggs.   Do not try
to instruct someone who is more experienced than you.
(Extremely casual; potentially rude.) □ PENELOPE: *I see
you have a flat tire there. The first thing you need to do
to fix a flat tire is. . . .* ALAN: *I've fixed more flats than
you've ever seen. Don't teach your grandmother to suck
eggs.* □ *Albert told the seasoned guitar player that she
was holding the guitar incorrectly. "Don't teach your
grandmother to suck eggs," she replied.*

Don't throw the baby out with the bathwater.   Do not
discard something valuable in your enthusiasm for getting rid of some useless thing associated with it. □ JILL:
*As long as I'm selling all the books Grandpa had, I might
as well sell the bookcases, too.* JANE: *Don't throw the baby
out with the bathwater. You can use the bookcases for
something else.* □ *In order to keep his campaign promise
to decrease state spending, the new governor abolished
several state agencies. Most of his constituents approved
of this at first, but when he began to cut funding for state
hospitals, people objected that he was throwing out the
baby with the bathwater.*

Dream of a funeral and you hear of a marriage.   If you
dream that a person has died, you will learn that person
is to be married. (This saying expresses a superstition.

Sometimes *wedding* is used instead of *marriage*.) ☐
ALAN: *I had a dream last night that my sister was killed.*
SANDRA: *Dream of a funeral and you hear of a marriage.*

Drink like a fish To drink alcohol excessively; to be in
the habit of drinking alcohol excessively. (Casual.) ☐ *Jeff
really drank like a fish at the party on Saturday.* ☐ *I
worry about Nancy; she drinks like a fish.*

Dry as dust Not at all engaging; completely unemotional.
☐ *The textbook for my history class is dry as dust.* ☐ *The
educational television show was supposed to be interesting to children, but most children found it dry as dust.*

Duck soup Very easy; an easy thing to do. (Casual.) ☐
For Maria, knitting a sweater is duck soup. ☐ JILL: *This
jar is stuck. Could you open it for me?* JANE: *Sure. Duck
soup.*

E

Early ripe, early rotten. AND **Soon ripe, soon rotten.** A child with extraordinary talent or intelligence will probably lose those qualities by the time he or she grows up. □ JILL: *Philip was such a fine violinist when he was little; I'm surprised he's become such a good-for-nothing adult.* JANE: *Early ripe, early rotten.* □ JANE: *You must be very proud of your little boy. He seems so mature for his age.* ELLEN: *I'm afraid it won't last. You know what they say: "Soon ripe, soon rotten."*

Early to bed and early to rise, makes a man healthy, wealthy, and wise. Going to bed early and waking up early is good for you. (You can use **Early to bed, early to rise** to describe someone who goes to bed early and wakes up early.) □ GRANDMOTHER: *I don't think it's good for you to be staying out so late, dear. Early to bed and early to rise—* GRANDSON: *Makes a man healthy, wealthy, and wise. Yeah, Grandma, I know.* □ HOST: *Don't leave so soon! The party's just beginning.* GUEST: *It's past my bedtime, I'm afraid.* HOST: *Early to bed, early to rise, huh?*

Easier said than done. It is easy to say that something should be done, but difficult to do that thing. □ SANDRA: *All we need to do now is shovel all the snow off the driveway.* ALAN: *Easier said than done.* □ JILL: *We can go to*

Florida if we can get cheap plane tickets. JANE: *Yes, but that's easier said than done.*

East is East and West is West (and never the twain shall meet). Two things are so different that they can never come together or agree. (From Rudyard Kipling's poem, "The Ballad of East and West.") □ *I had hoped that Andrew and I could be friends in spite of our political differences. But, in our case, I'm afraid that East is East and West is West.* □ *The successful conference between American and Japanese businessmen disproved the old saying that East is East and West is West and never the twain shall meet.*

East or west, home is best. See the following entry.

East, west, home's best. AND **East or west, home is best.** Home is the best place to be. □ JILL: *What was your favorite place on the tour?* JANE: *East, west, home's best, I think.* □ *You may think that traveling all the time is fun, but eventually you'll discover that east or west, home is best.*

Easy come, easy go. AND **Come easy, go easy.** You will probably lose anything that you get without effort; something that is come by with little effort can be lost without much grief. □ *Laura found a five-dollar bill in the street, but it fell out of her pocket later. "Easy come, easy go," she sighed when she discovered that it was gone.* □ *I won a blender in the school raffle, but my kids knocked it off the counter and broke it. Come easy, go easy.*

Eat, drink, and be merry, for tomorrow we die. Enjoy yourself whenever you can, because you may die soon. (**Eat, drink, and be merry** by itself is simply a way of encouraging people to enjoy themselves.) □ FRED: *No cake for me, thank you. I'm on a diet.* JANE: *But, Fred, this is a birthday party. Eat, drink, and be merry.* □

Natasha encouraged all her guests to eat, drink, and be merry, for tomorrow we die.

Eat someone out of house and home   To eat a very great deal; or, to cost too much to support. □ *When I invited my grandson to stay with me all summer, I wasn't aware he was going to eat me out of house and home.* □ *You can't possibly take in another stray cat. The twelve cats you already have are eating you out of house and home as it is.*

Eat to live, not live to eat.   Do not be gluttonous; eating should not be your favorite activity, but something you do to maintain your health. □ JILL: *I can't wait till lunch. I want to get a pizza with everything on it, and a chocolate soda, and then for dessert. . . .* JANE: *Eat to live, not live to eat, OK, Jill?* □ *"Eat to live, not live to eat," was the doctor's advice to Gene, who was dangerously overweight.*

Eavesdroppers never hear any good of themselves. AND **Listeners never hear any good of themselves.**   If you eavesdrop on people who are talking about you, chances are that you will hear them say unfavorable things about you. (Implies that you should not eavesdrop.) □ CHILD: *Mommy, I heard Suzy and Lisa talking about me, and they said I was a crybaby!* MOTHER: *That just goes to show you, dear, that eavesdroppers never hear any good of themselves.* □ *I knew that Mother and Dad had gone into the other room to discuss my situation, and I was tempted to put my ear to the door and listen to them, but I remembered that listeners never hear any good of themselves.*

Empty vessels make the most sound.   Foolish people make the most noise. □ *I suspect Brenda is not very smart. She chatters constantly, and as they say, empty vessels make the most sound.* □ ELLEN: *Mary's so viva-*

cious, always so talkative. FRED: *Yes. Empty vessels make the most noise.*

Enough is as good as a feast.   You do not need more than enough of anything. □ *We don't have much of a surplus of food for dinner tonight, but enough is as good as a feast.* □ SANDRA: *I wish I could offer you more lavish hospitality.* JANE: *Don't be silly. Enough is as good as a feast.*

Enough to keep body and soul together   Very little; only enough to survive. (Usually refers to money.) □ *When he worked for the library, Marshall only made enough to keep body and soul together.* □ *Maria's savings were just enough to keep body and soul together while she looked for another job.*

Escape by the skin of one's teeth   Just barely escape. (Also the cliché: **by the skin of one's teeth,** just barely.) □ *Lloyd escaped from the burning building by the skin of his teeth.* □ JILL: *Did Grace manage to catch her plane?* JANE: *By the skin of her teeth.*

Even a worm will turn.   Even a meek person will become angry if you abuse him or her too much. □ *You'd better stop maltreating Angela. She's a mild-mannered woman, but even a worm will turn.* □ JILL: *Did you hear Cathy yelling at Fred today? She finally told him to stop pestering her.* JANE: *I guess the worm has turned!*

(Even) the best of friends must part.   Even very good friends cannot stay together forever. □ CHILD: *I don't want Debby to move away. She's my best friend.* MOTHER: *Sometimes the best of friends must part, honey, even if they don't want to.* □ *Even the best of friends must part, so it shouldn't surprise you that you lose touch with your acquaintances after a while.*

Every cloud has a silver lining.   You can derive some benefit from every bad thing that happens to you. (You can also refer to the silver lining of a particular cloud, the benefit you can derive from a particular misfortune.) □ *I'm sorry your business is going badly, but don't despair. Every cloud has a silver lining.* □ *When Mary's friends visited her in the hospital, they tried to cheer her up, but Mary never could find the silver lining in the cloud of her illness.*

Every dog has his day. Everyone will be fortunate at least once; everyone will have at least a brief opportunity to be in power. □ JILL: *Eric really seems to enjoy being grand marshal of the parade.* JANE: *Every dog has his day, and I guess this is Eric's.* □ PENELOPE: *Emily won the lottery last month, and today she won a bicycle in the school raffle. I never win anything.* SANDRA: *Cheer up. Every dog has his day.*

Every family has a skeleton in the closet. Every family has an unpleasant secret. (Also the cliché: **a skeleton in the closet,** an unpleasant secret.) □ *Every family has a skeleton in the closet; for the Chapmans, it was their oldest son's criminal record.* □ *Although the Norrises seem very wholesome and aboveboard, I'm convinced that there's a skeleton in their closet.*

Every horse thinks its own pack heaviest. Everyone thinks he or she has the hardest work to do or the most difficult problems to overcome. □ JILL: *I can't believe Maria had the nerve to complain about her bad manicure as if it were a serious problem.* JANE: *You can't really blame her. Every horse thinks its own pack heaviest.* □ *When we were growing up, my sister and I each thought our own chores were harder than the other's. Every horse thinks its own pack heaviest.*

Every Jack has his Jill. Every man will eventually find a woman to be his romantic partner. □ BILL: *I'll never have a girlfriend. None of the girls I take out will agree to a second date.* FRED: *Cheer up; every Jack has his Jill.*

☐ *No one in town could imagine any woman loving Eustace, but every Jack has his Jill, and Eustace did find a wife.*

Every man for himself (and the devil take the hindmost). AND **Devil take the hindmost** Everyone has to fight for his or her own survival. (You can use this to describe an extremely competitive situation.) ☐ *At first we tried to help each other study for the exam, but soon it was every man for himself, and the devil take the hindmost.* ☐ *The inventors tried to collaborate, agreeing to share the profits from their invention, but they grew so suspicious of each other that each began to work separately, and devil take the hindmost.* ☐ *When the government collapsed, it was every man for himself.*

Every man has his price. It is possible to bribe anyone as long as you know what to bribe him or her with. ☐ HENCHMAN: *I've offered the judge half a million dollars to give you a light sentence, but he says he can't be bought.* GANGSTER: *Keep trying. Every man has his price.* ☐ *Every man has his price, and the townsfolk were shocked to discover just how low their mayor's price had been.*

Every man is the architect of his own fortune. Your own decisions and your own actions determine what your life will be like. ☐ *The teacher told us, "If you work hard, you can become whatever you want. Every man is the architect of his own fortune."* ☐ *You shouldn't blame other people for your problems. Every man is the architect of his own fortune.*

Every man to his taste. Everyone likes something different, and you should not condemn anyone for liking what he or she likes. (Can be used to remark that someone's tastes are different from yours, as in the first example.) ☐ JILL: *Why don't you get some decent neckties, Fred?* FRED: *What do you mean, decent? My ties are perfectly* *fine!* JILL: *Oh, well. Every man to his taste.* □ ELLEN: *People who like cats are much more discerning than people who like dogs, don't you think?* JANE: *Not necessarily. Everyone to his taste.*

Every tub must stand on its own bottom. AND **Let every tub stand on its own bottom.** Everyone must support himself or herself; people should be independent. □ *Emily did not want to join the other students, who were helping each other study for the exam. "Every tub must stand on its own bottom," she said.* □ *Don't ask me for help. Let every tub stand on its own bottom.*

Everybody loves a lord. People are attracted to the wealthy and powerful. □ *It seemed that the entire city had come to the airport to watch the duke's plane land. Everybody loves a lord.* □ *Although the prince was vulgar and unpleasant, he always received plenty of invitations to social gatherings; everybody loves a lord.*

Everything comes to him who waits. See *Good things come to him who waits.*

Evil be to him who evil thinks. May bad things happen to anyone who thinks evil things. (A curse against those who wish you harm. This is the English version of the French *Honi soit qui mal y pense,* the motto of the Most Noble Order of the Garter, a British order of knighthood.) □ *The secret brotherhood took an oath of loyalty and finished their meeting by declaring, "Evil be to him who evil thinks."* □ BILL: *There's no way in the world you can get that clock fixed by the time your wife comes home.* FRED: *Evil be to him who evil thinks!*

Example is better than precept. You will teach people more effectively by being a good example than you will by telling them what to do. □ FRED: *I don't know what's wrong with my employees. I can't get the idiots to be polite, no matter what I say.* SANDRA: *Keep in mind that ex-*

ample is better than precept. □ *Mother never lectured us; she just tried her best to be a good person, and we tried hard to be like her. She was living proof that example is better than precept.*

Experience is the best teacher. You will learn more from things that happen to you than you will from hearing about things that happen to other people. □ *I don't care how many books you read about how to run a business; experience is the best teacher.* □ *The nurse believed that experience was the best teacher when it came to developing a bedside manner, so she made sure that all her students spent a lot of time with patients.*

Experience is the father of wisdom. AND **Experience is the mother of wisdom.** The more that happens to you, the more you will learn. □ SON: *The teacher made a mistake in class today, and I corrected him. I had no idea it would make him so mad.* MOTHER: *Experience is the father of wisdom, dear, and now you're a little wiser about people and their pride.* □ *I never understood why supervisors got so frustrated with me until I became a supervisor and got frustrated with my subordinates. Experience was definitely the mother of wisdom, in my case.*

Experience is the mother of wisdom. See the previous entry.

Experience is the teacher of fools. Only fools do not learn from other people's mistakes and insist on repeating them. □ FATHER: *You should spend more time studying and less time having fun with your friends. If I had been a better student when I was your age, I'd have a better job now.* SON: *Oh, come on, Dad. School's worthless.* FATHER: *Don't make the same mistake I did! Experience is the teacher of fools.* □ *Mother warned me against marrying a man from such a different background. Well, experience is the teacher of fools.*

F

Fact is stranger than fiction. AND **Truth is stranger than fiction.** Things that really happen are harder to believe than stories that people invent. □ *Did you see the story in the newspaper about the criminal who attacks people with a toenail clipper? Fact is stranger than fiction!* □ JILL: *I can't believe someone's really selling candles shaped like ice-cream cones.* JANE: *Truth is stranger than fiction.*

Faint heart never won fair lady. A timid suitor never won his lady. (Used to encourage boys or men to be bold in courting women.) □ BILL: *I'd really like to go out with Alice, but what if she says no?* ALAN: *You won't know till you ask her. Faint heart never won fair lady.* □ *Don't be so shy about talking to Edith. Faint heart never won fair lady.*

Faith will move mountains. If you believe in what you are doing, you can overcome any obstacle. □ *Victoria's faith in her cause could move mountains.* □ *You may feel disheartened sometimes, but remember that faith will move mountains.*

Fall between two stools To fail because you cannot decide between two choices; for someone or something to be difficult to classify because the entity is not clearly one thing or another. □ *George could not make up his*

*mind whether he was in love with Anna or with Roberta.
He fell between two stools; while he hesitated, they both
found different boyfriends.* □ *I thought Lydia was going
to buy Mother a birthday present, and Lydia thought I
was going to. Mother's gift sort of fell between two stools.*

Familiarity breeds contempt. People do not respect
someone they know well enough to know his or her
faults. □ *The movie star doesn't let anyone get to know
him, because he knows that familiarity breeds contempt.* □ JILL: *I used to think Fred was an admirable
guy, but now that I work for him, I'm learning that he's
more or less a rat.* JANE: *Familiarity breeds contempt,
huh?*

Far from the madding crowd In a quiet, restful place.
(From Thomas Gray's poem, "Elegy Written in a Country
Churchyard.") □ *Julia sat daydreaming at her desk,
wishing she were far from the madding crowd.* □ SAN-
DRA: *Where shall we go this weekend?* ALAN: *Anywhere, as
long as it's far from the madding crowd.*

Feed a cold and starve a fever. You should feed someone who has a cold, and withhold food from someone
who has a fever; or, if you feed someone who has a cold,
he or she will develop a fever, and you will have to withhold food until the person gets better. □ JILL: *I don't feel
like going out to lunch with you. I have a cold.* JANE: *All
the more reason you should get something to eat. Feed a
cold and starve a fever, you know.* □ *I know you're hungry, but your fever's still high, and I have to feed a cold
and starve a fever.*

Feel something in one's bones To intuit something. □
*Something bad is going to happen today. I can just feel it
in my bones.* □ JILL: *I don't think we should go to Marcia's party.* JANE: *Why not?* JILL: *I can't really explain it.
I feel it in my bones.*

Fiddle while Rome burns   To do something frivolous during an emergency. □ *Because Dr. Hopkins played golf every Wednesday during the great epidemic, many people accused him of fiddling while Rome burned.* □ SECRETARY: *There's a team of investigative reporters outside, and they want to know what happened to all the money missing from the city treasury.* MAYOR: *I'll talk to them later. Right now I'm busy playing my new computer game.* SECRETARY: *How can you fiddle while Rome burns?*

Fields have eyes, and woods have ears.   Even though you are outside in an apparently empty landscape, someone may be eavesdropping on you. □ JILL: *You said you had a secret. Tell me.* JANE: *Not here.* JILL: *But there's nobody else in the park.* JANE: *Fields have eyes, and woods have ears.* □ *Rick and Celia pursued their courtship as they walked home from school together, forgetting that fields have eyes, and woods have ears.*

Fight fire with fire   Use against your opponent the same methods he or she is using against you. □ *After her opponent had spent several weeks slandering her, the candidate decided to fight fire with fire.* □ *When evangelists would come to our house and try to convert us, Mother would fight fire with fire and try to convert them to her religion.*

Fight tooth and nail   Fight with all your resources; fight as hard as possible. □ *The lobbyist fought tooth and nail for the bill to be passed into law.* □ *If you try to take custody of my children away from me, I will fight you tooth and nail.*

Finders keepers(, losers weepers).   If you find something, you are entitled to keep it. (This is a children's rhyme and sounds childish when used by adults.) □ BILL: *Hey! How come you're using my fountain pen?* FRED: *It's mine now. I found it on the floor—finders keepers, losers*

weepers. □ CHILD: *That's my hat. You can't have it.* PLAY-
MATE: *I found it. Finders keepers.*

Fine feathers make fine birds. If you dress elegantly,
people will think you are elegant. (Can be used ironically, to suggest that even though someone dresses well,
he or she is not a high-class person.) □ BILL: *I don't see
why I should have to wear a necktie for a job interview.*
JANE: *Fine feathers make fine birds.* □ ELLEN: *Bruce's
girlfriend looks terribly out of place in an evening
gown, doesn't she? I bet she's never been out of blue jeans
before in her life.* FRED: *Fine feathers make fine birds.*

Fine words butter no parsnips. Just because someone
promises something does not guarantee that he or she
will do it. (Can be used as a rebuke, implying that the
person you are addressing is promising something he or
she will not do, as in the second example.) □ PENELOPE:
*Tom promised he would buy me any house I want if I
marry him!* SANDRA: *Fine words butter no parsnips.* □
FRED: *Sweetheart, I'm very sorry I've been so short-
tempered. I'll never, never be like that anymore.* ELLEN:
Fine words butter no parsnips.

Fingers were made before forks. It is all right to eat
with one's fingers because people had to eat somehow
before there were forks. (You can use this to justify eating something with your fingers.) □ MOTHER: *Put that
chicken wing back on your plate and eat it properly,
with a knife and fork.* CHILD: *But Mom, fingers were
made before forks.* □ *I don't see why it's considered bad
manners to eat with your fingers. Fingers were made before forks.*

Fire is a good servant but a bad master. You must be
careful to keep fire under control so that it will not hurt
you. □ *Don't play with the candle flames, children. Fire
is a good servant but a bad master.* □ *At camp, we*

learned how to build and extinguish fires safely, since fire is a good servant but a bad master.

First catch your hare. Do not make plans about what you will do when you have something until you actually have it. □ JILL: *When I win the sports car in the raffle, I'll drive it out to California to see my brother, and then I'll take a trip down to Mexico, and then—* JANE: *First catch your hare. You don't have that sports car yet.* □ FRED: *When I buy my house on the beach, you can spend summers with me there.* ELLEN: *First catch your hare.*

First come, first served. The first people to arrive will be able to get the best choices. □ *You can't reserve a seat at the movie theater; it's strictly first come, first served.* □ *We should get to the book sale as soon as they open; it's first come, first served.*

First impressions are the most lasting. People will remember the way you appear when you first meet them, so it is important to be your best when you meet someone for the first time. □ *George spent two hours picking just the right clothes to wear when he met the influential lawyer, since he knew that first impressions are the most lasting.* □ *Andrew fervently hoped that first impressions would not be the most lasting with Elaine, since he had been boisterously drunk when he first met her.*

First see the light of day To be born; to come into being. (Can be said figuratively of books or ideas, as in the second example.) □ *My grandfather has taken care of me since I first saw the light of day.* □ *Vincent's collection of short stories first saw the light of day in a privately printed edition three years ago.*

First things first Do things in the proper order; do not skip things that you should do first. □ JILL: *Should we go to the museum first, or should we go shopping?* JANE: *Let's eat lunch before we discuss it. First things first.* □

First things first: read the directions carefully before you try to assemble the bookcase.

Flog a dead horse AND **Beat a dead horse** To insist on talking about something that no one is interested in, or that has already been thoroughly discussed. □ *The history teacher lectured us every day about the importance of studying history, until we begged him to stop flogging a dead horse.* □ JILL: *I think I'll write the company president another letter asking him to prohibit smoking in all the offices.* JANE: *There's no use beating a dead horse, Jill; he's already decided to let people smoke.*

Fool me once, shame on you; fool me twice, shame on me. After someone has tricked you once, you should be wary of him or her, so that that person cannot trick you again. □ FRED: *Would you like a can of peanuts?* SANDRA: *The last can of peanuts you gave me had a toy snake in it.* FRED: *This one really is peanuts.* SANDRA: *Fool me once, shame on you; fool me twice, shame on me.* □ *The last strawberries I bought from this market looked nice and red, but they tasted terribly bland. I won't buy strawberries here again. Fool me once, shame on you; fool me twice, shame on me.*

Fools rush in where angels fear to tread. Foolish people usually do not understand when a situation is dangerous, so they are not afraid to do things that would frighten more sensible people. □ ALAN: *Bob is too scared to go in and confront the boss, so I'm going to.* JANE: *Fools rush in where angels fear to tread.* □ *The firemen could tell that the burning house was about to collapse, and they hesitated to go inside. But Joe, unaware of the danger, ran in, grabbed the little boy, and brought him to safety. Fools rush in where angels fear to tread, and sometimes, as in this case, they get wonderful results.*

For want of a nail the shoe was lost; for want of a shoe the horse was lost; and for want of a horse the man was lost. Overlooking small details can have disastrous consequences. (You can quote any of the sentences in this proverb by themselves.) □ JILL: *I don't think we need to check our bicycle tires before we go for our ride.* JANE: *I disagree. For want of a nail the shoe was lost.* □ *Before we began the hike into the mountains, we checked our equipment painstakingly, remembering that for want of a horse the man was lost.*

Forewarned is forearmed. If you know about something beforehand, you can prepare for it. □ *Before you meet Lily, I should tell you that she's a little eccentric. Forewarned is forearmed, right?* □ *Check the temperature before you go outside. Forewarned is forearmed.*

Forgive and forget. You should not only forgive people for hurting you, you should also forget that they ever hurt you. □ *When my sister lost my favorite book, I was angry at her for weeks, but my mother finally convinced me to forgive and forget.* □ SANDRA: *Are you going to invite Sam to your party?* PENELOPE: *No way. Last year he laughed at my new skirt.* SANDRA: *Come on, Penelope, forgive and forget.*

Fortune favors the bold. See the following entry.

Fortune favors the brave. AND **Fortune favors the bold.** You will have good luck if you carry out your plans boldly. (Used to encourage people to carry out their plans.) □ *Fortune favors the bold, Vincent. Quit your day job and work on your novel full-time.* □ JILL: *Let's wait till next year before trying to start our own business.* JANE: *No. We'll do it this year. Fortune favors the brave.*

From the sublime to the ridiculous is only a step. Something grand can easily become very funny. (Also the cliché: **from the sublime to the ridiculous,** describing something grand turning into something funny.) ☐ *Vincent, I don't think you should include a bowl of breakfast cereal in your still-life painting. From the sublime to the ridiculous is only a step.* ☐ *The production of* Macbeth *went from the sublime to the ridiculous when Lady Macbeth came onstage in an old army uniform.*

G

Garbage in, garbage out. If you give nonsensical instructions to people or computers, those instructions will produce nonsensical results. □ JILL: *Why is my computer generating all this gibberish?* JANE: *You must have made a mistake in the program. Garbage in, garbage out.* □ *Ed insists that children are so ignorant nowadays because their teachers are incompetent. "Garbage in, garbage out," he says.*

Gather ye rosebuds while ye may. Enjoy yourself while you can, before you lose the opportunity or before you become too old. (From Robert Herrick's poem, "To the Virgins, to Make Much of Time.") □ PENELOPE: *Should I go out on a date with Robbie on Saturday, or should I stay home and study?* ELLEN: *Gather ye rosebuds while ye may.* □ *You ought to travel abroad now, while you're young, before you have responsibilities that might keep you from going. Gather ye rosebuds while ye may.*

Genius is an infinite capacity for taking pains. Genius is the quality of being exceedingly careful about everything you do. □ *If genius is an infinite capacity for taking pains, Marilyn certainly has it. She never overlooks a single detail that needs attention.* □ *If you want to be a great artist, you'll have to be more careful about your* *work. Genius is an infinite capacity for taking pains, after all.*

Genius is ten percent inspiration and ninety percent perspiration. People get brilliant results primarily by working hard, not because they have special inborn powers. □ CHILD: *Betty always does the best drawings in art class. She must be a genius.* FATHER: *If you worked hard, you could do just as well. Remember, genius is ten percent inspiration and ninety percent perspiration.* □ *Vincent got the inspiration for his novel in a momentary flash, but it took him two years of writing for eight hours a day to finish the book. He's a living example of the fact that genius is ten percent inspiration and ninety percent perspiration.*

Get down to brass tacks Do what everyone present has come together to do. (Casual.) □ *The members of the committee had exchanged pleasantries for ten minutes or so when the chairman suggested that they get down to brass tacks and discuss business.* □ FRED: *Hello, Ellen. You're looking lovely tonight.* ELLEN: *Let's get down to brass tacks, Fred. Do you have the money I asked you to bring?*

Get in on the ground floor Invest in an enterprise when it is just starting out, so that you will have influence over it when it expands. (Casual; associated with financial dealings.) □ *Jones is giving me a chance to get in on the ground floor of his new company.* □ *You can get in on the ground floor if you invest in our business now.*

Get it straight from the horse's mouth To get information from the person most directly involved. □ JILL: *Tracy is going to have a baby.* JANE: *Who told you that?* JILL: *I got it straight from the horse's mouth.* □ *There's a rumor that Randolph is moving to Alaska, but I won't believe it until I get it straight from the horse's mouth.*

Get up on the wrong side of the bed   To be in a bad mood for no obvious reason. (Asking someone ''Did you get up on the wrong side of the bed?'' is a playful way of remarking that the person is in a bad mood.) □ *Please forgive my little boy for being rude to you. He must have gotten up on the wrong side of the bed.* □ FRED: *I don't like those shoes you're wearing. The heels are too high for business attire. And I wish you'd get your suit cleaned more often.* SANDRA: *What's the matter with you? Did you get up on the wrong side of the bed?*

Give credit where credit is due.   To acknowledge someone's contribution or ability. □ JILL: *Sandra, that was a wonderful meal.* SANDRA: *I must give credit where credit is due; Alan helped with all of the cooking.* □ ELLEN: *Roger is pompous, petty, and immature. I think he's completely worthless.* JANE: *Now, Ellen, give credit where credit is due; he's also extremely smart.*

Give someone a dose of his own medicine   To mistreat or annoy someone in the same way that he or she mistreats or annoys other people. □ *Tom was in the habit of playing loud music when his neighbors were trying to sleep, until the night when they cranked up their stereo and gave him a dose of his own medicine.* □ *Don is always so rude to everyone; I wish someone would give him a dose of his own medicine.*

Give someone an inch and he'll take a mile.   See the following entry.

Give someone an inch and he'll take a yard. AND **Give someone an inch and he'll take a mile.**   Be generous to someone and the person will demand even more. (Describes someone who will take advantage of you if you are even a little kind to him or her.) □ *If you let Mark borrow your tools for this weekend, he'll wind up keeping them for years. Give him an inch and he'll take a* *mile.* □ *Lisa made the mistake of allowing George to use the office typewriter to type one personal letter, so now he uses it for all his personal typing. Give him an inch and he'll take a yard.*

Give someone enough rope and he'll hang himself. If you give someone the freedom to behave badly, eventually he or she will not be able to escape punishment. □ JILL: *I think Matilda's been stealing things out of my desk. Should I tell the boss?* JANE: *No; give her enough rope and she'll hang herself. One of these days she'll steal something important, the boss will find out for himself, and he'll fire her.* □ *Rather than reprimand their son for his reckless driving, Larry's parents decided that if they gave him enough rope he would hang himself. Sure enough, he was soon arrested for ignoring a stop sign, and the fine he had to pay convinced him to be more careful.*

Give someone the benefit of the doubt To assume that someone is acting in good faith even though it is possible that he or she is being dishonest. □ CUSTOMER: *I would like to exchange this toaster. When I got it home, I discovered that it was broken.* CLERK: *How do I know you didn't break it?* CUSTOMER: *Give me the benefit of the doubt.* □ STUDENT: *I'm sorry I haven't done my homework; my grandmother died last week and I was too busy going to the funeral.* TEACHER: *Your excuse sounds dubious, but I'll give you the benefit of the doubt.*

Give the devil his due To acknowledge the achievements or abilities of someone you do not like. □ *Arthur is a hateful person, but to give the devil his due, he is extremely intelligent.* □ *After telling us George's faults in great detail, Melinda grudgingly gave the devil his due and admitted that he was an efficient worker.*

Give the shirt off one's back   To be extremely generous; to give anything that is asked for, even when you do not have very much to give. □ *Tom would give any of his old army buddies the shirt off his back.* □ *You can always count on Mark when you're in trouble; he'd give you the shirt off his back.*

Give us the tools, and we will finish the job.   A reply to someone who wants you to do a task for which you lack the equipment. □ FRED: *When are you going to finish writing that computer program?* JILL: *When you get our computer fixed. Give us the tools, and we will finish the job.* □ *How am I supposed to wash the upstairs windows without a ladder? Give us the tools, and we will finish the job!*

Go from bad to worse   To deteriorate; to get worse. □ *Beth's health went from bad to worse after her operation.* □ *Dorothy's been going from bad to worse since she lost her job.*

Go like the wind   To go very fast. □ *Emily's sleek new bicycle can really go like the wind.* □ *The racehorse went like the wind, beating its nearest opponent by several lengths.*

Go over something with a fine-tooth comb. AND **Go through something with a fine-tooth comb.**   To examine something very thoroughly. □ SANDRA: *Did you find the error in our checkbook?* ALAN: *I've been through the accounts with a fine-tooth comb, but I still can't figure out where we made the mistake.* □ *The detective went over the apartment with a fine-tooth comb, but he was unable to find any of the burglar's fingerprints.*

Go through something with a fine-tooth comb   See the previous entry.

God helps them that help themselves. AND **God helps those who help themselves.**   You cannot rely on divine help, but must work yourself to get what you want. □ *You can't spend your days waiting for a good job to find you. God helps those that help themselves.* □ *If you want a better education, start studying. God helps those who help themselves.*

God takes soonest those he loveth best. Good people often die young. □ *The minister told the boy's grieving parents that God takes soonest those he loveth best.* □ *It may seem to us that Nancy was too young to die, but God takes soonest those he loveth best.*

God's in his heaven; all's right with the world. Everything is just as it should be. (You can use this proverb to express satisfaction, joy, or contentment.) □ *Now that my wife has returned from her long trip, God's in his heaven; all's right with the world.* □ SANDRA: *I finally fixed our TV set.* ALAN: *God's in his heaven; all's right with the world.*

Going to hell in a handbasket Deteriorating fast; becoming extremely bad. (Casual.) □ *With all the banks closing and businesses going bankrupt, the economy is going to hell in a handbasket.* □ *Phil's drinking is so bad, he's really going to hell in a handbasket.*

Gone (before) but not forgotten Dead but still remembered. (Describes someone who has died but who is not forgotten by the people who knew him or her. Most often used as an epitaph.) □ *On Mildred's gravestone was written, "Beloved wife and mother, gone but not forgotten."* □ *William was gone, but certainly not forgotten; his wife and children thought of him every day.*

Good fences make good neighbors. It is easier to be friendly with your neighbor if neither of you trespasses upon the other's property or privacy. □ *My mother warned me against spending all my time with my best friend. "Good fences make good neighbors," she said,*

"*and eventually you will both want some time alone.*" □
SANDRA: *The guy next door is letting his party guests
wander across our lawn again.* ALAN: *I guess we'll have
to build a fence there. Good fences make good neighbors,
like they say.*

Good men are scarce. AND **A good man is hard to find.**
There are only a few good people in the world. □ *Larry
is the best employee I've ever had, and I'll go to a good
deal of effort to keep him, because good men are scarce.*
□ *"I think you should marry John," Amanda advised
her daughter. "He's a good man, and a good man is hard
to find."*

Good riddance to bad rubbish! Good to be rid of that
person or thing! (Said when you hear that someone or
something you think is bad has been disposed of. Expresses your satisfaction that the bad thing is gone.) □
JILL: *Fred moved out of town; I guess I won't be seeing
him anymore.* JANE: *Good riddance to bad rubbish! I
never did like him.* □ ALAN: *I got such a bad stain on my
gray suit last night that I think I'll have to throw the suit
away.* SANDRA: *Good riddance to bad rubbish! That suit
made you look like an undertaker.*

Good seed makes a good crop. Starting with good materials will help you get good results. □ JILL: *Elsie and Jim
are going to have a baby.* JANE: *I'm sure it will be a good
child, since they're both such good people. Good seed
makes a good crop.* □ *I am sure Robert's business will
flourish. He's capable and honest, and good seed makes a
good crop.*

Good things come in small packages. See *The best
things come in small packages.*

Good things come to him who waits. AND **Everything
comes to him who waits.** You should be patient and
wait for what you want. □ FRED: *Why is it taking you so*

long to get dinner ready? Can't you hurry up? ELLEN: *Good things come to him who waits.* □ JILL: *I wish our train would get here.* JANE: *Everything comes to her who waits.*

Governments have long arms. See *Kings have long arms.*

Great minds think alike. Very intelligent people tend to come up with the same ideas at the same time. (Used playfully, to commend someone for expressing the same thing you were thinking of; implies that you are congratulating that person for being as smart as you are. Also **Great minds run in the same gutters**, a casual and jocular variant.) □ JILL: *Let's ride our bikes to the store instead of walking.* JANE: *I was just thinking we should do that, too.* JILL: *Great minds think alike.* □ ALAN: *If we call the office and tell them we're sick today, we could go to that ball game.* SANDRA: *My thoughts exactly. Great minds run in the same gutters.*

Great oaks from little acorns grow. Immense things can come from small sources. □ JANE: *I was thinking of opening a day-care center at our church, but one little day-care center won't do much toward making sure all the kids in town get taken care of.* SANDRA: *But if you start day-care at your church, lots of other churches might follow your example. Great oaks from little acorns grow.* □ *Don't tell lies, not even small ones. Great oaks from little acorns grow.*

Grist for someone's mill See the following entry.

Grist for the mill AND **Grist for someone's mill** Something useful or needed. □ *Vincent bases the novels he writes on his own experience, so everything that happens to him is grist for the mill.* □ *Ever since I started making patchwork quilts, every scrap of cloth I find is grist for the mill.*

H

Half a loaf is better than none. Getting only part of what you want is better than not getting anything. □ FRED: *How did your court case go?* ALAN: *Not good. I asked for $500, and the judge only awarded me $200.* FRED: *Half a loaf is better than none.* □ *Laura agreed to pose for Vincent, but she refused to pose in the nude. Vincent, deciding that half a loaf was better than none, painted her with her clothes on.*

Half the truth is often a whole lie. If you do not tell the whole truth, you can mislead people more than if you tell them an outright lie. □ ELLEN: *Is it really true that Fred took all that money out of our savings account to buy me a present?* JANE: *Well, it's sort of true.* ELLEN: *Be careful what you say. Half the truth is often a whole lie.* □ JILL: *You lied to me.* JANE: *I did not. Everything I said was true.* □ JILL: *But you didn't tell me the whole story. And half the truth is often a whole lie.*

Half the world knows not how the other half lives. You cannot understand what life is like for people who are different from you; often, rich people do not know what it is like to be poor, and poor people do not know what it is like to be rich. (Also the cliché: **the way the other half lives,** the way life is for someone who is different from you.) □ *Jim's family had never been very well-to-*

do. Until he spent school vacation at his friend Richard's country home, Jim was never aware that some people do not have to work for a living. He was also bewildered by the array of forks set by his plate at every meal. He had discovered that half the world knows not how the other half lives. □ *Tom decided to dress in secondhand clothes and spend the weekend among the homeless men in the warehouse district, to see how the other half lives.*

Handsome is as handsome does. It is more important to treat people well than to be good-looking; just because you are good-looking does not mean you are a good person. □ JILL: *Don't you sometimes wish that your husband were not so homely?* SANDRA: *Handsome is as handsome does, and I'd rather have Alan than any movie star.* □ JILL: *I'd like to get to know George better.* JANE: *Why?* JILL: *He's so handsome.* JANE: *Handsome is as handsome does. He's a very unpleasant person.*

Happy is the bride that the sun shines on. It is supposed to be good luck for the sun to shine on a couple on their wedding day. □ *Our wedding day was a sunny one, and most of my relatives made sure to remind me, "Happy is the bride that the sun shines on."* □ *I'm sure you'll have a wonderful married life. It's a fine, sunny day, and happy is the bride that the sun shines on.*

Happy is the country which has no history. Since history usually records only violent, unfortunate, or tumultuous events, a country with no history would be a country lucky enough to have no such unhappy events to record. □ *The history of our country is so full of greed, violence, and dishonesty; happy is the country which has no history.* □ *Brian says he would like to live in some obscure little country that no one's ever heard of, since happy is the country which has no history. The problem is, he can't find one.*

Hard words break no bones. Verbal abuse does not physically hurt you, and therefore you should not be very upset by it. (Can be used to reply to someone who is verbally abusing you.) □ JILL: *I can't believe some of the names Fred called me.* JANE: *Well, hard words break no bones.* □ FRED: *Idiot! Numbskull!* BILL: *Hard words break no bones.*

(Has the) cat got your tongue? Why are you not saying anything? (Often said by adults to children.) □ *Grandpa used to terrify me, both because he was big and fierce-looking and because he usually greeted me by bellowing, "Cat got your tongue?"* □ *Hi, Lisa! How are you? How's your husband? Are you surprised to see me? What's the matter, has the cat got your tongue?*

Haste makes waste. You do not save any time by working too fast; hurrying will cause you to make mistakes, and you will have to take extra time to do the job over again. □ JILL: *If I hurry, I can finish typing this paper before lunch.* JANE: *Be careful. Haste makes waste.* □ FRED: *Hurry up and get my car fixed.* ALAN: *Don't rush me. Haste makes waste.*

Haul someone over the coals. AND **Rake someone over the coals** To reprimand or punish someone severely. □ *The boss ordered Phil into her office and proceeded to haul him over the coals.* □ *I admit I made a mistake, but there's no need to rake me over the coals.*

Have a bee in one's bonnet To have an obsession about something. □ *Edward has a bee in his bonnet about cleanliness; he takes at least four showers every day.* □ *Paper clips are the bee in Lena's bonnet. If she sees a paper clip lying on the sidewalk she can't walk by without picking it up.*

Have a bone to pick (with someone) To have a complaint; to have something you want to argue about with someone. □ *I've got a bone to pick with you. Why did you leave your wet towels all over the bathroom floor?* □ ALAN: *Max called while you were out.* SANDRA: *What did he want?* ALAN: *He sounded as if he had a bone to pick.*

Have a chip on one's shoulder   To be belligerent; eager for a fight. □ *Be careful around Jill today. She's really got a chip on her shoulder.* □ FRED: *You're the most unreasonable person I've ever had to deal with. Are you trying to make me fire you?* JANE: *Boy, have you got a chip on your shoulder. Calm down.*

Have a finger in every pie   To be involved in many different affairs; to profit from many different enterprises. □ *Johnson wasn't just a newspaper editor; he had a finger in every pie, from politics to the fine arts.* □ *My boss does her best to have a finger in every pie in this corporation.*

Have an ace up one's sleeve   To have something concealed that will ensure that you win. □ *The basketball coach has an ace up his sleeve. The other team doesn't know that he hasn't put his best player in the game yet.* □ *My opponent thinks he has beaten me, but I have an ace up my sleeve.*

Have an axe to grind   To have a grievance that you constantly talk about or act upon, even when it is inappropriate to do so. □ JILL: *This columnist always blames political liberals for all the country's problems.* JANE: *Yes, he does have an axe to grind, doesn't he?* □ *It's not that I have an axe to grind; it's just that I think this issue is really important.*

Have bats in the belfry   To be crazy. (Casual. Also *bats, batty* crazy.) □ JILL: *Tony told me there's going to be an enormous earthquake here next month.* JANE: *Don't listen to Tony. He's got bats in the belfry.* □ *My job is enough to drive anyone bats.*

Have better (or other) fish to fry To have better (or other) things to do. (Somewhat casual.) □ *I can't stand around arguing with you all day. I have other fish to fry.* □ *After watching the uninspiring softball game for two innings, Jill decided she had better fish to fry and left the ballpark.*

Have one foot in the grave To be close to death; to be extremely ill. (Blunt; not polite to say about the person you are addressing or someone who is important to the person you are addressing.) □ JILL: *I went to see Eddie in the hospital yesterday.* JANE: *How is he?* JILL: *Looks like he's got one foot in the grave, I'm sorry to say.* □ *To hear Joe talk, you'd think his mother's got one foot in the grave, but in fact she's recovering nicely.*

Have second thoughts To regret or reverse an earlier decision. □ *Yesterday I was sure I wanted to resign from my job, but today I'm having second thoughts.* □ JILL: *We should buy our plane tickets soon, or the price will go up.* JANE: *I don't know, Jill; maybe we shouldn't take this trip.* JILL: *Don't tell me you're having second thoughts about going!*

Have the courage of one's convictions To be brave because you are doing what you believe is right. □ JILL: *Alice is so brave to speak out against the administration.* JANE: *Well, she has the courage of her convictions.* □ SCIENTIST: *Maybe I shouldn't publish my results. What if they're not right?* ASSISTANT: *Have the courage of your convictions. If you believe the results are right, publish them.*

Have too many irons in the fire To have too many commitments. □ *I'd love to go to Florida with you, but I've got too many irons in the fire to contemplate a pleasure trip right now.* □ *Don't volunteer to work at the hospital; you have too many irons in the fire already.*

Have too much of a good thing   To hurt yourself by over-indulging in something good. (Often used in the phrase, "You can have too much of a good thing.") □ *I've gained five pounds from all the holiday dinners I've eaten this month. I think I had too much of a good thing.* □ ALAN: *We're having such a good time at this resort, why don't we stay a month instead of just a week?* SANDRA: *I think we'd get bored with it if we stayed that long. You can have too much of a good thing, you know.*

He gives twice who gives quickly.   When someone asks you for something, it is more helpful to give something right away than to wait, even if you might be able to give more if you waited. □ *We need your contributions to help the victims of the hurricane. And remember: he gives twice who gives quickly.* □ *Morris didn't have all the money his sister asked for, but he sent what he had immediately, knowing that he gives twice who gives quickly.*

He lives long who lives well.   If you live virtuously, you will have a long life; a person who does not live virtuously is wasting his life. □ *The pastor, exhorting his congregation to live moral lives, said, "He lives long who lives well."* □ CHILD: *Why should I be good? It's hard, and nobody appreciates it.* FATHER: *Sometimes that's true, but he lives long who lives well.*

He that cannot obey cannot command.   If you want to become a leader, you should first learn how to follow someone else. □ *You may think you're impressing your boss by challenging every order he gives you, but it only makes you look incompetent. He that cannot obey cannot command.* □ *Jones can't seem to do anything I ask him to. He'll never get anywhere; he that cannot obey cannot command.*

He that hath a full purse never wanted a friend.   A rich person always has plenty of friends. □ JILL: *Ever since Joe won the lottery, he's been getting congratulations from friends and relatives he hasn't heard from in years.* JANE: *You know how it is. He that hath a full purse never wanted a friend.* □ *When Mark inherited his grandfather's millions, he discovered that he that hath a full purse never wanted a friend.*

He that is down need fear no fall.   If you have nothing, you cannot lose anything by taking a risk. □ *Jim spent his last ten dollars on lottery tickets, figuring that he who is down need fear no fall.* □ *The basketball team became more aggressive and daring after their long losing streak, since he that is down need fear no fall.*

He that would eat the kernel must crack the nut.   You have to work if you want to get anything good. □ *If you want to be a good pianist, you have to practice every day. He that would eat the kernel must crack the nut.* □ *Rebuilding this poor old house is a tough job, but he that would eat the kernel must crack the nut.*

He that would go to sea for pleasure, would go to hell for a pastime.   Being a sailor is so unpleasant that anyone who would do it for fun must be crazy. □ OLD SAILOR: *Why did you decide to go to sea?* YOUNG SAILOR: *I thought it would be fun.* OLD SAILOR: *He that would go to sea for pleasure, would go to hell for a pastime.* □ *After I got out of school, I thought I might have a good time if I joined the Navy. My uncle, who had been a sailor, laughed, "He that would go to sea for pleasure, would go to hell for a pastime."*

He that would have eggs must endure the cackling of hens.   You must be willing to endure unpleasant, irritating things in order to get what you want. □ PENELOPE: *I'm tired of working after school. All the customers at the* *store are so rude.* MOTHER: *But you wanted money to buy a car. He that would have eggs must endure the cackling of hens, dear.* □ *Because they were jealous of her good grades, Maria's fellow law students spread malicious rumors about her. This sometimes daunted Maria, but she was determined to become a lawyer. She knew that he that would have eggs must endure the cackling of hens.*

He that would the daughter win, must with the mother first begin. If you want to marry a woman, you should find a way to impress her mother, so that the mother will favor her marrying you. □ HARRY: *I think I want to marry Gina.* BILL: *Don't propose to her until you're sure her mother is on your side. He that would the daughter win, must with the mother first begin.* □ *When you take flowers to your girlfriend, make sure to take some to her mother as well. Remember, he that would the daughter win, must with the mother first begin.*

He travels fastest who travels alone. It is easier to achieve your goals if you do not have a spouse, children, or other connections to consider. □ *I love you, but I can't ask you to marry me. I've got ambitions, and he travels fastest who travels alone.* □ JILL: *Don't go yet! Wait for me to get ready.* JANE: *But you always take at least half an hour. No wonder they always say that he travels fastest who travels alone.*

He who begins many things, finishes but few. If you start a lot of projects, you will not have time and energy to complete them all. (Can be used to warn someone against starting too many projects.) □ VINCENT: *I've got ideas for six different novels to write, and then of course I want to paint Elaine's portrait, and. . . .* ALAN: *Don't be so ambitious. Remember, he who begins many things, finishes but few.* □ *Sarah's room is littered with sweaters and mittens she started to knit but never finished, a* testament to the fact that *she who begins many things, finishes but few.*

He who excuses himself accuses himself. By apologizing for something, you admit that you did it. □ *Maybe I should tell my boss I'm sorry for breaking the copy machine. On the other hand, he who excuses himself accuses himself.* □ JILL: *I spilled paint all over Sandra's books. I'd better apologize to her.* JANE: *But she doesn't know it was you who did that. She who excuses herself accuses herself, you know.*

He who fights and runs away, may live to fight another day. It may be cowardly to run away from a fight, but running away gives you a better chance of surviving. □ SANDRA: *What happened to you?* ALAN: *Two men just beat me up and took my wallet away.* SANDRA: *Did you try to get the wallet back?* ALAN: *Let's just say I believe that he who fights and runs away, may live to fight another day.* □ *The school bully told Phillip to meet him in the playground after school, but Phillip didn't keep the appointment. When his friends called him a coward, Phillip shrugged and said, "He who fights and runs away, may live to fight another day."*

He who hesitates is lost. People should act decisively. □ JILL: *Should I apply for that job? At first I thought I definitely should, but now I don't know.* . . . JANE: *She who hesitates is lost.* □ *Call that girl and ask her out. Call her right now. He who hesitates is lost.*

He who laughs last, laughs best. See the following entry.

He who laughs last, laughs longest. AND **He who laughs last, laughs best.** If someone does something nasty to you, that person may feel satisfaction, but you will feel even more satisfaction if you get revenge on that person. (Also the cliché: **to have the last laugh** or **get the last laugh**, to get revenge.) □ *Joe pulled a dirty trick on me,* *but I'll get him back. He who laughs last, laughs best.* □ *Mary put a frog in my bed last night, but tonight I'm going to get the last laugh.*

He who pays the piper calls the tune.   If you are paying for someone's services, you can dictate exactly what you want that person to do. □ *When Mrs. Dalton told the artist what she wanted her portrait to look like, the artist cringed to think that anyone could have such bad taste. Still, he who pays the piper calls the tune, and Mrs. Dalton got what she wanted.* □ JILL: *Did you see that TV program about drilling for oil? They made the oil companies look like heroes.* JANE: *That's because the oil companies sponsored the program. He who pays the piper calls the tune.*

He who rides a tiger is afraid to dismount.   Sometimes it is more dangerous to stop doing a dangerous thing than it is to continue doing it. □ JILL: *You shouldn't take out another loan. You're already too far in debt.* JANE: *If I don't take out a loan, I can't make the payments on the loans I already have. You know how it is—she who rides a tiger is afraid to dismount.* □ JOE: *I can't stop lying to my parents about my grades. If I tell them that I'm failing, they'll kill me.* BILL: *He who rides a tiger is afraid to dismount, huh?*

He who sups with the devil should have a long spoon.
If you have dealings with dangerous people, you must be careful that they do not harm you. □ JILL: *Why are you going out to lunch with Chris so often? You know the horrible things he did to Melissa.* JANE: *He may be able to help me advance my career.* JILL: *Just remember that he who sups with the devil should have a long spoon.* □ *If you're going to hang out with that disreputable bunch of people, keep in mind that he who sups with the devil should have a long spoon.*

He who would climb the ladder must begin at the bottom. If you want to gain high status, you must start with low status and slowly work upwards. □ *After you graduate from college, don't expect your first job to be glamorous and well paying. He who would climb the ladder must begin at the bottom.* □ *Although Thomas hoped to become a famous journalist, he didn't mind working for a small-town newspaper at first. "He who would climb the ladder must begin at the bottom," he said.*

Heaven protects children, sailors, and drunken men. Children, sailors, and drunks often escape being injured in dangerous situations. (*Sailors* is sometimes omitted from the list, and *drunkards* or *drunks* can be used instead of *drunken men*. Often used to express amazement that a child, sailor, or drunk person has not been injured.) □ Jill: *Did you hear? A little girl fell out of a second-floor window in our apartment building.* Jane: *Was she killed?* Jill: *She wasn't even hurt.* Jane: *Heaven protects children, sailors, and drunken men.* □ *Arthur was so drunk he shouldn't even have been conscious, but he managed to drive home without hurting himself or anyone else; heaven protects children and drunkards.*

Hell hath no fury like a woman scorned. There is nothing as unpleasant as a woman who has been offended or whose love has not been returned. □ *When Mary Ann discovered that George was not in love with her, George discovered that hell hath no fury like a woman scorned.* □ Bill: *I'm getting tired of going out with Sylvia; I think I'll tell her we're through.* Fred: *Be careful. Hell hath no fury like a woman scorned, you know.*

Here today, (and) gone tomorrow. Available now, but soon to be gone. (Used to describe something that does not last—often an opportunity). □ *The stores near my house don't stay in business very long—here today, and* *gone tomorrow.* □ *If you want this carpet, buy it now. This sale price is here today, gone tomorrow.*

Here's mud in your eye! Drink up! (Said before taking a drink, in order to encourage someone with you to begin drinking too. Very casual.) □ *As he lifted his glass, Sam said, "Here's mud in your eye!"* □ *Lisa poured cocktails for everyone, then said, "Here's mud in your eye!" and took a sip of hers.*

Hide one's light under a bushel To conceal one's abilities. (Biblical.) □ *I don't believe Gloria is all that inept; I think she hides her light under a bushel.* □ *When the other children began to tease Nancy for being a "brain," Nancy hid her light under a bushel, deliberately performing badly in class.*

History repeats itself. The same kinds of events seem to happen over and over. □ *It seems that history is about to repeat itself for that poor country; it is about to be invaded again.* □ ALAN: *The country is headed for an economic depression.* SANDRA: *How do you know?* ALAN: *History repeats itself. The conditions now are just like the conditions before the last major depression.*

Hit the nail on the head To discern and state the crucial point. □ JILL: *Once we've found office space in an area we like, we can start our own business.* JANE: *So the first thing we need to do is figure out how much we can afford to pay for rent.* JILL: *Yes, you've hit the nail on the head. How much we can afford will determine what neighborhoods we should look in for offices.* □ *Last night we were discussing ways of recruiting more men to join our ballet class. Amy hit the nail on the head when she remarked that we'll need some way to convince men that ballet dancing is not effeminate.*

Hitch your wagon to a star. Always aspire to do great things; do not set pessimistic goals. (From Ralph Waldo

Emerson's essay, "Civilization.") □ *The speaker who delivered the high-school commencement address challenged the graduating students to hitch their wagons to a star.* □ VINCENT: *What do you want to be when you grow up?* CHILD: *I used to want to be a great actor, but my dad told me hardly anybody gets to be an actor, so now I have to pick something else.* VINCENT: *Nonsense. If you want to be an actor, then do your best to be an actor. Hitch your wagon to a star!*

Hoist with one's own petard   Hurt by something devised to hurt someone else. □ *Fred planned to play a trick on Allan, so he filled his cigar box with exploding cigars. However, he wound up hoist with his own petard; later on, he forgot about the trick cigars and lit one himself.* □ *Emily convinced everyone in the office that not every employee needed to be invited to every office party; she felt sure that the others would consequently exclude Beatrice, against whom she had a grudge. But she was hoist by her own petard in the end, since she herself suddenly stopped receiving party invitations.*

Hoist your sail when the wind is fair.   Begin a project when circumstances are the most favorable. □ *Don't ask your mother for permission now; she's in a bad mood. Hoist your sail when the wind is fair.* □ *Wait until the economy has stabilized before trying to start your own business. Hoist your sail when the wind is fair.*

Home is where the heart is.   People long to be at home; or, your home is whatever place you long to be. □ *I've had a lovely time visiting you, but home is where the heart is, and I think it's time I went back.* □ *If home is where the heart is, then my home is my parents' old house. I've never loved my own apartment the way I love their place.*

Honesty is the best policy. You should always tell the truth, even when it seems as if it would be useful to tell a lie. □ JILL: *I borrowed Jane's white blouse without asking her, and then I spilled tomato sauce on it. Should I tell her what happened, or should I just put the blouse back in her closet and hope she won't notice?* SANDRA: *Honesty is the best policy.* □ FRED: *I forgot that today is Ellen's birthday! What excuse should I give her?* JANE: *Honesty is the best policy.*

Hope deferred makes the heart sick. AND **Hope deferred maketh the heart sick.** If you have to wait a long time for something you want, you will become despairing. (Biblical.) □ *Charlie waited so long for the woman he loved that he decided he didn't want to love anybody. Hope deferred makes the heart sick.* □ JILL: *When am I going to get a promotion?* FRED: *Eventually.* JILL: *Hope deferred maketh the heart sick, Fred.*

Hope deferred maketh the heart sick. See the previous entry.

Hope for the best and prepare for the worst. You should have a cheerful attitude, but make sure you are ready for disaster. □ *While my father was in the hospital after his heart attack, we hoped for the best and prepared for the worst.* □ *When you study for a major exam, hope for the best and prepare for the worst. That is to say, don't make yourself anxious by worrying that it will be too difficult, but review your material as if you expect the exam to be extremely hard.*

Hope is a good breakfast but a bad supper. It is good to start the day feeling hopeful, but if none of the things you hope for come to pass by the end of the day, you will feel disappointed. (Can be used to warn someone against hoping for something that is unlikely to happen.) □ PENELOPE: *I hope Tommy will call me today.* SANDRA: *Hope is* *a good breakfast but a bad supper.* □ *Lisa began the day hoping that she would find work, and by the end of the day she had learned that hope is a good breakfast but a bad supper.*

Hope springs eternal (in the human breast). People will continue to hope even though they have evidence that things cannot possibly turn out the way they want. (From Alexander Pope's poem, "Essay on Man." Sometimes used to remark that you believe someone's situation is hopeless, as in the first example.) □ JILL: *The boss may have turned me down the first twelve times I asked for a raise, but this time I really think she'll give it to me.* JANE: *Hope springs eternal in the human breast.* □ ALAN: *You're not still trying to teach the dog to shake hands!* SANDRA: *Hope springs eternal.*

How the mighty have fallen. A jovial or mocking way of remarking that someone is doing something that he or she used to consider very demeaning. □ JILL: *Ever since Fred's wife left him, he has had to cook his own meals.* JANE: *Well! How the mighty have fallen!* □ *When Dan lost his money, he had to sell his expensive sports car. Now he drives an ugly old sedan. How the mighty have fallen.*

Hunger is the best sauce. Everything tastes especially good when you are hungry, because you are so eager to eat it. □ *After our twenty-mile hike, we stopped at a little roadside restaurant. It may have been that they made the most delicious food in the world there, or it may have been that hunger was the best sauce.* □ SANDRA: *Dinner is marvelous, Alan! I don't mind having waited till nine o'clock for you to finish cooking it.* ALAN: *Oh, it only tastes good because you had to wait. Hunger is the best sauce.*

I

I am not my brother's keeper. AND **Am I my brother's keeper?** You are not responsible for another person's doings or whereabouts. (Biblical. Also, *I am not someone's keeper.*) □ Fred: *Where's Robert?* Jane: *Am I my brother's keeper?* □ Jill: *How could you let Sandra run off like that?* Alan: *I'm not my brother's keeper.*

I would not touch it with a ten-foot pole. I would not have anything to do with it under any circumstances. (Said about something you think is untrustworthy, as in the first example, or in response to a remark that seems to invite a nasty reply, as in the second example. The British version is "I would not touch it with a barge-pole.") □ Jill: *This advertisement says I can buy land in Florida for a small investment. Do you think I should?* Jane: *I wouldn't touch it with a ten-foot pole.* □ Jane: *Can you believe this? Jill said she thinks I'm bossy. You don't think I'm bossy, do you?* Sandra: *I wouldn't touch that with a ten-foot pole.*

Idle folk have the least leisure. See the following entry.

Idle people have the least leisure. AND **Idle folk have the least leisure.** If you are not energetic and hard-working, you will never have any free time, since you will have to spend all your time finishing your work. □ *My grandmother always told me not to dawdle, since* *idle people have the least leisure.* □ JILL: *Every time I pass by Emily's desk, she's always staring out the window as if she has nothing to do. But whenever I ask her to lunch, she says she has too much work.* JANE: *She's a case of idle folk having the least leisure, I suspect.*

Idleness is the root of all evil. If you have no useful work to do, you will think of harmful things to do in order to amuse yourself. □ CHILD: *Why do you make me do so many chores?* FATHER: *Idleness is the root of all evil.* □ *Whenever Alice had some free time, she would try to find some useful thing to do around the house, since she believed that idleness is the root of all evil.*

If a thing is worth doing, it's worth doing well. If you are going to do something, do it as well as you possibly can. □ JILL: *Do we have to wash the walls before we paint them? It seems like such a lot of extra work.* FRED: *Yes, we have to. The paint won't stick properly otherwise. If a thing is worth doing, it's worth doing well.* □ *Bruce never did sloppy work. He believed that if something is worth doing, it's worth doing well.*

If anything can go wrong, it will. Every possible disaster will occur, whether you have prepared for it or not. (This saying is also referred to as "Murphy's Law.") □ FRED: *Your car should be fine now, as long as the battery doesn't die.* ALAN: *Then we'd better put a new battery in. If anything can go wrong, it will; so let's make sure it can't go wrong.* □ *I think this is going to be a bad day. If anything can go wrong, it will.*

If at first you don't succeed, try, try again. You have to keep trying until you get what you want. □ JILL: *I spent all morning trying to fix the computer, and it still won't work.* JANE: *If at first you don't succeed, try, try again.* □ *You'll learn that dance step eventually. If at first you don't succeed, try, try again.*

If God did not exist, it would be necessary to invent Him. People need a deity to worship. (This is an English translation of a quote from Voltaire. It is often parodied, using a person's name instead of *God* and implying that the person is somehow necessary.) □ *The atheist tried to convince Jerry that God does not exist, and that people should not waste their time worshiping Him. "But you can't stop people from worshiping God," Jerry replied. "If God did not exist, it would be necessary to invent Him." □ The unscrupulous mayor was such a convenient scapegoat for the city's problems that if she had not existed, it would have been necessary to invent her.*

If "ifs" and "ands" were pots and pans (there'd be no work for tinkers' hands). Wishing for things is useless. (Often said in reply to someone who says something beginning with "If only. . . .") □ DAUGHTER: *If only we didn't have to move out of town, I'd be the happiest girl in the world.* GRANDMOTHER: *If "ifs" and "ands" were pots and pans, there'd be no work for tinkers' hands.* □ JILL: *If Fred were more considerate, this would be a pretty decent office to work in.* JANE: *If "ifs" and "ands" were pots and pans. . . .*

If the mountain will not come to Mahomet, Mahomet must go to the mountain. If things do not change the way you want them to, you must adjust to the way they are. (*Mohammed* is often used instead of *Mahomet.* Also *the mountain has come to Mahomet,* something or someone that you would not expect to travel has arrived. There are many variations of this proverb. See the examples.) □ *The president won't see me so I will have to go to his office. If the mountain will not come to Mahomet, Mahomet must go to the mountain.* □ *If Caroline can't leave the hospital on her birthday, we'll have to take her birthday party to the hospital. If the mountain won't come to Mahomet, Mahomet will have to go to the mountain.* □

It's true I don't usually leave my home, but if you can't come to see me, I'll have to come see you. The mountain will come to Mohammed.

If the shoe fits(, wear it). An unflattering remark applies to you, so you should accept it. (Slightly rude.) □ FRED: *Hey, Jill, how's your love life?* JILL: *I don't like busybodies, Fred.* FRED: *Are you calling me a busybody?* JANE: *If the shoe fits, wear it.* □ ELLEN: *The professor told me I can't write!* BILL: *If the shoe fits, Ellen.*

If the truth were known If people knew how something really was, instead of how it appears to be. □ *If the truth were known, people wouldn't shop at that store. Its owners aren't as honest as they seem.* □ SAM: *You're always polite to Fred, but you don't really like him, do you?* ALAN: *Well, no, if the truth were known.*

If (the) worst comes to (the) worst In the worst possible circumstances; if the worst possible thing should happen. □ *We should be able to catch the four-thirty train, but if the worst comes to the worst, we could get a taxi and still get into town on time.* □ *Of course, I hope that your wife's health recovers, but if worst comes to worst, I want you to know that we'd be happy to have you stay with us.*

If two ride on a horse, one must ride behind. When two people do something together, one of them will be the leader and the other will have to be subordinate. □ SANDRA: *How come every time we get together, we always do what you want to do, and never do what I want to do?* ELLEN: *Well, dear, if two ride on a horse, one must ride behind.* □ *Grandma said, "Don't fool yourself thinking you'll have an equitable marriage. If two ride on a horse, one must ride behind."*

If wishes were horses, then beggars would ride. People make a lot of wishes, but wishing is useless. □ JILL: *If*

*I were Queen of the World, I would make sure that every-
one had enough to eat.* JANE: *And if wishes were horses,
then beggars would ride.* □ ALAN: *I sure wish I had one of
those expensive cameras.* SANDRA: *If wishes were horses,
then beggars would ride.*

If you can't be good, be careful.   If you are going to do
immoral things, make sure they are not dangerous; or, if
you are going to do something immoral, make sure to
keep it secret. (Sometimes used as a flippant way of saying good-bye.) □ *Be a good girl on your vacation trip. Or
if you can't be good, be careful.* □ *Ernest likes to close his
letters with, "If you can't be good, be careful."*

If you can't beat them, join them. AND **If you can't lick
'em, join 'em.**   If you have to give up fighting some
group, band together with them. (The "lick" version is
casual.) □ JILL: *I just got a kitten.* JANE: *I can't believe it!
You used to hate people who owned cats.* JILL: *If you can't
beat them, join them.* □ ALAN: *I hear you're a Republi-
can now.* FRED: *Yeah, I figured, if you can't lick 'em, join
'em.*

If you can't lick 'em, join 'em.   See the previous entry.

If you can't stand the heat, get out of the kitchen.   If
the pressures of some situation are too much for you,
you should leave that situation. (Somewhat insulting;
implies that the person you are addressing is not strong
enough to tolerate pressure.) □ ALAN: *I didn't think being a stockbroker could be so stressful.* FRED: *If you can't
stand the heat, get out of the kitchen.* □ JILL: *This exercise class is too tough; the teacher should let us slow
down.* JANE: *If you can't stand the heat, get out of the
kitchen.*

If you don't like it, (you can) lump it.   Things cannot be
changed to suit your preferences. □ *We're having fish
for dinner tonight. And if you don't like it, you can*

lump it. □ *We're going to go visit Aunt Sally this weekend. If you don't like it, lump it.*

If you don't make mistakes you don't make anything. If you try to do something, you will likely make mistakes; the only way to make no mistakes is to avoid trying to do anything. (Can be used to console someone who has made a mistake.) □ ALAN: *I'm sorry there's no dessert. I tried to make a cake, but I messed it up.* SANDRA: *That's OK, dear; if you don't make mistakes, you don't make anything.* □ *It's a shame that you ruined the sweater you were making, but if you don't make mistakes, you don't make anything.*

If you lie down with dogs, you will get up with fleas. If you associate with bad people, you will acquire their faults. □ GRANDDAUGHTER: *It's not fair. I'm starting to get a bad reputation just because I'm friends with Suzy and she has a bad reputation.* GRANDMOTHER: *It's only natural. People think that if you lie down with dogs, you will get up with fleas.* □ *If you keep hanging out with those dishonest boys, I won't trust you anymore. If you lie down with dogs, you will get up with fleas.*

If you play with fire you get burned. If you do something dangerous, you will get hurt. (Also the cliché: **to play with fire,** to do something dangerous or risky.) □ *Joe said, "I have no sympathy for race-car drivers who get injured. They should know that if you play with fire you get burned." □ My mother always told us that experimenting with hard drugs was playing with fire.*

If you run after two hares you will catch neither. You cannot do two things successfully at the same time. □ FRED: *I can be successful in business and get involved in raising my kids at the same time.* ALAN: *Don't be so sure. If you run after two hares you will catch neither.* □ VANESSA: *If I want to pursue my acting career, I'll have to* *take more days off to go to auditions. But I want to get ahead in the office, too.* JANE: *If you run after two hares you will catch neither.*

If you want a thing done well, do it yourself. You cannot rely on other people to do things properly for you. (Sometimes *right* is used instead of *well*.) □ *I asked my son to dice the vegetables for me, but he's cut them into chunks too big to use. I should have known: if you want a thing done well, do it yourself.* □ *Laura wouldn't trust professional auto mechanics, but did all her own car repair. "If you want something done right, do it yourself," she said.*

If you want peace, (you must) prepare for war. If a country is well armed, its opponents will be less likely to attack it. □ *Max was always arguing with those of his friends who believed in disarmament. "Getting rid of our weapons won't promote peace," he would say. "If you want peace, you must prepare for war." □ The politician argued that the country needed more munitions factories. "If you want peace, prepare for war," he said.*

If you would be well served, serve yourself. You should do things for yourself, since you cannot trust other people to do them exactly the way you want. □ *I would never hire a maid, because a maid wouldn't clean things the way I want them cleaned. Like they say: if you would be well served, serve yourself.* □ ALAN: *That mechanic always does a horrible job of fixing my car.* SANDRA: *If you would be well served, serve yourself, dear.*

If you're born to be hanged then you'll never be drowned. If you escape one disaster, it must be because you are destined for a different kind of disaster. (Sometimes used literally, to warn someone who has escaped drowning against gloating over his or her luck.) □ *When their ship was trapped in a terrible storm, Ellen* *told her husband that she feared they would die. "Don't worry," he replied with a yawn, "if you're born to be hanged then you'll never be drowned."* □ FRED: *A pipe burst in the subway line this morning, and I barely escaped drowning!* JANE: *If you're born to be hanged then you'll never be drowned, I guess.*

Ignorance (of the law) is no excuse (for breaking it). Even if you do not know that something is against the law, you can still be punished for doing it. □ POLICE OFFICER: *I'm giving you a speeding ticket.* MOTORIST: *But I didn't know I was exceeding the speed limit!* POLICE OFFICER: *Ignorance of the law is no excuse for breaking it.* □ *Terry protested that he didn't know it was illegal to break the windows of an abandoned building, but the judge informed him that ignorance of the law was no excuse.*

Imitation is the sincerest form of flattery. Copying someone is flattering because it shows you want to be like that person. □ CHILD: *Susie's doing everything I do. Make her stop.* MOTHER: *Don't be cross with her. Imitation is the sincerest form of flattery.* □ *Imitation may be the sincerest form of flattery, but I don't feel flattered when Mary copies my answers to the homework.*

In (at) one ear and out (of) the other Heard but not remembered. (Used to describe something that someone does not listen to.) □ ELLEN: *Did you tell Junior to be careful with the car when he drives it?* FRED: *Yes, but I think it went in one ear and out the other.* □ *The teacher felt that everything she told her students was in one ear and out the other.*

In like a lion, out like a lamb. See *March comes in like a lion, and goes out like a lamb.*

In the country of the blind, the one-eyed man is king. A person who is not particularly capable can attain a powerful position if the people around him or her are even less capable. □ JILL: *How on earth did Joe get promoted to be head of his department? He's such a blunderer!* JANE: *In the country of the blind, the one-eyed man is king.* □ *Matthew liked to work among people who, in his opinion, were not as smart as he was, since he had heard that in the country of the blind, the one-eyed man is king.*

In this day and age Nowadays; in modern times. □ JILL: *I heard that Anna became a nun.* JANE: *Do people still become nuns in this day and age?* □ *Nobody should have to live without indoor plumbing in this day and age.*

It is a long lane that has no turning. Bad times cannot continue forever; things will soon improve. □ NANCY: *It's been six months, and neither one of us can find work. I'm afraid we're going to starve to death.* BILL: *Don't despair, honey. It is a long lane that has no turning.* □ *Your luck has been bad for a long time, but it is a long lane that has no turning. I'm sure things will change soon.*

It is a poor heart that never rejoices. AND **It is a sad heart that never rejoices.** Even a habitually sad person cannot be sad all the time. (Sometimes used to indicate that a habitually sad person is happy about something.) □ JILL: *I've never seen Sam smile before, but today, at his retirement party, he smiled.* JANE: *It is a poor heart that never rejoices.* □ ALAN: *I think Phil is only happy when he's drunk.* SANDRA: *It is a sad heart that never rejoices.*

It is a sad heart that never rejoices. See the previous entry.

It is a wise child that knows its own father. You can never have certain proof that a certain man is your father. (Implies that the child in question might be illegitimate.) □ *It is a wise child that knows its own father, but Emily is so much like her dad that there's very little uncertainty.* □ BILL: *Your name is Joe Avery; are you Charles Avery's son?* JOE: *That's what my mother always told me, though it's a wise child that knows its own father.*

It is better to be born lucky than rich. If you are born rich, you may lose your money, but if you are born lucky, you will always get what you need or want just by chance. □ *Maybe your family doesn't have a lot of money, but you are lucky, you know. And it's better to be born lucky than rich.* □ *When Joseph was fifteen, his parents lost all their money. That was when he decided it would have been better to be born lucky than rich.*

It is better to give than to receive. AND **It is more blessed to give than to receive.** It is more virtuous to give things than to get them. (Biblical.) □ *Susan told her children, "Instead of thinking so much about what you want for your birthday, think about what to give your brothers and sisters for their birthdays. Remember, it is better to give than to receive."* □ *Our charity encourages you to share the good things you have. It is more blessed to give than to receive.*

It is better to travel hopefully than to arrive. You should enjoy the process of doing something, rather than anticipate the result of doing it. □ BILL: *I can't wait till I get my high school diploma.* FRED: *You should concentrate on enjoying high school instead. It is better to travel hopefully than to arrive.* □ *I like cooking food almost as much as I like eating what I cook. It's better to travel hopefully than to arrive, after all.*

It is better to wear out than to rust out. It is better to work until you die than to be idle just because you are old. □ NANCY: *Grandma, you shouldn't work so hard. You're not young anymore, you know.* GRANDMOTHER:

Thanks for your concern, dear, but I plan to keep work-ing. It's better to wear out than to rust out. □ BILL: *You really ought to relax. I'm afraid you'll kill yourself with too much work.* NANCY: *So what? It's better to wear out than to rust out.*

It is easier to tear down than to build up.   Destroying things is easier than building them. □ *The new town hall had taken four years to erect, but the vandals wrecked it in only one night, proving once again that it is easier to tear down than to build up.* □ JILL: *That poor politician —he served honestly and well for all those years and now his career is ruined by one little scandal.* JANE: *It is eas-ier to tear down than to build up.*

It is easy to be wise after the event.   After you see the consequences of a decision, it is easy to tell if the deci-sion was good, but it is also too late, since the conse-quences have already happened. □ JILL: *I should never have invited Aunt Betsy to stay with me; I haven't had a peaceful moment since she got here.* JANE: *Well, it's easy to be wise after the event.* □ ALAN: *I had a feeling that we should have bought tickets ahead of time. Now we're here, and the theater is sold out.* SANDRA: *If that's what you thought, you should have said so before. It's easy to be wise after the event.*

It is more blessed to give than to receive.   See *It is bet-ter to give than to receive.*

It is never too late to learn.   You can always learn some-thing new. □ ALAN: *Help me make the salad dressing.* SANDRA: *But I don't know anything about making salad dressing.* ALAN: *It's never too late to learn.* □ *Grandma decided to take a course in using computers. "It's never too late to learn," she said.*

It is never too late to mend.   It is never too late to apolo-gize for something you have done or try to repair something you have done wrong. □ PENELOPE: *I still miss Tony, but it's been a year since our big fight and we haven't spoken to each other since.* MOTHER: *Well, it's never too late to mend; why don't you call him up and apologize?* □ JILL: *Sandra will never forgive me for messing up her presentation. And now it's too late to even say I'm sorry.* JANE: *Nonsense. It's never too late to mend.*

It is not work that kills, but worry. Working hard will not hurt you, but worrying too much is bad for your health. □ NANCY: *You've been working so many hours every day, I'm afraid you'll get sick.* BILL: *It's not work that kills, but worry.* □ *When I was unemployed, I worried all the time and was in terrible health; now, I may be working seven days a week, but I've never felt better. Positive proof that it is not work that kills, but worry.*

It is the pace that kills. Trying to do too much too fast is bad for you. □ *You're putting yourself under too much stress by trying to knit that whole outfit in time for your sister's birthday. It is the pace that kills, you know.* □ NANCY: *I hate college.* BILL: *Why? Is the subject material too difficult?* NANCY: *No, they just expect me to learn too much of it too fast. It is the pace that kills.*

It never hurts to ask. You do not risk anything by asking someone for a favor. (Usually used to suggest asking a favor.) □ ALAN: *Do you think Jill would look after our house while we're on vacation?* SANDRA: *It never hurts to ask.* □ *Maybe Bill will help me. It can't hurt to ask, in any case.*

It never rains but it pours. Good (or bad) things do not just happen a few at a time, but in large numbers all at once. □ FRED: *I can't believe this. This morning I had a flat tire. When I went to the garage to get the tire patched, I discovered I didn't have any money, and I couldn't even charge it because my credit card's expired.* JANE: *It never* *rains but it pours.* □ *More nice things happened to me today than happened in this whole last year. It never rains but it pours.*

It takes all kinds (to make a world). There are many different kinds of people, and you should not condemn them for being different. (Often used to indicate that some person seems very strange.) □ JILL: *Eleanor's trying another fad diet. This week she's sprinkling dried algae on all her food.* JANE: *It takes all kinds.* □ CHILD: *Mommy, I saw a weird man today. He was walking down the street singing real loud. I wish they'd put weird people like that in jail, so they can't scare me.* MOTHER: *Now, now, honey, it takes all kinds to make a world.*

It takes money to make money. In order to make money, you must first have some money to invest. □ *I've been reading a lot of books about how to become wealthy, and they all make it depressingly clear that it takes money to make money.* □ BILL: *For a negligible investment of $1,000, I'll give you a controlling share of my company.* JANE: *I don't have $1,000 to throw away on your harebrained scheme.* BILL: *You'll never get rich with that attitude. It takes money to make money.*

It takes two to make a bargain. Both parties in a negotiation must agree in order for the negotiation to be successful. □ JILL: *You'll give me a ride to work every day this week, like we agreed, won't you?* JANE: *Wait a minute. I only said I'd give you a ride to work today. It takes two to make a bargain.* □ ELLEN: *We decided you should make dinner tonight, right?* FRED: *No, we didn't decide that; you decided that. It takes two to make a bargain.*

It takes two to make a quarrel. An argument is never only one person's fault; if the other person refuses to participate, there cannot be an argument. □ PENELOPE: *I*

think Mimi ought to apologize for arguing with me.
MOTHER: *It takes two to make a quarrel, dear. Maybe you
ought to apologize to her.* □ JILL: *Why are you always so
quarrelsome?* JANE: *Hey, it's not just my fault. It takes
two to make a quarrel.*

It takes two to tango. Some things cannot be accom-
plished by one person acting alone. (Often accusatory;
implies that the person about whom you say it is cooper-
ating to produce some unpleasant situation.) □ ALAN:
You're always arguing! Stop arguing all the time. JANE: *I
can't argue all by myself. It takes two to tango.* □ FRED:
Did you hear? Janice got herself pregnant. JILL: *What do
you mean "got herself pregnant"? It takes two to tango.*

It's (all) Greek to me. Something is incomprehensible. □
*Can you explain what this paragraph in the lease
means? Legal language is all Greek to me.* □ *I can't figure out this diagram for how to assemble my bicycle. It's
all Greek to me.*

It's always darkest just before the dawn. See *The darkest hour is just before the dawn.*

It's an ill bird that fouls its own nest. Only a foolish or
dishonorable person would bring dishonor to himself or
herself or his or her surroundings; only a bad person
would ruin the place where he or she lives. (Also the cliché: **to foul one's own nest,** to discredit oneself; to ruin
the place where one lives.) □ *I don't like my new neighbor. Not only does he never mow his lawn, he covers it
with all kinds of trash. It's an ill bird that fouls its own
nest.* □ *Don't you ever sweep your floors? I know you
like to have a casual life style, but this isn't just casual—
it's fouling your own nest.*

It's an ill wind that blows nobody (any) good. Even
misfortune can benefit someone or something; a calamity for one person usually benefits somebody else. □ *The*

tremendous hailstorm left gaping holes in most of the roofs in town, so many families were homeless. The roofing repairman, however, made plenty of money fixing those holes. It's an ill wind that blows nobody any good. □ JILL: *The oil shortage is hurting everybody.* JANE: *Everybody except the people who own oil wells.* JILL: *That's true. It's an ill wind that blows nobody good.*

It's ill waiting for dead men's shoes. You should not be eager for someone to die so that you inherit something. □ FRED: *Uncle Eddie promised me his collection of chess sets when he dies.* ELLEN: *It's ill waiting for dead men's shoes.* □ PHIL: *Why should I bother to learn some kind of trade? I'll be rich when Grandpa dies and leaves me all his money.* ALAN: *It's ill waiting for dead men's shoes.*

It's no use crying over spilled milk. AND **Don't cry over spilled milk.** Do not be upset about making a mistake that you cannot change. □ *I know you don't like your new haircut, but you can't change it now. It's no use crying over spilled milk.* □ *OK, so you broke the drill I lent you. Don't cry over spilled milk.*

It's not the heat, it's the humidity. When the air is damp, hot days feel even hotter and more miserable. □ JILL: *I hope the air conditioning is fixed soon; the heat is unbearable in here.* JANE: *It's not the heat, it's the humidity.* □ ALAN: *I thought the summers were hot when I was growing up in New Mexico, but they're even hotter here in Iowa.* SANDRA: *The climate is moister here; it's not the heat, it's the humidity.*

It's six of one, half a dozen of another. Two options are equivalent as far as you are concerned. □ *To get downtown, we can either take the highway or the side streets.*

It's six of one, half a dozen of another, since both routes take the same amount of time. □ JILL: *Would you rather peel the carrots or wash the lettuce?* JANE: *It's six of one, half a dozen of the other.*

J

Judge not, lest ye be judged. AND **Judge not, that ye be not judged.** If you condemn other people, then they will have the right to condemn you, so it is best not to condemn them. (Biblical.) □ JILL: *I'm sure Gloria is the one who's been stealing from petty cash. She's so sloppy, nasty, and ill-mannered. Don't you think she'd be capable of theft?* JANE: *Judge not, lest ye be judged.* □ VINCENT: *Fred is an evil human being. He eats meat, so he contributes to the torture and slaughter of innocent animals. He ought to be tortured instead.* ALAN: *Oh, Vincent, judge not, that ye be not judged.*

Judge not, that ye be not judged. See the previous entry.

K

Keep a stiff upper lip. Act as though you are not upset; do not let unpleasant things upset you. (English people are stereotypically supposed to be very good at keeping a stiff upper lip.) □ *Even though he was only three years old, Jonathan kept a stiff upper lip the whole time he was in the hospital recovering from his surgery.* □ JILL: *Sometimes this job frustrates me so much I could just break down in tears.* JANE: *Keep a stiff upper lip. Things are bound to improve.*

Keep a thing seven years and you'll (always) find a use for it. If you keep a seemingly useless thing for seven years, you will supposedly have some occasion to use it during that time. □ JILL: *My mother sent me a four-foot-tall ceramic vase for my birthday. What can I possibly use it for?* JANE: *Keep it seven years and you'll find some use for it.* □ BILL: *I think I'll throw out most of these knickknacks before I move.* ALAN: *You should keep them seven years, so you can find a use for them.* BILL: *But I won't have enough space in my new apartment to keep them for seven years!*

Keep no more cats than will catch mice. Do not support anyone who does not or cannot do something useful for you in return. □ ELLEN: *My son came home after he graduated from college. That was six months ago, and he still* *doesn't have a job or help me around the house or any-thing.* SANDRA: *Insist that he move out; keep no more cats than will catch mice.* □ *Phil fired his secretary when she became too crippled from arthritis to type. "I keep no more cats than will catch mice," he said.*

Keep one's nose to the grindstone. To work hard and con-stantly. □ SON: *I'll never get good grades. I might as well not even study.* MOTHER: *Don't give up yet. I'm sure that if you just keep your nose to the grindstone, you'll get the results you want.* □ *Mary kept her nose to the grindstone while her friends were out enjoying themselves.*

Keep up with the Joneses To have everything in the lat-est style. □ *Because Mrs. Fraser was determined to keep up with the Joneses at all costs, she pressured her hus-band to get the highest-paying job possible.* □ *Don't worry so much about keeping up with the Joneses. You can be perfectly happy without an entirely new ward-robe every season.*

Keep your shop and your shop will keep you. If you work hard at running your business, then your business will always make enough of a profit to support you. □ *When Grandpa turned his hardware store over to me, he said, "It's hard work, but it's a good living. Keep the shop and the shop will keep you."* □ *Nellie advised me, "If you want to be independent, open some kind of store. Keep your shop and your shop will keep you."*

Kill the goose that lays the golden egg(s). To destroy something that is profitable to you. □ *Fred's wife knew he wasn't happy in his job, even though it paid well; still, she felt that advising him to leave it would be kill-ing the goose that laid the golden eggs.* □ BILL: *Renting out my apartment building is so much trouble, maybe I'll sell the whole thing.* FRED: *Don't kill the goose that lays the golden egg!*

Kill two birds with one stone To accomplish two things with one action. □ *For Miranda, mowing the lawn always killed two birds with one stone, in that it kept her lawn looking tidy and provided her with a good day's exercise too.* □ *If I bake potato bread, that will kill two birds with one stone. It will use up my leftover potatoes as well as being my contribution to the bake sale.*

Kings have long arms. AND **Governments have long arms.** Those who are in power can always catch and punish people who have opposed them, no matter how far away those opponents may go. (Also the cliché: **the long arm of the law,** the law's, or police force's, power to catch people who have tried to escape by going far away.) □ *After his attempt to assassinate the king, the prince sailed to a distant country, although his wife warned him it would be to no avail. "Kings have long arms," she reminded him.* □ *The outlaw spent his whole life running from state to state, but eventually the long arm of the law caught up with him.*

Know thyself. Be aware of your own limitations; know what you are capable of doing. (This was the motto inscribed on the temple of Apollo at Delphi.) □ *The motto of the ballet corps was "Know thyself"; every dancer was expected to know how far she could stretch, and not hurt herself by trying to exceed her limits.* □ *"Know thyself,"* the high school guidance counselor admonished us, *"and try to find a career that makes the most of your abilities."*

Know which side one's bread is buttered on To be aware of where your money comes from; to be loyal to the person or thing that will benefit you the most. □ WIFE: *Please be sure not to upset Grandma. You know we can't do without the money she sends us every month.* HUSBAND: *Don't worry. I know which side my bread is buttered on.* □ *Knowing which side her bread was but-*

tered on, Linda supported Julie's faction instead of Mark's. Although Mark was her friend, Julie was in a position to promote Linda.

Knowledge is power.   The more you know, the more you can control. □ *My mother insisted that all her children learn the basics of car repair. "Knowledge is power," she said, "and the more you know about cars, the less likely you are to fall victim to incompetent mechanics."* □ CHILD: *How come I have to study history? I don't care what all those dead people did hundreds of years ago.* MOTHER: *Knowledge is power. If you know something about the past, it may help you to anticipate the future.*

L

Laugh all the way to the bank   To gloat over having done something that made a lot of money. (Usually said only of a third person.) □ *Jones sold his worthless property for a large price; now he's laughing all the way to the bank.* □ *The criminal felt no remorse for having defrauded so many people. In fact, she laughed all the way to the bank.*

Laugh and the world laughs with you; weep and you weep alone.   When you are happy, people will want to be around you and share your happiness, but when you are sad, people will avoid you. □ NANCY: *When Harry and I were dating, all our friends invited us places and called to say hello. Now that we've broken up, they treat me as if I don't exist.* JANE: *Laugh and the world laughs with you; weep and you weep alone.* □ *Laugh and the world laughs with you; weep and you weep alone—I hate that. I need people around me more when I'm in a bad mood, to cheer me up.*

Laugh out of the other side of one's mouth   To be upset when someone gets revenge on you. □ *Phil played a dirty trick on me, but he'll be laughing out of the other side of his mouth when I get through with him.* □ *That was really low-down, what Gina did to you. I think you should make her laugh out of the other side of her mouth.*

Leave no stone unturned   To search in every conceivable place. □ *The detective pledged to leave no stone unturned in her search for the kidnapped heir.* □ *We left no stone unturned in our attempt to find the necklace Andrea had lost.*

Leave well enough alone.   If something is satisfactory, do not try to change it. □ *I don't think you need to put on any more makeup. Leave well enough alone.* □ *The children seem to be playing together nicely without any interference from us. Let's leave well enough alone.*

Lend your money and lose your friend.   You should not lend money to your friends; if you do, either you will have to bother your friend to repay the loan, which will make your friend resent you, or your friend will not repay the loan, which will make you resent your friend. □ Jill: *Can you loan me five dollars for lunch?* Jane: *Sorry. I believe in that old saying, "Lend your money and lose your friend."* □ Bill: *Joe needs a hundred dollars to pay his landlord. I'm thinking about lending it to him.* Alan: *Lend your money and lose your friend.*

Let bygones be bygones.   Forgive someone for something he or she did in the past. □ Jill: *Why don't you want to invite Ellen to your party?* Jane: *She was rude to me at the office picnic.* Jill: *But that was six months ago. Let bygones be bygones.* □ *Nancy held a grudge against her teacher for a long time, but she finally decided to let bygones be bygones.*

Let every tub stand on its own bottom.   See *Every tub must stand on its own bottom.*

Let sleeping dogs lie.   Do not instigate trouble; leave something alone if it might cause trouble. □ Jill: *Should I ask the boss if he's upset at my coming in late in the mornings?* Jane: *If he hasn't said anything about it, just let sleeping dogs lie.* □ *I thought I would ask Anna if she* *wanted me to pay her back right away, but then I decided to let sleeping dogs lie.*

Let the buyer beware. When you buy something, you must take precautions against being cheated, because you cannot trust merchants to be honest about what they sell. □ *Let the buyer beware when shopping for a used car.* □ *Several of the lamps among those Wayne offered for sale were broken. "If a customer isn't smart enough to try a lamp before he buys it, that's his problem," Wayne argued. "Let the buyer beware."*

Let the cat out of the bag To tell a secret; to let something slip out that you are not supposed to reveal. □ *My mother didn't tell me she was coming for a visit; she wanted to surprise me. But my sister let the cat out of the bag.* □ *Marvin didn't want anyone to know that he was engaged, but to judge from the way all his friends were congratulating him, someone must have let the cat out of the bag.*

Let the chips fall where they may. Let something happen regardless of the consequences and no matter what happens. □ *I'm going to tell Ellen the truth about her husband, let the chips fall where they may.* □ *Kathy decided to risk her money on the investment, and let the chips fall where they may.*

Let the cobbler stick to his last. Do not advise someone in matters outside your area of expertise. □ *Whenever Allan, who is a lawyer, tried to give Vincent suggestions about how to write his novel, Vincent would say, "Let the cobbler stick to his last."* □ BILL: *I don't think you should put so much oregano in the spaghetti sauce.* NANCY: *You're a construction worker, not a chef. Let the cobbler stick to his last.*

Let the dead bury the dead. Do not try to revive old grievances; forget about past conflicts. (Biblical.) □ *The*

Nelson family and the Hopkins family had been feuding for decades, but when Andrew Nelson and Louise Hopkins declared that they wanted to get married, their families decided to let the dead bury the dead. □ *Some citizens opposed signing a trade agreement with a country against whom we had once fought a war, but most people felt we should let the dead bury the dead.*

Let them eat cake.   A joking disclaimer of responsibility for some group of people. (Supposed to have been said by Marie Antoinette when she heard that the common people had no bread.) □ FRED: *The budget will allow each one of our managers to get a substantial holiday bonus.* SANDRA: *And what about the rest of the employees?* FRED: *Let them eat cake!* □ ELLEN: *I am going to invite all the good students to a lovely party at my home.* SANDRA: *And the students who aren't so good?* ELLEN: *Let them eat cake.*

Life begins at forty.   By the time you are forty years old, you have enough experience and skill to do what you want to do with your life. □ ALAN: *Why are you so depressed?* SANDRA: *Tomorrow's my fortieth birthday.* ALAN: *Cheer up! Life begins at forty.* □ *For Pete, life began at forty, because by that time he had enough financial security to enjoy himself now and then, rather than having to work all the time.*

Life is just a bowl of cherries.   Everything is going well; life is carefree. (Often used ironically, as in the second example.) □ *The real estate salesman tried to convince us that life in the suburbs is just a bowl of cherries.* □ JILL: *Hi, Jane. How are you?* JANE: *Oh, my alarm clock didn't go off this morning, and then my car wouldn't start, and I missed the bus and got to work late, and I just found out my rent's going up fifty dollars a month. Life is just a bowl of cherries.*

Life is short and time is swift. You should enjoy life as much as possible, because it does not last very long. □ JILL: *Want to go to the movies with me?* JANE: *Oh, I don't know; I should probably stay at work and finish a few things.* JILL: *Come on, Jane, life is short and time is swift.* □ *Don't stay at home tonight watching TV; come out with us and enjoy walking in the good weather while it lasts. Life is short and time is swift.*

Life isn't all beer and skittles. Life is not pleasurable all the time; you cannot always be having fun. □ *I don't really mind going back to work when my vacation is over. Life isn't all beer and skittles, and I enjoy my fun that much more because I have work to compare it to.* □ *When George's parents stopped supporting him, George suddenly discovered that life isn't all beer and skittles.*

Lightning never strikes (the same place) twice. The same unpredictable thing never happens to the same person twice. □ JILL: *I'm scared to drive ever since that truck hit my car.* ALAN: *Don't worry. Lightning never strikes the same place twice.* □ *It's strange, but I feel safer since my apartment was robbed; I figure lightning never strikes the same place twice.*

Like a bat out of hell Extremely fast. (Very casual.) □ *I was walking down Main Street when I saw this cop car come screaming by like a bat out of hell.* □ *When I saw that the kitchen was on fire, I tore out of the house like a bat out of hell.*

Like a bull in a china shop Very clumsy in a delicate situation. □ *I never know what to say to the mourners at a funeral. I feel like a bull in a china shop, trampling on their feelings without even meaning to.* □ *After five minutes in the outdoor market, Lester felt like a bull in a china shop; in reaching for an orange, he had managed to tumble down several elaborate pyramids of fruit.*

Like a bump on a log Completely inert. (Derogatory. Often used in the phrase "to sit there like a bump on a log.") □ *Don't just sit there like a bump on a log; give me a hand!* □ *You can never tell what Julia thinks of something; she just sits there like a bump on a log.*

Like breeds like. People tend to raise children who are like them; something tends to give rise to things that resemble it. □ JILL: *I think Fred's little boy is going to be just as disagreeable as Fred.* JANE: *That's no surprise. Like breeds like.* □ *The professor's students all write papers like the ones the professor writes. Like breeds like.*

Like death warmed over Very pale; weary; weak. (Casual.) □ *I only got two hours' sleep last night, and today I feel like death warmed over.* □ *I wonder what's wrong with Julie; she looks like death warmed over.*

Like father, like son Fathers and sons resemble each other; sons tend to do what their fathers did before them. □ JILL: *George's father smoked all the time, and now George is smoking excessively, too.* JANE: *Like father, like son, eh?* □ *I think my son will grow up tall, just like his father. Like father, like son.*

Like greased lightning Extremely fast. □ *After my uncle modified the car, it could go like greased lightning.* □ *Jimmy's horse runs like greased lightning.*

Like mother, like daughter Daughters resemble their mothers; daughters tend to do what their mothers did before them. □ *My mother loved sweets, and every time my father saw me with a cookie in my hand, he would sigh, "Like mother, like daughter."* □ JILL: *Gina's beautiful.* JANE: *Like mother, like daughter; her mother's gorgeous, too.*

Like rats abandoning a sinking ship See *Rats abandon a sinking ship.*

Like the wind See *(As) swift as the wind.*

Like two peas in a pod Quite similar. □ *Andrea and her cousin Laura are just like two peas in a pod; you can hardly tell them apart.* □ *After so many years of marriage, John and Mary have really grown to resemble one another, so that now they're like two peas in a pod.*

Listeners never hear any good of themselves. See *Eavesdroppers never hear any good of themselves.*

Little and often fills the purse. If you get a little bit of money frequently, you will always have enough. □ JILL: *I don't think I'll ever be able to save very much; I can only afford to save such a little bit of money from every paycheck.* JANE: *Ah, but little and often fills the purse.* □ *The handyman did not disdain small jobs offered by people in his neighborhood, since he knew that little and often fills the purse.*

Little pitchers have big ears. Children like to listen to adult conversations and can understand a lot of what they hear. (Use this to warn another adult not to talk about something because there is a child present.) □ *I started to tell Mary about the date I had on Saturday, but she interrupted me, saying, "Little pitchers have big ears," and looking pointedly at her six-year-old daughter, who was in the room with us.* □ *I'd rather you didn't gossip about the office in front of my kids. Little pitchers have big ears.*

Little strokes fell great oaks. You can complete a large, intimidating task by steadily doing small parts of it. □ JILL: *How can I possibly write a fifty-page report in two months?* JANE: *Just write a little bit every day. Little strokes fell great oaks.* □ *Debbie was daunted by the prospect of fixing up the old house, but she reminded herself that little strokes fell great oaks. "I'll start by scraping the old wallpaper off the walls," she decided, "and then I'll keep at it, one job at a time."*

Little thieves are hanged, but great ones escape. Truly expert criminals are never caught. □ *Everyone's making such a fuss because they convicted that bank robber, but he must not have been a very dangerous criminal. Little thieves are hanged, but great ones escape.* □ ALAN: *Rogers can't have been a very great thief.* SANDRA: *How can you say that? He stole half a million dollars!* ALAN: *But they caught him, didn't they? Little thieves are hanged, but great ones escape.*

Little things please little minds. AND **Small things please small minds.** People who are not intelligent are pleased by trivial things. (Implies that the person you are talking about is not intelligent.) □ FRED: *Why are you so happy?* ELLEN: *I found a perfectly good ballpoint pen on the sidewalk today.* FRED: *Huh. Little things please little minds.* □ JILL: *Nathaniel's been awfully cheerful today.* JANE: *Yes, his favorite TV show is on tonight.* JILL: *Little things please little minds, they say.*

Live by the sword, die by the sword. If you use violence against other people, you can expect to have violence used against you; or, you can expect to become a victim of whatever means you use to get what you want. (Biblical.) □ *The gang leader who organized so many murders was eventually murdered himself. Live by the sword, die by the sword.* □ *Bill liked to spread damaging gossip about other people, until he lost all his friends because of some gossip that was spread about him. Live by the sword, die by the sword.*

Lock the stable door after the horse is stolen See *Shut the stable door after the horse has bolted.*

Look before you leap. Think carefully about what you are about to do before you do it. □ *I'm not saying you shouldn't sign the lease for that apartment. I'm just saying you should look before you leap.* □ JILL: *I'm thinking* *about going to night school.* JANE: *Are you sure you can spare the time and the money? Look before you leap.*

Look for a needle in a haystack   To look for something in a situation where it will be extremely difficult to find. (Usually used in the phrase, "like looking for a needle in a haystack," implying that your present search will be extremely difficult.) □ *Trying to find a particular book in Eleanor's enormous, chaotic library was like looking for a needle in a haystack.* □ *I wanted a spoon that matched my silverware pattern, so I went to the antique sale to see if I could buy one. It soon became apparent that looking for one particular kind of spoon among the thousands of silver spoons they had for sale was going to be like looking for a needle in a haystack.*

Love begets love.   If you behave lovingly to other people, they will behave lovingly to you. □ CHILD: *I hate Tammy! She's always mean to me.* FATHER: *If you're nicer to her, maybe she'll change her ways. Love begets love.* □ *In Eileen's case, evidently love begets love. She's kind to everybody, and in return, even the most hateful people are kind to her.*

Love is blind.   If you love someone, you cannot see any faults in that person. □ JILL: *I don't understand why Joanna likes Tom. He's inconsiderate, he's vain, and he isn't even good-looking.* JANE: *Love is blind.* □ JILL: *How can you put up with Tom? He's so rude to you.* SANDRA: *What do you mean? He's never rude.* JILL: *Love is blind.*

Love makes the world go round.   Life is more pleasant when people treat each other lovingly. □ *Come on, guys, stop fighting with each other all the time. Love makes the world go round.* □ *Linda is always patient and kind to everyone. She's a living example of how love makes the world go round.*

Love me, love my dog. If you love someone, you should accept everything and everyone that the person loves. □ JILL: *I wish you'd keep your dog out of the house when I come over.* JANE: *Love me, love my dog.* □ *Most of Alice's friends didn't like her sister, but they accepted her because Alice insisted, "Love me, love my dog."*

Love will find a way. People who are in love will overcome any obstacles in order to be together. (Sometimes used ironically, to suggest that someone is in love with whatever he or she is struggling to be near, as in the second example.) □ JILL: *I feel so sorry for Lily and Craig. They just got engaged, and now his job is transferring him across the country.* JANE: *Love will find a way, I'm sure.* □ ALAN: *Fred's feeling discouraged because he didn't get the loan he needed to buy the sports car he wants.* BILL: *I'm sure he'll get that car eventually. Love will find a way.*

Lucky at cards, unlucky in love If you frequently win at card games, you will not have happy love affairs. (Can imply the converse, that if you do not win at card games, you will have happy love affairs.) □ FRED: *I wish I was George. He always wins tons of money at our poker games.* ALAN: *Don't be jealous of him. Lucky at cards, unlucky in love.* □ JILL: *I won every game of gin rummy I played yesterday.* JANE: *I'm sorry to hear that.* JILL: *Why?* JANE: *You know what they say—lucky at cards, unlucky in love.*

M

Make a clean breast of it   To confess to something; to tell the truth. □ *Jill decided to make a clean breast of it and tell Alan that she was the one who dented his car.* □ JANE: *I borrowed Jill's watch without asking her, and then I lost it! What can I tell her to keep her from getting angry?* ELLEN: *If I were you, I'd make a clean breast of it. She may get upset at first, but not as upset as she'd be if you lied and she found out the truth later.*

Make a long story short   To sum up or come to the point of a story you are telling. □ *First thing this morning, the phone rang, and it was my cousin, telling me about a baby shower she had been to, and right after she hung up, the carpet cleaners came and started steam-cleaning all the carpets, and I had to supervise them, and—to make a long story short, I never got a chance to eat breakfast today.* □ *Monica spent fifteen minutes telling us her grievances against the dentist, and then said, "To make a long story short, I'm looking for another dentist now."*

Make a mountain out of a molehill   To exaggerate something; to react to a small problem as if it were a large problem. □ *Just because Rita didn't invite you to her party doesn't mean she hates you. You're making a mountain out of a molehill.* □ PENELOPE: *I know I failed* *my geometry exam today. This is the end of my academic career. I might as well drop out of school.* SANDRA: *Don't make a mountain out of a molehill.*

Make a virtue of necessity To do what you have to do cheerfully or willingly. □ *When Bill's mother became sick, there was no one but Bill to take care of her, so Bill made a virtue of necessity and resolved to enjoy their time together.* □ *Sandra did not enjoy wearing business attire, but when her work demanded it, she made a virtue of necessity.*

Make haste slowly. Act quickly, but not so quickly that you make careless mistakes. □ SANDRA: *Why are you throwing your clothes around the room?* ALAN: *You told me to get my things packed in a hurry.* SANDRA: *Yes, but make haste slowly; otherwise we'll have to spend an hour cleaning up the mess you make.* □ *The students in the first-aid class had to learn to make haste slowly when treating an injury, since mistakes could endanger the patient's life.*

Make hay while the sun shines. If you have an opportunity to do something, do it before the opportunity expires. □ SANDRA: *While my husband's out of town, I'm going to watch all the movies he wouldn't take me to see.* JANE: *Why not? Make hay while the sun shines.* □ *As long as you're unemployed, you might as well use your spare time to clean the house thoroughly. Make hay while the sun shines.*

Make one turn (over) in one's grave Do something that would have deeply offended someone who is now dead. (Often the dead person referred to is someone famous.) □ *Tonight's rendition of the* Jupiter Symphony *was enough to make Mozart turn over in his grave.* □ *The careless way you treat your grandmother's china is making her turn in her grave, I'm sure.*

Make the best of a bad job To try to salvage something from a ruined situation. □ *When the dry cleaners ruined Mrs. Anderson's coat, they made the best of a bad job by offering to buy her another one.* □ ALAN: *Oh, no! I burned all the cookies I was going to take to the party.* SANDRA: *Well, we'll have to make the best of a bad job. See if you can cover up the burned parts with frosting.*

Man does not live by bread alone. In order to survive, people need more than physical things like food and shelter; they also need mental or spiritual things like satisfaction and love. (Biblical.) □ *It's not enough to donate food to the hungry. Man does not live by bread alone.* □ ALAN: *I'm so miserable.* JILL: *How can you be miserable? You've got a good place to live, plenty to eat, nice clothes . . . .* ALAN: *But man does not live by bread alone.*

Man proposes, God disposes. People may make plans, but they cannot control the outcome of their plans. □ *Leslie hopes to become a lawyer, but man proposes, God disposes.* □ JILL: *Are you really going to be able to finish writing your novel by the end of the year?* VINCENT: *Man proposes, God disposes.*

Many a true word is spoken in jest. AND **There's many a true word spoken in jest.** Just because something is said as a joke, it can still be true. □ FRED: *Why did you make a joke about my being stingy? Do you really think I'm cheap?* ELLEN: *Of course not, don't be silly. It was just a joke.* FRED: *But many a true word is spoken in jest.* □ SANDRA: *Don't be upset because I said you're fat. I was only joking.* ALAN: *But there's many a true word spoken in jest.*

Many are called but few are chosen. Many people may want something, but only a few people get it. (Biblical.) □ *When it comes to getting into a good college, many are called but few are chosen.* □ JILL: *I've always wanted to* *be independently wealthy.* JANE: *Many are called, but few are chosen.*

Many hands make light work. If everyone helps with a large task, it will get done easily and quickly. □ *Cleaning up the banquet room won't take long if we all help; many hands make light work.* □ *You do have a lot of dishes to wash, but you also have all of us to help you, and many hands make light work.*

March comes in like a lion, and goes out like a lamb. AND **In like a lion, out like a lamb.** The month of March usually starts with cold, unpleasant weather, but ends mild and pleasant. (Either part of the proverb can be used alone.) □ *March certainly is coming in like a lion this year; there's been a snowstorm every day this week.* □ JILL: *Today is March twenty-fifth, and it's beautiful and warm outside, when just two weeks ago, everything was covered with ice.* JANE: *In like a lion and out like a lamb, all right.*

Marriages are made in heaven. You cannot foretell who will marry whom. Two people may love each other very much but may end up not marrying each other, and two people who do not even know each other may marry each other in the end. (Also **a marriage made in heaven; a match made in heaven,** a very happy or harmonious marriage or partnership.) □ *When Tom and Eliza got engaged, no one doubted they would get married, but within a few months, they broke it off and each married someone else. Marriages are made in heaven.* □ *The partnership of George and Ira Gershwin was a match made in heaven; they wrote such beautiful songs.*

Marry in haste, (and) repent at leisure. If you marry someone you do not know well, or decide to marry someone without first carefully considering what you are doing, you will probably regret it for a long time. □ *Anna* *wanted some time to consider Sam's proposal of marriage; she had heard the saying, "Marry in haste, and repent at leisure."* □ BETSY: *John and I decided we'd just get married last weekend. What do you think?* GRANDMOTHER: *Marry in haste, repent at leisure.*

Men are blind in their own cause. If you believe in something very fervently, you will not recognize the flaws in what you believe or the dangers associated with it. □ *Lawrence joined the political organization because he believed in its avowed purpose. He would not believe that its leaders were running it only to profit themselves, though that was obvious to everyone else. Men are blind in their own cause.* □ JILL: *Lyle is so intent on converting people to his religion, that he doesn't see that his constant preaching is alienating his friends.* JANE: *Men are blind in their own cause.*

Men make houses, women make homes. Men are often the ones who build or acquire houses for their families, but women provide the things that make a house into a home. □ *When William moved into his own apartment, his mother insisted on choosing and arranging the furniture and decorations for him. "Men make houses, women make homes," she said, "and I want you to have a home as nice as the one you grew up in."* □ *Daniel had no interest in helping his wife search for curtains, rugs, or other amenities for their new home. "That's your job," he said. "Men make houses, women make homes, right?"*

Might makes right. The stronger of two opponents will always control the situation. □ CHILD: *How come the country with the biggest army always tells the other countries what to do?* FATHER: *Might makes right.* □ *Nobody agrees with Andy's ideas, but he's the most powerful person in the office, so we have to do what he says anyway. Might makes right.*

Mind one's p's and q's. To behave properly; to display good manners. □ *When you children go to visit Aunt Muriel, you'll have to mind your p's and q's; not like at home, where I let you do as you please.* □ *We'd better mind our p's and q's for this new teacher; I hear he's very strict.*

Mind your own business! Do not pry into my affairs! (Slightly rude.) □ JILL: *How was your date with that architect?* JANE: *Mind your own business!* □ FRED: *Are you planning to go to the bank tonight?* ELLEN: *Mind your own business!*

Misery loves company. Unhappy people like other people to be unhappy too. □ JILL: *Why is Linda criticizing everybody today?* JANE: *Her boss criticized her this morning, and misery loves company.* □ *I should probably feel bad because my sister is so depressed, but I'm pretty depressed myself. Misery loves company.*

Misfortunes never come singly. Bad things tend to happen in groups. □ *I already told you that my wife lost her job. Well, misfortunes never come singly; our house was robbed last night.* □ *Alicia slipped and fell on the icy sidewalk, and while she was struggling to get up, her keys fell through a grating into the sewer. Misfortunes never come singly.*

Moderation in all things. Do not do anything too much or too little. □ *Felicia always ate sparingly. "Moderation in all things," she told herself.* □ JANE: *I think you watch too much TV.* JILL: *So you think I shouldn't watch any?* JILL: *No, just watch a reasonable amount. Moderation in all things.*

Monday's child is fair of face. A child born on Monday will be good-looking. (This comes from a rhyme that tells what children will be like, according to which day they are born: "Monday's child is fair of face,/Tuesday's child is full of grace,/Wednesday's child is full of woe,/ Thursday's child has far to go,/Friday's child is loving and giving,/Saturday's child works hard for a living,/But a child that is born on the Sabbath day/Is blithe and bonny, good and gay.'') □ *Joan is so pretty, she must be a Monday's child. Monday's child is fair of face.* □ JANE: *What day were you born on?* FRED: *Monday. Why?* JANE: *That's a surprise. Monday's child is fair of face, and that does not describe you at all.*

Money burns a hole in someone's pocket. Someone is very eager to spend his or her money; extra money in the possession of some people almost demands to be spent. □ *Leonard never could save any money; it always burned a hole in his pocket.* □ *Let's go shopping. I just got paid, and the money is burning a hole in my pocket.*

Money does not grow on trees. It is not easy to get money. (Casual. Implies that the person you are addressing spends money too easily.) □ CHILD: *Can I have ten dollars to go to the movies?* FATHER: *Ten dollars?! Money doesn't grow on trees.* □ *No, I don't think we ought to buy a new set of living-room furniture. Money doesn't grow on trees.*

Money is power. If you have money, you can get things and do things. □ *Emily wanted a career that would make her a lot of money, since money is power.* □ *The revolutionaries knew they would need money in order to overthrow the government. They believed that money is power.*

Money is the root of all evil. AND **The love of money is the root of all evil.** People do many evil things in order to get rich. (Biblical.) □ FRED: *I know I could make more money if I just knew the right things to invest in.* ELLEN: *Don't worry so much about money. It's the root of all evil, after all.* □ *As the newspapers continued to report*

*the dastardly things the wealthy young banker had done
to become even wealthier, people shook their heads and
remarked, "The love of money is the root of all evil."*

Monkey see, monkey do. Children imitate what they see
other people doing. (Playful.) □ *I don't let my children
watch TV programs that show kids being disrespectful to
their elders. I know what would happen if I did: monkey
see, monkey do.* □ *When Bert's son saw Bert shaving, he
wanted to shave, too. Monkey see, monkey do.*

More haste, less speed Do not do things in such a hurry
that you make mistakes. (Used to request someone to act
less hurriedly.) □ JILL: *I'm trying to call the police, but I
keep getting wrong numbers!* JANE: *That's because you're
dialing so fast. More haste, less speed.* □ *I know you
want to finish that sweater by Joe's birthday, but you're
knitting so fast that you make mistakes. More haste, less
speed.*

Morning dreams come true. If you dream something in
the morning, it will really happen. (According to this superstition.) □ JILL: *This morning I dreamed that the office burned down.* JANE: *We'd better get out of here, then.
You know what they say: morning dreams come true.* □
*As I was sleeping through the sound of my alarm clock
this morning, I dreamed I was late to work. That morning dream definitely came true.*

Moving three times is as bad as a fire. If you move your
household three times, you will lose or damage as many
things as a fire in your house would have destroyed or
damaged. □ *Having to move again is bad enough without my mother clucking, "Moving three times is as bad
as a fire."* □ FRED: *The company is transferring me
again.* ELLEN: *But we can't make another move! Moving
three times is as bad as a fire.*

Much ado about nothing A lot of commotion about something unimportant. □ *Every single newspaper and TV station gave extensive coverage to the First Lady's cosmetic surgery. Much ado about nothing, if you ask me.* □ *So many people protested the movie that I expected it to be very offensive, but, really, the protests were much ado about nothing.*

Murder will out. Murder will always be discovered; a bad deed will be found out. □ *Horace thought he had disposed of his victim in such a way that no one would ever discover his crime, but murder will out.* □ *For many years, we had assumed that the old man had died a natural death, but eventually evidence to the contrary did surface; murder will out.*

My cup runneth over. I have received so many benefits that I cannot contain them all. (Said when you feel overcome because many good things have happened to you.) □ *This week, I finished paying off my mortgage, my eyesight improved, and my first grandchild was born. My cup runneth over.* □ *Janet was speechless with happiness when she saw how many of her friends and relatives had joined together to give her a surprise party. "My cup runneth over," she finally said.*

N

Nature abhors a vacuum. If there is a gap, something will fill it. □ JILL: *As soon as the beggar who used to work that corner left, another one showed up.* JANE: *Nature abhors a vacuum.* □ ELLEN: *I'm so glad that silly fashion magazine went out of business.* SANDRA: *I'm sorry to tell you, but they've started another one. Nature abhors a vacuum.*

Necessity is the mother of invention. When people really need to do something, they will figure out a way to do it. □ SANDRA: *How can you possibly make that recipe? We don't have half the ingredients it calls for.* ALAN: *Necessity is the mother of invention.* □ *When the fan belt on Linda's car broke in the middle of the desert, Linda used her stockings as a replacement. Necessity is the mother of invention.*

Necessity knows no law. If you are desperate, you may have to do illegal things. □ *The judge was inclined to be lenient with the young criminals; they had only picked pockets because they couldn't make enough money by honest means to both pay their rent and buy something to eat. "Necessity knows no law," he thought to himself.* □ *I'm an honest person by nature, but I lost my job, and my kids needed food and clothes, and it seemed like the* best way to get money was to deal in illegal drugs. *Necessity knows no law.*

Needs must when the devil drives. When you are desperate, you must do things you ordinarily would not do. □ *Bill usually avoided asking Fred for favors, but this time no one else could help him, so he had to. Needs must when the devil drives.* □ *We're going to have to get an enormous loan to pay for your mother's surgery. I hate to go into debt, but needs must when the devil drives.*

Neither a borrower nor a lender be. It is difficult to be friends with someone who owes you money or with someone to whom you owe something, so it is better not to borrow or lend in the first place. □ *After losing several of my favorite books because I didn't have the nerve to insist that my friends return them, I learned that it is best to neither a borrower nor a lender be.* □ JILL: *George said he would pay me back with loads of interest if I could lend him some money for some stock he wants to buy. Do you think I should?* JANE: *Neither a borrower nor a lender be, particularly if George is the person you're lending to. His get-rich-quick schemes never work out.*

Neither rhyme nor reason Without logic, order, or planning. (Describes something disorganized. Usually appears in the expressions "there was neither rhyme nor reason to something" or "something had neither rhyme nor reason.") □ *There seems to be neither rhyme nor reason to Gerald's filing system.* □ *The novel's plot had neither rhyme nor reason.*

Never a dull moment Things are always exciting around here. (Describes an exciting or hectic situation.) □ *Every time I visit Jean, she has dozens of things planned for us to do: parties and theaters to attend, restaurants to try, scenic places to see. Never a dull moment.* □ ALAN: *How was work today?* SANDRA: *First of all, my boss called me* *in to yell at me. Then I had to fire one of my subordinates. And then my desk chair broke when I sat down on it. Never a dull moment.*

Never ask pardon before you are accused.   Do not apologize for something if nobody knows that you did it, because by apologizing, you are admitting that you did it. □ ALAN: *Should I apologize to Sandra for losing the necktie she gave me?* JANE: *Wait and see if she asks you what happened to the necktie. Never ask pardon before you are accused.* □ STUDENT: *I'm sorry I'm late to class.* TEACHER: *Are you late? I didn't notice. That just goes to show you that you should never ask pardon before you are accused.*

Never halloo till you are out of the woods.   Do not rejoice until you are certain that your problems are over. □ JILL: *Now that I have a full-time job, I'm certain to be able to pay all my debts.* JANE: *But it's just a temporary job; it may not last long. Never halloo till you are out of the woods.* □ PENELOPE: *I got an A on the last math quiz; I think I'm going to pass my math class!* ALAN: *You still need to pass the final exam. Never halloo till you are out of the woods.*

Never make a threat you cannot carry out.   You should not threaten to do something you cannot do; otherwise, people will not believe you are serious when you threaten. □ BILL: *If you don't stop being rude to me, I'll have you fired!* JANE: *Never make a threat you cannot carry out.* □ DAUGHTER: *Unless you let me go out with Timothy, I'll run away and get my own apartment.* FATHER: *Never make a threat you can't carry out.*

Never say die.   Do not give up. □ JILL: *I don't think I can finish this project in time.* JANE: *Never say die.* □ ALAN: *It's no use. I can't make my checkbook balance.* SANDRA: *Never say die!*

Never speak ill of the dead. You should not say bad things about dead people. □ *Your Uncle Phil had a lot of faults, but there's no reason to talk about them now that he's gone. Never speak ill of the dead.* □ *I hate to speak ill of the dead, but Cecilia was a mean woman, God rest her soul.*

Never tell tales out of school. Do not tell secrets; do not gossip. □ TIM: *Did Penelope let you kiss her on your date last night?* KEITH: *I never tell tales out of school.* □ FRED: *I just learned something really scandalous about the president of our company.* ELLEN: *Well, I don't want to hear it. You shouldn't tell tales out of school.*

Never trouble trouble till trouble troubles you. If you think something might cause trouble, leave it alone and wait until it actually causes trouble. □ ELLEN: *My daughter's teacher is going to be troublesome, I can tell. Maybe I should go to the school and talk to her.* JANE: *Why not wait till she actually does something? Never trouble trouble till trouble troubles you.* □ NANCY: *I think I made a mistake in one of my calculations. I should probably tell the boss.* BILL: *No, just wait and see if he notices. Never trouble trouble till trouble troubles you.*

New brooms sweep clean. AND **A new broom sweeps-clean.** Someone who is new in a particular job will do a very good job at first, to prove how competent he or she is, but will eventually get more and more lax. □ JILL: *That new supervisor is awfully strict.* JANE: *New brooms sweep clean.* □ *The new teacher immediately flunked three of the laziest students. "A new broom sweeps clean," one of the students shrugged.*

Nice guys finish last. You will never be able to get what you want by being kind and considerate. (Not everyone agrees with this idea.) □ *The unscrupulous salesman advised me, "Don't worry if you have to lie about the* *product to get the customer to buy it. Nice guys finish last.* □ *Larry couldn't interest any of the girls in going out with him, even though they all said he was a "nice guy." "I guess nice guys finish last," he sighed.*

Nineteen to the dozen   Very rapidly or energetically. □ *Whenever I get together with my cousins, we always gossip away nineteen to the dozen.* □ *While Alan got the other ingredients, Sandra was chopping up potatoes nineteen to the dozen.*

No man can serve two masters.   You cannot work for two different people, organizations, or purposes in good faith, because you will end up favoring one over the other. (Biblical.) □ *Al tried going to school and working, both full-time, but soon discovered that he could not serve two masters.* □ VINCENT: *I just got a job as a waiter. I figure I can do that in the evenings, and work on my poetry during the days.* ALAN: *But, Vincent, no man can serve two masters.*

No news is good news.   If you do not hear from someone, assume that all is well with him or her. □ FRED: *I wonder if Jill is doing all right in her new job.* JANE: *No news is good news.* □ SANDRA: *I'm worried about my sister. She hasn't called me for months.* ALAN: *No news is good news, right?*

No one is indispensable.   Anyone may become unnecessary; anyone may lose his or her job. □ FRED: *You can't fire me. I'm absolutely necessary to this company.* NANCY: *No one is indispensable, Fred.* □ *The housekeeper was sure that her employer would always need her, but she discovered that no one is indispensable.*

No one is infallible.   Everyone makes mistakes. □ FRED: *I used to trust my broker, but he told me to buy this stock, which turned out to be worthless!* SANDRA: *Well, no one is infallible.* □ JILL: *You told me you knew the way to Alan's* *house, but following your directions has gotten us completely lost.* JANE: *No one is infallible.*

No pain, no gain If you want to improve, you must work so hard that it hurts. (Casual. Associated with sports and physical exercise.) □ PLAYER: *I can't do any more push-ups. My muscles hurt.* COACH: *No pain, no gain.* □ *Come on, everybody! Run one more lap! No pain, no gain!*

No sooner said than done Something will be done right away. □ JILL: *Can I help you out?* JANE: *Yes! Put these files in alphabetical order.* JILL: *No sooner said than done.* □ *The service at the hotel was really remarkable. Everything we asked for was no sooner said than done.*

None but the brave deserve the fair. Only a courageous and gallant man deserves a beautiful woman; only the best deserves the best. □ *Stop making excuses and just call Gina. None but the brave deserve the fair.* □ BILL: *Nora will never go out with me again. I really bored her on our date.* FRED: *Then try again! None but the brave deserve the fair.*

Not able to get something for love or money Not able to get something at any price; completely unable to get. □ *Oranges were so scarce last winter that you couldn't get them for love or money.* □ *I wanted to go to the concert, but I couldn't get a ticket for love or money.*

Not able to make head or tail of something Not able to understand something at all. □ *I couldn't make head or tail of the professor's geology lecture this morning.* □ *Can you help me fill out my tax forms? I can't make head or tail of the instructions.*

Not enough room to swing a cat Very little room. (A way of describing a cramped place, usually a room. Casual.) □ *Is this room your whole apartment? There isn't enough room to swing a cat!* □ *The hotel advertised its*

*spacious rooms, but in reality there wasn't room enough
in them to swing a cat.*

Not one's cup of tea Not one's choice or preference.
(Used to describe an activity you do not enjoy. Can sound
somewhat affected.) □ *You three visit the museum without me. Looking at fussy old paintings is not my cup of
tea.* □ *Going to church, Mary said, was not her cup of
tea.*

Not to know someone from Adam To be completely unfamiliar with someone; not to know someone by sight at
all. □ JILL: *Did you see the head of the company come
through our office this morning?* JANE: *I'm not sure. I
wouldn't know the head of the company from Adam.* □
*My sister told me I should drop in on her old friend when
I'm in New York, but her friend doesn't know me from
Adam, so I don't think there would be any point in my
dropping in.*

Not to let the grass grow under one's feet To begin
something without delay and carry it out industriously.
□ SANDRA: *Last night I told Alan that we needed a new
bookshelf, and he had built one by the time I got home today.* JILL: *Boy, he doesn't let the grass grow under his feet.*
□ *Mary didn't let the grass grow under her feet when she
was looking for a job. She would get the "help wanted"
section of the paper every morning, and spend the afternoons applying for all the advertised jobs she was qualified for.*

Not worth a hill of beans Worthless. (Casual and somewhat countrified.) □ *Arthur's asking $20,000 for that
property, and it isn't worth a hill of beans.* □ BILL: *I
promise you, once we're married, I'll never look at another woman.* NANCY: *Your promises aren't worth a hill
of beans.*

Not worth the paper it's written on Meaningless or without authority. (Describes a worthless document.) □ *That contract isn't worth the paper it's written on. All the signatures are forged.* □ *Don't buy stock in that company. It's not worth the paper it's written on.*

Nothing comes of nothing. Everything has a source; or, if you contribute nothing, you will get nothing. □ JILL: *Why are you so depressed today?* JANE: *No reason.* JILL: *There has to be a reason. Nothing comes of nothing.* □ *I'm not surprised you did so poorly in school; you haven't been putting in any effort. Nothing comes of nothing.*

Nothing is certain but death and taxes. Everything in life is unpredictable, except that you can be sure you will die and you will have to pay taxes. (You can also refer to *death and taxes* as the only certain things in life.) □ SON: *I can't believe how much tax money is being withheld from my paycheck!* FATHER: *Welcome to adult life, where nothing is certain but death and taxes.* □ ELLEN: *I just know I'm going to get this job. I'm certain of it.* JANE: *You never know. Nothing is certain but death and taxes.*

Nothing is certain but the unforeseen. You cannot foresee what will happen. □ JILL: *Now that we've got a new boss, this is certain to be a nicer place to work.* JANE: *Nothing is certain but the unforeseen.* □ *It does seem likely that we will lose the election, but who knows? Nothing is certain but the unforeseen.*

Nothing is given so freely as advice. People will give you advice more willingly than they give you anything else. □ *Although no one in my family was willing to give me a loan, they all had suggestions about how I could get the money from elsewhere. Nothing is given so freely as advice.* □ *Don't hesitate to ask people what they* *think you ought to do. Nothing is given so freely as advice.*

Nothing so bad but (it) might have been worse. Although bad things do happen, they are not as bad as other things you can imagine that might have happened. □ JOAN: *This is like a nightmare! My house burned down —I lost everything!* NANCY: *At least you and your family are safe. Nothing so bad but might have been worse.* □ *My bicycle tire blew out, but at least it blew out within walking distance of a repair shop. Nothing so bad but it might have been worse.*

Nothing succeeds like success. If you have succeeded in the past, you will continue to be successful in the future. □ *After Alan's brilliant courtroom victory, everyone wanted to be his client. Nothing succeeds like success.* □ *I'm sure you and your wife will be happily married for many, many years. After all, you've been happy together for a number of years already, and nothing succeeds like success.*

Nothing to boast about Ordinary; mediocre. □ *In high school, my grades were acceptable, but they were nothing to boast about.* □ JILL: *Does this town have a good library?* NANCY: *It's nothing to boast about.*

Nothing to write home about Mediocre; not as good as you expected. □ *I went to that new restaurant last night. It's nothing to write home about.* □ JILL: *I went to see a movie last night.* JANE: *How was it?* JILL: *Nothing to write home about.*

Nothing ventured, nothing gained. If you do not take risks, you will never accomplish anything. □ BILL: *Should I ask my boss for a promotion?* SANDRA: *Nothing ventured, nothing gained.* □ *I think I'll audition for a part in that play. Nothing ventured, nothing gained.*

Nuttier than a fruitcake See *(As) nutty as a fruitcake.*

O

Old habits die hard.   People find it difficult to change their accustomed behavior. □ *Joan retired last year, but she still gets up as early as she used to when she had to go to work. Old habits die hard.* □ *Even though my daughter has left home, I still set a place at table for her every night. Old habits die hard.*

Once a priest, always a priest AND **Once a whore, always a whore**   A person who has done a certain kind of job will always have the characteristics of people who do that job, even after he or she no longer does that kind of work. (This can be applied to many different occupations.) □ ALAN: *My cousin left the clergy, but boy! He still preaches at me all the time.* JANE: *Once a priest, always a priest, huh?* □ SANDRA: *Sshh! Don't talk so loud.* JILL: *You can stop hushing people, Sandra; you haven't worked in a library for the last three years.* SANDRA: *I can't help it. Once a librarian, always a librarian.*

Once a whore, always a whore   See the previous entry.

Once bitten, twice shy   When something has hurt you once, you tend to avoid it. □ JILL: *Let's go ride the roller coaster.* JANE: *No, thanks. I got really sick on one of those once—once bitten, twice shy.* □ *I once sent in money for something I saw advertised in the back of a magazine, but the merchandise was of such poor quality I was* *sorry I'd bought it. I'll never buy anything that way again; once bitten, twice shy.*

Once in a blue moon Very seldom. □ JILL: *Does your husband ever bring you flowers?* ELLEN: *Once in a blue moon.* □ *Once in a blue moon, I buy a fashion magazine, just to see what people are wearing.*

One cannot be in two places at once. You cannot be in more than one place or do more than one thing at the same time. □ CHILD: *Mom! Mom! Come help me wash my hair!* MOTHER: *Just a minute! I'm putting clean sheets on your bed right now, and I can't be in two places at once.* □ JILL: *Where's Laura? I told her I need her to come to this meeting!* JANE: *But you just sent her to the office supply store to get something for you. She can't be in two places at once.*

One cannot love and be wise. People often fall in love with someone with whom they are not compatible or behave foolishly when they are in love. □ JILL: *George stood outside Jenny's house all night in the rain, hoping to get a glimpse of her. Wasn't that a silly thing to do?* JANE: *One cannot love and be wise.* □ *My son and his girlfriend have decided to get married in the spring. I don't think that's wise, since they won't have enough money saved by then to set up house. But then, one cannot love and be wise.*

One good turn deserves another. If someone does you a favor, you should do a favor for that person in return. □ JILL: *Thanks for the ride.* JANE: *It's the least I can do after you helped me wash the car last week. One good turn deserves another.* □ CHILD: *I don't want to help Grandma go shopping.* FATHER: *But she helped you with your homework yesterday. And one good turn deserves another.*

One hand for oneself and one for the ship. When you are on a ship, always use one hand to steady yourself, and one to work; likewise, always put some effort into safeguarding yourself as well as into working. □ *The old sailor chastised us for forgetting to hold onto something during the rough weather. "One hand for yourself and one for the ship," he bellowed.* □ *This company expects you to work hard, but not so hard that you hurt yourself. One hand for yourself and one for the ship.*

One has to draw the line somewhere. It is necessary to set limits and enforce them. □ ELLEN: *This is the fifth night this week that my son has stayed out too late.* SAN-DRA: *Why not punish him, then? You have to draw the line somewhere.* □ *I am a fairly easy-going employer, but I cannot allow my employees to take two hours for lunch. I have to draw the line somewhere.*

One law for the rich and another for the poor Rich people are sometimes able to escape without punishment when they commit crimes, while poor people are usually punished. □ JILL: *The banker who embezzled all that money was sentenced today. He only has to do charity work. But the janitor who helped him will have to go to jail.* JANE: *Sounds like one law for the rich and another for the poor.* □ *It doesn't seem fair—rich people can avoid paying their taxes and not get in trouble, but poor people are always punished if they don't pay. We shouldn't have one law for the rich and another for the poor.*

One man's loss is another man's gain. When one person loses something, another person gets it. (You can substitute appropriate names or pronouns for the phrases *one man's* and *another man's,* as in the second example.) □ *Melvin found a five-dollar bill on the sidewalk. "One man's loss is another man's gain," he thought to himself, as he took the money.* □ JANE: *Andy just got fired.* JILL: *I know. And Andy's loss is my gain; I'm getting promoted to his job!*

One man's meat is another man's poison. Something that one person likes may be distasteful to someone else. ☐ FRED: *What do you mean you don't like French fries? They're the best food in the world!* ALAN: *One man's meat is another man's poison.* ☐ JILL: *I don't understand why Don doesn't like to read science fiction. It's the most interesting thing to read.* JANE: *One man's meat is another man's poison.*

One might as well be hanged for a sheep as for a lamb. If you have decided to do something that will have unpleasant consequences, do it to the largest degree possible, so that you will feel that the punishment was worth it. ☐ *Andrew knew he couldn't afford a gold watch, but he decided to use his credit card to get one anyway. Then he told himself, "One might as well be hanged for a sheep as for a lamb," and bought the most expensive watch in the jewelry store.* ☐ FRED: *I think I'll have a chocolate bar.* JANE: *I thought your diet didn't allow you to eat candy.* FRED: *It doesn't; I've decided to splurge.* JANE: *Then don't just have a chocolate bar; have a whole box of chocolates. You might as well be hanged for a sheep as for a lamb.*

One of these days is none of these days. If you say you will do something "one of these days," you probably do not seriously intend to do it, and therefore it will not get done. ☐ ALAN: *When are you going to fix the garage door?* SANDRA: *One of these days.* ALAN: *One of these days is none of these days.* ☐ JILL: *One of these days, I'll pay you the money I owe you.* JANE: *One of these days is none of these days.*

One swallow does not a summer make. See the following entry.

One swallow does not make a summer. AND **One swallow does not a summer make.** You should not assume that something is true just because you have seen one piece of evidence for it. □ AMANDA: *I got a good grade on this quiz! My troubles in school are over.* NANCY: *One swallow does not a summer make.* □ SANDRA: *I think we'll be able to sell a lot of things today. I've already sold a television set.* JOHN: *One swallow doesn't make a summer.*

One's bark is worse than one's bite.   Someone makes a lot of harsh-sounding threats but never carries them out. □ *Don't get upset at anything my father says. His bark is worse than his bite.* □ JILL: *Lisa says she's going to sue me for letting my dog dig up her rosebushes.* JOHN: *Don't pay any attention. Her bark is worse than her bite.*

One's heart is in one's mouth   You are afraid or apprehensive. (Also the cliché: **with one's heart in one's mouth,** afraid or apprehensive, and **have one's heart in one's mouth,** to be afraid or apprehensive.) □ *As I entered the job interview, my heart was in my mouth.* □ *While the surgeons worked to save her husband, Alicia paced in the hospital waiting room with her heart in her mouth.*

(Only) time will tell.   You will only know the outcome after time has passed. □ JILL: *Do you think Bill and Nancy will have a happy marriage?* JOHN: *Only time will tell.* □ *I'm not sure yet if our advertising campaign was a success. Time will tell.*

(Open) confession is good for the soul.   If you have done something wrong, you will feel better if you confess that you did it. □ *You ought to tell Dad that you broke his radio. Open confession is good for the soul.* □ PENELOPE: *I've been so upset about cheating on the exam that I haven't been sleeping nights.* SAM: *You can do something about it; confession is good for the soul.*

Opportunity knocks but once.   You will only have one chance to do something important or profitable. (You can say **opportunity knocks** to signal that someone's chance to do something important is here right now.) □ *Investing in my business may be your only chance to make money. Come on. Opportunity knocks but once.* □ *When Nancy got a scholarship offer from a college far away, her parents encouraged her to go, even though they didn't like the thought of her moving so far from home. "Opportunity knocks but once," they said, "and this may be your only chance to get a good education."*

Opportunity makes a thief.   Anyone would steal, given a chance to do so without being punished. □ JANE: *I used to think Greta was a good person, but I just found out she steals office supplies from work.* JILL: *Don't judge her so harshly. Opportunity makes a thief.* □ *Mr. Cooper thought of himself as a moral man. But opportunity makes a thief, and here he had the opportunity to steal thousands of dollars undetected.*

Other times, other manners   Different generations or eras have different customs. □ *Clarice thought her grandchildren addressed their friends in startlingly rude terms. "But then," she reflected, "other times, other manners."* □ EDNA: *The young folks today are so shocking. Why, when I was their age, you wouldn't kiss your husband in public, let alone some of the things these children do!* ALONSO: *Other times, other manners.*

Out of sight, out of mind.   If you do not see something frequently, you will forget about it. (Sometimes used to imply that you will forget about people who have moved away.) □ *Ever since I moved, none of my old friends have gotten in touch with me. It's out of sight, out of mind with them, evidently.* □ *My electric bill somehow got moved to the bottom of the stack on my desk, and I forgot all about paying it. Out of sight, out of mind.*

Out of the frying pan into the fire. From a bad situation to an even worse one. □ *Joseph went out of the frying pan and into the fire by running away from home. Living on his own was much more difficult than living with his parents had been.* □ *I thought my new job would be less stressful than my old one, but I seem to have jumped out of the frying pan into the fire.*

Out of the mouths of babes What a remarkable thing for a child to say. (You can say this to another adult, or as an aside to yourself, after a child says something unusually pertinent.) □ *Mr. and Mrs. Doyle were quietly bickering in the kitchen when their seven-year-old daughter came in and said, "You guys should get counseling." After a surprised pause, Mrs. Doyle remarked, "Out of the mouths of babes."* □ CHILD: *Don't eat so much candy, Mommy. Candy is bad for your teeth.* MOTHER: *Out of the mouths of babes.*

P

Paddle one's own canoe Be independent; take care of yourself. (Casual.) □ *I've had to paddle my own canoe ever since I left home.* □ *I can't support you anymore; paddle your own canoe.*

Patience is a virtue. It is good to be patient. □ JILL: *I wish Mary would hurry up and call me back!* JANE: *Patience is a virtue.* □ FRED: *The doctor has kept us waiting for half an hour! If he doesn't call us into his office pretty soon, I may do something violent.* ELLEN: *Calm down, dear. Patience is a virtue.*

Pay the piper To pay for something; to pay what you owe. (Implies that you have avoided paying for as long as possible but cannot avoid it any longer.) □ *Linda frequently worked for a week at a time without much food or sleep. Eventually she had to pay the piper. She got so worn-out and sick that she could no longer work that hard.* □ *I once played truant from school for three days. I had a lot of fun, but it came time to pay the piper when the principal told my mother what I had done.*

Pay through the nose To pay an exorbitant price. (Casual.) □ JILL: *Did you get tickets to the concert?* JOHN: *Yes, but I had to pay through the nose.* □ *Don't buy your clothes at that fancy store, unless you want to pay through the nose.*

Penny wise and pound foolish   Thrifty with small sums and foolish with large sums. (Describes someone who will go to a lot of trouble and expense to save a little money. Even in the U.S., the reference is to British pounds sterling.) ☐ *Belinda saved box tops from twelve boxes of cereal and spent three dollars on postage for the cereal company to send her a free picture frame. She could have gotten the same picture frame at the department store for $2.50. Penny wise and pound foolish.* ☐ SAM: *If we drive to six different grocery stores, we'll get the best bargains on everything we buy.* ALAN: *But with gasoline so expensive, that's penny wise and pound foolish.*

People who live in glass houses shouldn't throw stones.   You should not criticize other people for having the same faults that you yourself have. ☐ JILL: *Richard sure was drinking a lot at the office party.* JANE: *I noticed you had quite a few cocktails yourself. People who live in glass houses shouldn't throw stones.* ☐ ELLEN: *I really hate Josephine. She's mean and unforgiving and uncharitable, and she's always saying nasty things about me.* BILL: *People who live in glass houses shouldn't throw stones.*

Physician, heal thyself.   Do not rebuke someone for a fault or problem you have yourself. (Biblical.) ☐ ELLEN: *You're such a spendthrift. You should go on a strict budget.* FRED: *But you manage money even worse than I do! Physician, heal thyself.* ☐ SANDRA: *You look like you're gaining weight. You should probably get more exercise.* ALAN: *Physician, heal thyself. You're getting a little pudgy, too.*

Politics makes strange bedfellows.   People who would normally dislike and avoid one another will work together if they think it is politically useful to do so. ☐ JILL: *I never would have thought that genteel, aristocratic candidate would pick such a rabble-rousing, rough-mannered running mate.* JANE: *Politics makes strange*

bedfellows. □ *I think MacAllister is a reprehensible person, but he and I both agree that there ought to be
stronger laws against pollution, so we work together. It's
another example of politics making strange bedfellows.*

Possession is nine-tenths of the law. If you actually
possess something, you have a stronger legal claim to
owning it than someone who merely says it belongs to
him or her. □ *Dana may say he owns this house, but we
actually live in it, and possession is nine-tenths of the
law.* □ *Even though Joe stole the jewelry, he figured he
could claim to own it, since he actually had it, and possession is nine-tenths of the law.*

Pour oil on troubled waters To soothe people who are
arguing. (Oil can be poured on stormy seas to calm the
water.) □ *Every time Joseph and his brother argued, Joseph's wife would invariably be the one to pour oil on the
troubled waters.* □ *Everyone in the family depended on
Margaret to pour oil on troubled waters whenever there
was a quarrel.*

Poverty is no sin. See the following entry.

Poverty is not a crime. AND **Poverty is no sin.** You
should not condemn someone for being poor. □ ELLEN: *I
wish there were a law to make all those poor people move
out of our neighborhood.* JIM: *Poverty is not a crime, Ellen.* □ NED: *I could never be friends with Michael. He
hardly makes any money.* ALAN: *But poverty is no sin.*

Practice makes perfect. Doing something over and over
again is the only way to learn to do it well. □ JILL: *I'm not
going to try to play the piano anymore. I always make so
many mistakes.* JANE: *Don't give up. Practice makes perfect.* □ CHILD: *How come you're so good at peeling potatoes?* FATHER: *Practice makes perfect.*

Practice what you preach. You yourself should do the
things you advise other people to do. □ FRED: *You should*

eat more vegetables; your diet is appalling. JANE: *But you aren't eating any vegetables. Practice what you preach.* □ *Dad always told us we should only watch an hour of television every day, but we all knew he didn't practice what he preached.*

Pretty is as pretty does. It is more important to treat people well than to be good-looking; just because you are good-looking does not mean you are a good person. (Said only of girls and women.) □ DAUGHTER: *I wish I were as pretty as Joanne.* MOTHER: *Pretty is as pretty does, and if you are nice to people they will like you just as much as they like her.* □ *Janice may have a pretty face, but pretty is as pretty does; the way she behaves isn't pretty at all.*

Prevention is better than cure. It is better to try to keep a bad thing from happening than it is to fix the bad thing once it has happened. □ *If we spend more money on education, so that children learn to be responsible citizens, we won't have to spend so much money on prisons. Prevention is better than cure.* □ *When I was young, I hated to brush my teeth, until the year when I had to have fifteen cavities filled. Since then, I've decided that prevention is better than cure.*

Pride goes before a fall. AND **Pride goeth before a fall.** If you are too proud and overconfident, you will make mistakes leading to your defeat. (Biblical.) □ PENELOPE: *I'm the best student in my History class. I'm sure I can pass the exam without studying very hard.* SAM: *Be careful. Pride goes before a fall, you know.* □ *David thinks he's such a skilled driver that the police will never catch him speeding, but pride goeth before a fall.*

Pride goeth before a fall. See the previous entry.

Procrastination is the thief of time. If you put off doing what you ought to do, you will end up not having enough time to do it properly. □ JIM: *Have you started* *looking for a job yet?* JANE: *Oh, that can wait till tomorrow.* JIM: *Procrastination is the thief of time.* □ *I really shouldn't delay working on my research paper any longer. Procrastination is the thief of time.*

Promises are like piecrust, made to be broken. It is useless to make promises, because people always break their promises. □ *Lisa made Andrew promise not to drink anymore, but promises are like piecrust, made to be broken.* □ JOHN: *You promised me you'd have the work finished in time!* FRED: *Promises are like piecrust, made to be broken.*

Pull oneself up by the bootstraps AND **Pull oneself up by one's bootstraps** To start out with nothing and succeed through hard work, without help from anyone else. □ *After his store burned down, Johnson pulled himself up by the bootstraps and soon had enough money to start another business.* □ *Uncle John thinks that poor people should pull themselves up by their bootstraps and not rely on the government for help.*

Pull the wool over someone's eyes To fool someone. □ *Don't try to pull the wool over my eyes. I know you've been smoking in your bedroom.* □ *It was easy to pull the wool over Aunt Emma's eyes—she was extremely gullible.*

Punctuality is the soul of business. You should be on time for all your business appointments. □ *The office manager insisted on everyone's coming to work on time, not a minute late. "Punctuality is the soul of business," she said.* □ *Josephine always met her clients exactly when she said she would, which gave them the impression that she was extremely businesslike, since punctuality is the soul of business.*

Put one's best foot forward To behave exceptionally well. □ *Always put your best foot forward when you go* *to a job interview.* □ *I want you to put your best foot forward when you meet Ms. Lucas; she's very influential and could help us a lot.*

Put one's foot down To set a limit that you are not willing to alter. □ *Dan was working until eight o'clock every night until his wife put her foot down.* □ *When all of the students began to neglect their homework, the teacher decided it was time to put his foot down.*

Put one's foot in it Inadvertently to do something rude, unwise, or awkward. □ *I really put my foot in it when I asked Mrs. Stephens how her husband was; I didn't know he died last week.* □ Jill: *I can't believe Marie wore a fur coat to the Anti-Animal-Cruelty meeting.* Jane: *Yes, she put her foot in it, all right.*

Put one's shoulder to the wheel To start working hard at something. □ *If you want to graduate with honors, you'll have to put your shoulder to the wheel and improve your grades.* □ *James cheerfully put his shoulder to the wheel and helped out whenever there was a difficult job to do.*

Put something on the line To risk something, especially money; to pay or put up money. □ *Megan put all of her savings on the line when she started her own business.* □ *I can't keep putting off my landlord with promises to pay. He wants me to put some money on the line.*

Put that in your pipe and smoke it! Acknowledge that you do not know the truth, and I do. (Emphatic and rude.) □ Ellen: *You're worthless! You never help me around the house!* Fred: *That's not true! I've cleaned the bathroom every week!* Ellen: *You have?* Fred: *Yeah, put that in your pipe and smoke it!* □ Jim: *Don't lecture me about John Donne. I know more about John Donne than you do. He was one of the greatest English poets of the eighteenth century.* John: *Eighteenth century?! He died* *in 1631!* JIM: *Really?* JOHN: *Yeah! Put that in your pipe and smoke it!*

Put your money where your mouth is. Be willing to risk something for what you say you believe. (Can be used to challenge someone to place a bet on what he or she has just said.) □ FRED: *I think Vincent is one of the most brilliant young writers today.* JANE: *Have you ever bought one of his books?* FRED: *Well, no. . . .* JANE: *Put your money where your mouth is, Fred.* □ *When Bill declared that his favorite football team was bound to win Monday's game, his friends said, "Put your money where your mouth is."*

Put your trust in God, and keep your powder dry. Have faith that God will make sure that you win a conflict, but be prepared to fight well and vigorously. (Supposed to have been said by Oliver Cromwell; *powder* means gunpowder.) □ BILL: *Am I going to win my lawsuit?* ALAN: *All you can do is put your trust in God, and keep your powder dry.* □ *Before the big game, the coach told the team that he was sure they would win, but they had better work hard. He told them, in effect, to put their trust in God, and keep their powder dry.*

R

Rain cats and dogs To rain extremely hard. (Casual.) □ *You can't go outside now; it's raining cats and dogs.* □ *Even though it was raining cats and dogs, Gordon went outside without an umbrella.*

Rake someone over the coals See *Haul someone over the coals.*

Rats abandon a sinking ship. AND **Like rats abandoning a sinking ship** You can tell when something is about to fail because large numbers of people begin to leave it. (Can imply that the people who leave are "rats," that is, selfish and disloyal.) □ JILL: *The company next door must be going bankrupt.* JANE: *How do you know?* JILL: *All its employees are resigning. Rats abandon a sinking ship.* □ *After the play got bad reviews, the cast members all went looking for other jobs, like rats abandoning a sinking ship.*

Razor-sharp See *(As) sharp as a razor.*

Read between the lines. Understand what someone is implying. □ JILL: *What did Jenny say?* JANE: *She thinks I did a horrible job on that report.* JILL: *She said that?* JANE: *Not in so many words, but I could read between the lines.* □ *On the surface, the annual report makes it sound as if the company is doing very well, but if you* *read between the lines, you can tell that it's in extreme financial trouble.*

Read someone like a(n open) book. To be able to tell what someone desires or intends even though that person has not said anything. (It is not polite to tell someone that you can read him or her like a book.) □ FRED: *All right, all right, I'll change my necktie if you don't like it.* ELLEN: *But I didn't say anything about your necktie!* FRED: *You didn't have to. I can read you like a book.* □ JILL: *Joe's planning to go on vacation next week and leave us all this work to do.* JANE: *How do you know?* JILL: *I can read him like an open book.*

Revenge is a dish best served cold. It is very satisfying to get revenge a long time after the event for which you want revenge. □ *I don't mind waiting to get revenge on Greg; I'll wait ten years if I have to. Revenge is a dish best served cold.* □ *Don't be in a hurry to avenge yourself on Bernie. Revenge is a dish best served cold.*

Revenge is sweet. It is very pleasurable to revenge yourself on someone. □ JILL: *Remember when Tom left me for another woman? Well, she just left him, and he asked me out on a date. I told him I had better things to do.* JANE: *Revenge is sweet, huh?* □ *When I was little, my father used to wake me up on Saturdays by squirting me with a water pistol. The last time I went to visit him, I sneaked up on him on Saturday morning and squirted him with my water pistol. Revenge is sweet.*

Ring down the curtain To cause something to end. □ *One of our neighbors rang down the curtain on our party by calling the police.* □ *After thirty years of writing novels about the same detective, Edward decided it was time to ring down the curtain on that particular character.*

177

Rob Peter to pay Paul To take from one person to give to another. □ NANCY: *I won't have enough fabric for the quilt I'm making for Beth. I'll have to take some from what I was going to use for Joan's quilt.* BILL: *Isn't that just robbing Peter to pay Paul?* □ JILL: *Can you lend me ten dollars? I owe it to Maureen.* JANE: *Talk about robbing Peter to pay Paul!*

Rock-solid See *(As) solid as a rock.*

Rock-steady See *(As) steady as a rock.*

Rome was not built in a day. It takes a lot of time to achieve something important. □ JILL: *We've been painting the house all day, and there's still so much to do!* JANE: *Be patient. Rome wasn't built in a day.* □ PROFESSOR: *When will you finish your research project?* STUDENT: *It'll take me a while. Rome wasn't built in a day, you know.*

Rose-red See *(As) red as a rose.*

Ruby-red See *(As) red as a ruby.*

S

Save for a rainy day To save something, usually money, for a time when you need it. □ *I'm sending you some money; if there's nothing you need to spend it on right now, save it for a rainy day.* □ JILL: *I'm going to spend my annual bonus on a weekend trip.* JANE: *I think I'll save mine for a rainy day.*

Scarcer than hen's teeth See *(As) scarce as hen's teeth.*

See no evil, hear no evil, speak no evil. Ignore any evil that you come in contact with; be virtuous even though there is evil around you. (Often represented by three monkeys, one of which is covering his eyes, one his ears, and one his mouth.) □ JILL: *Do you have any idea why Fred is staying in the office so late every night?* JANE: *Not me. Like the three little monkeys, I see no evil, hear no evil, speak no evil.* □ CHILD: *At school today, some of the kids were saying bad words about the teacher!* GRAND-MOTHER: *Well, you just ignore them. See no evil, hear no evil, speak no evil.*

Seeing is believing. It is hard to believe something you have not seen. (Implies that you will not believe the thing under discussion until you have seen it.) □ JILL: *They say Melissa has become a wonderful housekeeper now that she has her own apartment.* JANE: *Seeing is be-lieving.* □ *I really didn't think that Jerry's girlfriend* *could be as pretty as he said she was, but seeing is believing.*

Seek and ye shall find. If you want something, you must look for it. (Biblical. Can imply that the only thing you need to do to get something is look for it.) □ *The bookstore on the corner is an excellent one. Any book you want, just seek and ye shall find.* □ *When Sonia mourned that she wanted a better-paying job, her friend tossed her the "help wanted" section of the newspaper and said, "Seek and ye shall find."*

Seize the bull by the horns. AND **Take the bull by the horns.** Confront a problem boldly and directly. □ *When Jenny thought someone was following her down the alley, she seized the bull by the horns. "What do you want?" she demanded, turning to face the man behind her.* □ *The upstairs neighbors had their stereo on too loud again. "Let's wait and see if they turn it down," said Sandra. "No," said Alan, "I'm going to seize the bull by the horns." And he went upstairs to demand that they quiet down.*

Self-praise is no recommendation. If you praise yourself, people will think that you are boastful and will not respect you. □ VINCENT: *My new novel is the most powerful book ever written about the disintegration of the American family.* ALAN: *Self-praise is no recommendation.* □ *After listening to the lawyer brag about his achievements for a solid half hour, I decided I would find someone else to handle my case. Self-praise is no recommendation.*

Self-preservation is the first law of nature. Every living thing will fight to survive; it is natural to think of yourself first. □ JILL: *I can't believe you told the boss that the project failure was all my fault. How could you be so selfish?* FRED: *Self-preservation is the first law of nature.*

☐ *When Joe's best friend was arrested, Joe pretended not to know him. "Perhaps it wasn't very loyal of me," he thought, "but self-preservation is the first law of nature."*

Separate the men from the boys To decide which people are strong and capable and which are weak; to be a stringent test. (Frequently paraphrased for females, as in the second example.) ☐ *The coach promised us that the football training program would separate the men from the boys.* ☐ *"This exam," the professor promised, "will separate the men from the boys and the women from the girls."*

Separate the sheep from the goats To distinguish the good from the bad. (Biblical.) ☐ *Since you are conducting the job interviews, you will be responsible for separating the sheep from the goats.* ☐ *It is difficult to know what companies are good to invest in, but our brokerage firm is quite experienced in separating the sheep from the goats.*

Separate the wheat from the chaff To separate what is useful or valuable from what is worthless. ☐ *When it comes to books, time will separate the wheat from the chaff. Good books will have lasting appeal, and the rest will be forgotten.* ☐ *The managers hoped that the new procedure for evaluating employees would separate the wheat from the chaff.*

Set a beggar on horseback, and he'll ride to the devil. If a poor person becomes wealthy, he or she will quickly become corrupt. ☐ JILL: *Since Phil inherited all that money, all he does is go to parties and take drugs.* JANE: *Yep. Set a beggar on horseback, and he'll ride to the devil.* ☐ *George was awarded a hundred thousand dollars in damages from his lawsuit, which was probably more than he could have expected to earn in ten years. But instead of investing it, he managed to gamble it all away* *on poker games. Set a beggar on horseback, and he'll ride to the devil.*

Set a thief to catch a thief.   The best person to catch a thief is another thief, because he or she knows how thieves think. □ *The government set a thief to catch a thief, hiring a stockbroker convicted of fraudulent practices to entrap the stockbroker they were investigating for fraud.* □ JILL: *How are we ever going to find out who's been stealing from petty cash?* JANE: *Call up Suzy and ask her opinion.* JILL: *But she was fired for stealing from petty cash!* JANE: *Exactly. Set a thief to catch a thief.*

Share and share alike.   To share fairly and evenly. (Used to describe a situation in which everyone divides something equally; often used to instruct people to share.) □ *Jimmy, you can't have all the apples. Share and share alike.* □ *When our business began to make a profit, we agreed that everyone would get an equal percentage, share and share alike.*

Ships that pass in the night   People who meet each other only once, or people who meet but do not become very intimate. (From Henry Wadsworth Longfellow's poem, "Tales of a Wayside Inn.") □ *I had hoped to see Felicia again after the wonderful day we spent together, but we were only ships that pass in the night.* □ *Lillian and I are cousins, but we've always been ships that pass in the night.*

Shoot first, ask questions later.   Assume that everyone you encounter is hostile to you; or, take action, even though you do not know enough to be sure if it is the right action. □ *The self-defense instructor said, "When someone is following you down a deserted street at night, don't ask him what he wants. Shoot first, ask questions later."* □ *If the foreman saw that one of the workers was working slowly, he didn't stop to find out if the worker* *was sick or unhappy; he just fired him. He believed in shooting first and asking questions later.*

Short reckonings make long friends. If you borrow something from a friend, pay it back as soon as possible, so that the two of you remain friendly. □ *Now that you've finished using Bert's saw, take it right back to him. Short reckonings make long friends.* □ *When Linda gave me a loan, I paid it back within two weeks, since short reckonings make long friends.*

Shrouds have no pockets. You cannot take any material goods with you when you die. □ *Why are you so miserly? Shrouds have no pockets, you know.* □ *You should use your money to enjoy yourself while you're alive. Shrouds have no pockets.*

Shut the stable door after the horse has bolted. AND **Lock the stable door after the horse is stolen.** To try to prevent something that has already happened; to act too late. □ *When Ray heard that the bank had failed, he tried to withdraw his money, but there was no money to withdraw. He was shutting the stable door after the horse had bolted.* □ *Jenny has stopped smoking since the doctor told her that her lungs were in bad shape, but I'm afraid she's locking the stable door after the horse is stolen.*

Silence gives consent. If you do not object to what someone says or does, you can be assumed to agree with or condone it. □ JILL: *What did Fred say when you told him we were thinking about leaving the office early?* JANE: *He didn't say anything.* JILL: *Then he must not mind if we go. Silence gives consent.* □ *Since their mother had never reprimanded them for staying up late at night, the children assumed that silence gave consent. Consequently, they were very surprised one night when* *she spanked them for refusing to go to bed at eight o'clock.*

Silence is golden.   Silence is often good or desirable. (You can use this phrase to advise someone to be silent.) □ *Jerry has two teenage children who play the radio all day. He knows that silence is golden.* □ *Hush! Silence is golden.*

Sing before breakfast, you'll cry before night. AND **Sing before breakfast, you'll cry before supper.**   If you wake up feeling very happy, your mood will change before the end of the day. □ JILL: *I woke up in such a good mood today. I don't even know why, but everything seems good.* JANE: *Sing before breakfast, you'll cry before night.* □ ALAN: *Good morning, dear! Isn't it a wonderful day? I feel great.* SANDRA: *Sing before breakfast, you'll cry before supper.*

Sing before breakfast, you'll cry before supper.   See the previous entry.

Sleep like a log   To sleep very well and deeply. □ *Julia was so worn-out from hiking all morning that she knew she would sleep like a log that night.* □ SANDRA: *Did you sleep well?* ALAN: *Yes, like a log.*

Sleep like a top   To sleep soundly. (British.) □ *I feel very refreshed this morning, since I slept like a top last night.* □ JILL: *Did you sleep well?* JANE: *Like a top.*

Slow and steady wins the race.   If you work slowly but constantly, you will succeed better than if you work fast for a short while and do not continue. (Associated with Aesop's fable of "The Tortoise and the Hare.") □ *Now that you've made a good start on your project, don't get lazy. Slow and steady wins the race.* □ *Joy only had a little bit of time to spend sewing every day, but she worked steadily, and soon had finished a beautiful quilt. Slow and steady wins the race.*

Slow but sure AND **Slowly but surely**   Slow but unstoppable. □ *Vincent's progress on his novel was slow but sure.* □ *Nancy is finishing the paint job on her house, slowly but surely.*

Slower than molasses in January   See *(As) slow as molasses in January.*

Small things please small minds.   See *Little things please little minds.*

Snow-white   See *(As) white as snow.*

So many countries, so many customs   People in different countries have different ways of behaving. □ *In the last place I visited, it was considered rude to put your hands on the table at dinner, but here, it's rude to keep them under the table. So many countries, so many customs.* □ *When Judy took her trip around the world, she learned that she had to dress very differently in every country in order to be considered modest. So many countries, so many customs.*

Someone cannot see beyond the end of his nose.   Someone is not perceptive; someone is unaware of what is happening around him or her. (Somewhat casual.) □ SANDRA: *I think you ought to reprimand Elizabeth for coming in late so often.* FRED: *Has she been coming in late? I didn't notice.* SANDRA: *Sometimes I think you can't see beyond the end of your nose.* □ *Melissa really can't see beyond the end of her nose; it took her a month to notice that the building next to her house had been knocked down.*

Someone is not out of the woods yet.   Someone's problems are not yet over. □ JILL: *Has Eddie recovered from his surgery?* JANE: *He's not out of the woods yet, I'm afraid.* □ *I have paid most of my debts, but I'm not out of the woods yet.*

Someone puts his pants on one leg at a time. The person named is only human; the person named is an ordinary person. □ PENELOPE: *That man is my favorite movie star. Don't you think he's just divine?* SANDRA: *Oh, I don't know. I imagine he puts his pants on one leg at a time.* □ *You don't need to be so extreme about admiring Mr. Graves. He puts his pants on one leg at a time, like everybody else.*

Someone will get his (or hers). Someone will be punished for his or her misdeeds. (Casual.) □ JILL: *It seems like Fred can do any evil thing he wants.* JANE: *Don't worry. He'll get his.* □ *You may think you will always profit by your life of crime, but you'll get yours.*

Something is better than nothing. It is better to get only some of what you want than to get nothing at all. (Also the cliché: **better than nothing,** a way to describe something that is not exactly what you want, or not as much as you want.) □ FRED: *I only got $50 for all those books I sold.* JANE: *Something is better than nothing.* □ JILL: *Is your camera very good?* JANE: *It's better than nothing.*

Something is rotten in (the state of) Denmark. Something suspicious is going on. (From Shakespeare's play, *Hamlet.*) □ JIM: *Look, there's a light on in the office, even though it's way past the time everyone should have left.* JOHN: *Something is rotten in the state of Denmark.* □ SANDRA: *I wonder why Fred is coming in so late every morning.* JANE: *Something is rotten in Denmark.*

Soon ripe, soon rotten. See *Early ripe, early rotten.*

Sow the wind and reap the whirlwind To start some kind of trouble that grows much larger than you planned. (Biblical.) □ *Our enemy has sown the wind by provoking this war, and they will reap the whirlwind when we vanquish them.* □ JILL: *Bruce was only trying* *to play a practical joke with the office computer, but his joke program did so much damage that he's been fired.* JANE: *Sounds like he sowed the wind and reaped the whirlwind.*

Spare the rod and spoil the child. You should punish a child when he or she misbehaves, because if you do not, the child will grow up expecting everyone to indulge him or her. □ *Audrey's father believed literally that to spare the rod was to spoil the child; he paddled her vigorously every time she disobeyed him.* □ SANDRA: *How can you allow your little boy to be so rude?* ELLEN: *It distresses me to punish him.* SANDRA: *I can understand that, but spare the rod and spoil the child.*

Speak of the devil (and in he walks). AND **Talk of the devil (and he is sure to appear).** Talk about a certain person, and that person appears. (Used when someone appears whom you have just been talking about.) □ ALAN: *I haven't seen Bob for weeks.* SANDRA: *Look, here comes Bob right now.* ALAN: *Well, speak of the devil.* □ *Hi, there. We were just talking about you. Speak of the devil and in he walks.*

Stand the test of time To be well regarded; to last for a long time. □ *Bill and Nancy just celebrated their fiftieth wedding anniversary. Their marriage has stood the test of time.* □ *The singer's work was not popular while she was alive, but it has stood the test of time.*

Sticks and stones may break my bones, but words will never hurt me. You do not hurt me by calling me names. (A reply to someone who has called you names. Primarily used by children; sounds childish when used by adults.) □ BROTHER: *You're stupid and mean, and everybody hates you!* SISTER: *Sticks and stones may break my bones, but words will never hurt me.* □ SANDRA: *You're the most irresponsible person I know. And you're* *completely selfish.* FRED: *Sticks and stones may break my bones, but words will never hurt me.*

Still waters run deep. Quiet people are probably very thoughtful; they think a lot more than they say. □ JILL: *I get the impression that Nathan is not very smart. He never says anything.* JANE: *Don't be so sure. Still waters run deep, you know.* □ *Nina was a quiet child. "Still waters run deep," her grandmother used to say about her.*

Stolen fruit is sweetest. AND **Stolen pleasures are sweetest.** People often enjoy illicit things just because they are illicit. □ *To judge from the number of his extra-marital affairs, John must believe that stolen pleasures are sweetest.* □ JILL: *When I was a kid, I used to steal cherries from our neighbor's tree, and I've never had any other cherries that tasted as good.* JANE: *Stolen fruit is sweetest, huh?*

Stolen pleasures are sweetest. See the previous entry.

Strain at gnats and swallow camels To criticize other people for minor offenses while ignoring major offenses. (Biblical.) □ *Fred is always yelling at his secretary because sometimes her shoes are scuffed or her skirts are too short, but he ignores the messy state of his office. You might say he strains at gnats and swallows camels.* □ JILL: *Look at that. Edward is combing his hair at his desk. How unprofessional.* JANE: *Don't strain at gnats and swallow camels. There are worse problems than that around here.*

Stretch your arm no further than your sleeve will reach. Do not spend more money than you have. □ PENELOPE: *I can get enough money for college if I take out several loans.* BILL: *I'd advise against it. Stretch your arm no further than your sleeve will reach.* □ *Although Nancy really wanted a stereo, she knew she couldn't* *really afford it, and she never stretched her arm further than her sleeve would reach.*

Strike while the iron is hot. When you have an opportunity to do something, do it before you lose your chance. □ *This is the best time in the last ten years to buy a house. Strike while the iron is hot.* □ *Ask Lisa for a favor now, while she's in a good mood. Strike while the iron is hot.*

Sufficient unto the day is the evil thereof. You should not worry about things that might happen in the future; it is enough to worry about things that are happening today. (Biblical.) □ SANDRA: *I can't get to sleep; I keep thinking about the interview I have to do tomorrow.* ALAN: *If the interview is tomorrow, worry about it tomorrow. Sufficient unto the day is the evil thereof.* □ JILL: *What if I don't have enough money to pay my rent next month?* JANE: *Then you'll take care of it next month. Sufficient unto the day is the evil thereof.*

Sweeter than honey See *(As) sweet as honey.*

T

Take the bit between one's teeth   To take the initiative; to work determinedly.   □ *If you want to finish this project in time, you'll have to take the bit between your teeth.*   □ *We had practically decided to cancel the town festival when Muriel took the bit between her teeth and got the festival completely organized.*

Take the bitter with the sweet   To accept the bad things as well as the good things that happen. (Implies that the bad and good things you are talking about are very serious or important.)   □ *If you intend to get married, you must be prepared to take the bitter with the sweet.*   □ *When Susan learned that her young son was going to die from his disease, we were all amazed by the serenity with which she took the bitter with the sweet.*

Take the bull by the horns.   See *Seize the bull by the horns.*

Take the goods the gods provide.   If you have good fortune, enjoy it and use it to your advantage.   □ FRANCES: *I feel I have an unfair advantage over other people in the violin contest. After all, my parents were able to give me lessons with the very best teachers when I was young.* ALAN: *Frances, take the goods the gods provide.*   □ GEORGE: *The only reason I do so well as a model is that I* *was born with good looks. I didn't do anything to deserve my success.* BILL: *Take the goods the gods provide.*

Take the rough with the smooth   To accept difficult as well as easy times. □ *Don't give up on your business just because you lost money this month. You have to take the rough with the smooth.* □ *Lisa often felt frustrated with her studies, but took the rough with the smooth without complaining.*

Take the wind out of someone's sails   To destroy someone's enthusiasm or pride. □ *Rachel was eagerly telling us about her plans to start her own business when George took the wind out of her sails by remarking that nine out of ten small businesses go bankrupt within the first year.* □ *It seemed that Mrs. Cooper was going to spend all afternoon telling us how well her daughter had done in school, until Mrs. Johnson took the wind out of her sails by describing the more impressive academic feats of her children.*

Talk is cheap.   It is easier to say you will do something than to actually do it. (Saying this in response to someone who promises you something implies that you do not believe that person will keep the promise.) □ *My boss keeps saying she'll give me a raise, but talk is cheap.* □ *You've been promising me a new dishwasher for five years now. Talk is cheap.*

Talk of the devil (and he is sure to appear).   See *Speak of the devil (and in he walks).*

Tar someone with the same brush   To condemn someone for the same reason as you condemn someone else, whether that condemnation is justified or not. □ *Kendall and Moffat were close associates, so when Kendall was found to be practicing dishonestly, Moffat was tarred with the same brush.* □ *Having known one law-*

yer who was unprincipled and greedy, Sally tarred all lawyers with the same brush.

Tastes differ. Different people like different things. □ FRED: *Bill always goes out with such stupid girls. I can't understand why.* ALAN: *Tastes differ.* □ SANDRA: *How can you not like Ethiopian food? Everybody likes Ethiopian food!* ALAN: *Tastes differ, Sandra.*

Tell the truth and shame the devil. To tell the truth even though you have strong reasons for concealing it. □ JILL: *Have you been using my computer without asking permission?* JANE: *Uh . . . no. . . .* JILL: *Come on, Jane, tell the truth and shame the devil.* □ *I was afraid you would think badly of me if I told you that I'm a janitor, but now I feel I ought to tell the truth and shame the devil.*

That's the pot calling the kettle black. See *The pot is calling the kettle black.*

That's the way the ball bounces. AND **That's the way the cookie crumbles.** You cannot control everything that happens to you; you should accept the bad things that happen. (The ''cookie'' version is more casual.) □ BILL: *I bought a hundred lottery tickets this week, but I still didn't win!* ALAN: *That's the way the ball bounces.* □ *I was planning to have fun on my vacation, but I've been sick the whole time. I guess that's just the way the cookie crumbles.*

That's the way the cookie crumbles. See the previous entry.

The age of miracles is past. Supernatural events do not happen nowadays. □ SANDRA: *Maybe our car will suddenly start working again.* ALAN: *I don't think so. The age of miracles is past.* □ *I'm afraid your kitty won't come back to life. The age of miracles is past.*

The best defense is a good offense. If you attack your opponents, they will be so busy fighting off your attack that they will not be able to attack you. (Often associated with sports. Pronounce *defense* with the accent on the first syllable, so that it sounds similar to *offense*.) □ *The team mostly practiced offensive moves, because the coach believed that the best defense is a good offense.* □ *Jim knew that it was good to drive defensively, and he also knew that the best defense is a good offense, so he always tried to pass other drivers before they could pass him.*

The best is the enemy of the good. If you are too ambitious and try to make something better than you are capable of, you may ruin it. □ VINCENT: *After I revise it a few more times, my novel will be the best ever written.* ALAN: *I don't think you should revise it any more. Remember, the best is the enemy of the good.* □ *In fundraising as in other areas, the best is the enemy of the good. If you ask someone for a larger contribution than he can possibly give, he may give you nothing at all.*

The best-laid plans of mice and men oft go astray. AND **The best-laid schemes of mice and men gang aft agley.** Things often go wrong even though you have carefully planned what you are going to do. (The *gang aft agley* version is in Scots dialect, and comes from Robert Burns' poem "To a Mouse.") □ JILL: *This isn't fair. I reserved a hotel room for us three weeks ago, and now the clerk says he has no record of our reservation, and he doesn't think we'll be able to find anyplace else to stay on such short notice. So much for our fun weekend in the city.* JANE: *Well, these things happen. The best-laid plans of mice and men oft go astray.* □ *I had all the arrangements made for my party, and then the guest of honor got sick and I had to call the whole thing off. The best-laid schemes of mice and men gang aft agley.*

The best-laid schemes of mice and men gang aft agley. See the previous entry.

The best things come in small packages. AND **Good things come in small packages.** Small packages often contain valuable things. (Sometimes said of small people.) □ JILL: *I'm upset at George. He only gave me this tiny box for my birthday.* JANE: *Don't get upset till you know what's in it. Good things come in small packages.* □ CHILD: *I hate being so short.* GRANDMOTHER: *You shouldn't. The best things come in small packages.*

The best things in life are free. The most satisfying experiences do not cost any money. □ *Don't be gloomy because you're broke. The best things in life are free.* □ *Yesterday I took my children to the zoo. We didn't spend a penny, but we had a wonderful time. The best things in life are free.*

The bigger they are, the harder they fall. When prominent people fail, their failure is dramatic. □ *That man used to be a famous politician, but after the newspapers reported that he cheated on his wife, he lost his office and he can't get any kind of job. The bigger they are, the harder they fall.* □ *Jackson used to be the wealthiest person in the country, but he lost every cent of his money in the stock market crash. The bigger they are, the harder they fall.*

The biggest frog in the puddle AND **The biggest toad in the puddle** The most important or powerful person in some small, unimportant group. □ JILL: *Elaine seems to be obsessed with becoming class president.* JANE: *Yes, she really wants to be the biggest frog in the puddle.* □ *The people in my office don't care about doing their work; mostly they compete over who will be the biggest toad in the puddle.*

The biggest toad in the puddle See the previous entry.

The blind leading the blind A case of someone who is not capable of dealing with the situation guiding someone else who is not capable of dealing with it. □ JILL: *Arthur is helping me fill out my tax forms this year.* JANE: *Is he a tax expert?* JILL: *He read a book about income tax once.* JANE: *Sounds to me like the blind leading the blind.* □ *Nathan offered to be my guide through Philadelphia, but since he'd never been there before either, it was a case of the blind leading the blind.*

The bread always falls on the buttered side. When things go wrong, they go completely wrong. □ *Not only did my phone break, but it broke today—today of all days, when I'm expecting a really important call. The bread always falls on the buttered side.* □ *When the painting fell off the wall, it landed on a priceless porcelain vase and broke it. The bread always falls on the buttered side.*

The busiest men have the most leisure. AND **Busiest men find the most time.** Industrious people get their work done efficiently and therefore have time to do what they want. □ FRED: *How does Phil do it? He produces more than the rest of us, but he also manages to pursue all his hobbies.* ALAN: *The busiest men have the most leisure.* □ *As the town's only doctor, Bert worked extremely hard, yet he always had time to play with his children and go out with his wife. The busiest men find the most time.*

The calm before the storm The quiet period before something violent or disastrous happens. (Often refers to a person's emotions, as in the first example.) □ *Vera was sweet and smiling all morning, but those of us who knew her could tell that it was just the calm before the storm.* □ *Everyone hoped that the political upheaval was over, but the brief lull turned out to be the calm before the storm.*

The chickens come home to roost You have to face the consequences of your mistakes or bad deeds. □ JILL:

Emily found out that I said she was incompetent, and now she won't recommend me for that job. JANE: *The chickens have come home to roost, I see.* □ *For Henry, the chickens came home to roost the day his mother discovered the dent he had put in the family car.*

The child is father of the man. People's personalities form when they are children; a person will have the same qualities as an adult that he or she had as a child. (From William Wordsworth's poem, "My Heart Leaps Up.") □ JILL: *Ellen's little boy is so unpleasant.* JANE: *Yes, and just think, the child is father of the man.* □ *In Bill's case, the child was father of the man; he never lost his childhood delight in observing nature.*

The course of true love never did run smooth. People in love with each other often have to overcome difficulties in order to be together. (From Shakespeare's play, *A Midsummer Night's Dream*.) □ JILL: *What am I going to do? My boyfriend's job is transferring him to Texas, and I have to stay here.* JANE: *The course of true love never did run smooth.* □ SANDRA: *Beatrice and George seem to be fighting a lot lately. Do you suppose they're breaking up?* ALAN: *Not necessarily. The course of true love never did run smooth.*

The customer is always right. In order to keep customers happy, the people who serve them should always obey their wishes. (Often cited as a principle of good business dealings; customers sometimes say it to the people serving them in order to try to get good service.) □ CUSTOMER: *Excuse me, waiter. I didn't order a salad; why did you bring me one?* WAITER: *I'm sorry, sir, but you did order a salad.* CUSTOMER: *No, I didn't.* WAITER: *Yes, you did.* CUSTOMER: *Don't argue with me; haven't you heard that the customer is always right?* □ *When I began working at the gift shop, my boss told me, "Remember, the cus-*

tomer is always right, no matter how stupid or rude you may think he is being."

The darkest hour is just before the dawn. AND **It's always darkest just before the dawn.** When things are extremely bad, it may signal that they are about to get much better. □ JILL: *I feel like giving up. I don't have a job, my boyfriend left me, and they're raising the rent for my apartment.* JANE: *It's always darkest just before the dawn.* □ *For Brenda, the darkest hour was just before the dawn; within a week of the day she despairingly resolved to give up acting, she learned that she had gotten a part in a popular show.*

The devil can cite Scripture for his own purpose. See the following entry.

The devil can quote Scripture for his own purpose. AND **The devil can cite Scripture for his own purpose.** Evil people sometimes try to win the confidence of good people by quoting persuasive passages of Scripture; just because someone can quote Scripture to support his or her argument does not mean that the argument is virtuous. (*Scripture* usually refers to the Bible, but it can refer to other revered writings.) □ JILL: *You shouldn't go to work today. Even Jesus didn't think people should go to work. Remember how he said the lilies of the field were OK even though they didn't work?* JANE: *I also remember that the devil can cite Scripture for his own purpose.* □ SADIE: *Dad, you really ought to give me permission to go out with Nathan. He's such a polite boy, and he can even quote the Bible.* FATHER: *The devil can quote Scripture for his own purpose.*

The devil finds work for idle hands to do. If you do not have useful work to do, you will be tempted to do frivolous or harmful things to get rid of your boredom. □ *Knowing that the devil finds work for idle hands to do,*

Elizabeth always made sure that her children had plenty of chores to keep them occupied. □ During my school vacations when I was too young to get a job, the devil found work for my idle hands to do. I was always getting into trouble.

The devil is not so black as he is painted.   No one is as bad as people say he is. (Implies that people are saying too many bad things about someone.) □ JILL: *I think Roger must be the worst idiot in the world. Joe said Roger always parks his car in someone else's space, and Sandra says he's always rude.* JANE: *Give the guy a chance. The devil is not so black as he is painted.* □ *I can't believe that actress is as coldhearted as the gossip columns say she is. The devil is not so black as he is painted.*

The devil looks after his own.   Evil people are often prosperous or well taken care of. (Implies that they must be getting their prosperity from the devil, since they are not earning it by being good and deserving.) □ SANDRA: *I don't understand why the corner store is still in business. They cheat everybody!* ALAN: *Well, the devil looks after his own.* □ JILL: *How come Fletcher keeps getting promoted? Everyone knows he's cruel and dishonest.* JANE: *The devil looks after his own.*

The devil to pay   Severe and unpleasant consequences. (Usually **someone has the devil to pay** or **there will be the devil to pay.**) □ *There'll be the devil to pay if my wife finds out about my gambling.* □ *Joe had the devil to pay when his thefts were discovered.*

The devil's children have the devil's luck.   Evil people often seem to have good luck. □ *The police thought they had trapped the murderer, but he escaped. The devil's children have the devil's luck.* □ *Despite his shameless* *business practices, John prospered. The devil's children have the devil's luck.*

The difficult is done at once; the impossible takes a little longer. Tasks that are only difficult are done immediately, harder tasks take longer. (Describes a very competent group or person.) □ *The secretary in our office is extremely capable. She has a little sign on her desk that says, "The difficult is done at once; the impossible takes a little longer." In her case, it's not a joke.* □ PATRON: *I'm looking for a certain book; I'm afraid I can't remember the author or the title, but it had to do with photography, and the cover was light blue. Can you help me find it?* LIBRARIAN: *The difficult is done at once; the impossible takes a little longer.*

The early bird catches the worm. If you wake up and get to work early, you will succeed. (Sometimes used to remark that someone is awake and working surprisingly early, as in the second example.) □ FRED: *What are you doing in the office at 7:30 A.M.?* JANE: *The early bird catches the worm.* □ *I didn't expect to see you studying at the library at this hour of the morning. The early bird catches the worm, huh?*

The end justifies the means. You can use bad or immoral methods as long as you accomplish something good by using them. (Not everyone agrees with this idea.) □ *Lucy got money for the orphanage by embezzling it from the firm where she worked. "The end justifies the means," she told herself.* □ *The politician clearly believed that the end justifies the means, since he used all kinds of nefarious means to get elected.*

The exception proves the rule. Something that does not follow a rule shows that the rule exists. (Often used facetiously, to justify some rule you have proposed but which someone else has listed exceptions to. Also the cliché:

the exception that proves the rule, someone or something that does not follow a rule or trend. From a Latin phrase meaning that an exception tests a rule.) □ ELLEN: *Men are always rude.* SANDRA: *But Alan's always polite. And Larry and Ted are polite, too.* ELLEN: *They're just the exceptions that prove the rule.* □ BILL: *All the shows on TV are aimed at people with low intelligence.* ALAN: *What about that news program you like to watch?* BILL: *The exception proves the rule.*

The family that prays together stays together. Families who observe religion together will not break apart through divorce or estrangement. (This saying was invented as a slogan for the Catholic Church in the 1940s. One of its many humorous variants is "The family that plays together stays together.") □ *Mother believed that the family that prays together stays together and insisted that we all say prayers every night.* □ *Let's take our vacation together this year! The family that plays together stays together.*

The fat is in the fire. Matters have come to a crisis; trouble is about to start. □ BROTHER: *Mom found out that we broke the clock.* SISTER: *Uh-oh. The fat's in the fire now.* □ *The fat is in the fire at work; we're nowhere near finishing the project, but the deadline is in two days.*

The female of the species is more deadly than the male. In many animal species, the female is poisonous and the male is not, and, by analogy, women are more dangerous than men. □ *The TV show about famous women murderers evidently wanted to prove that the female of the species is more deadly than the male.* □ BILL: *My old girlfriend's been threatening me ever since I broke up with her, but she's too small and weak to do me any harm.* FRED: *I'd be careful if I were you. The female of the species is more deadly than the male.*

The first hundred years are the hardest. The first hundred years of your life are the hardest, and after that, you can expect things to get easier; in other words, your whole life will probably be difficult. (A jocular, ironic way to console someone who is having difficulties.) □ *Don't worry; things are bound to improve for you. The first hundred years are the hardest.* □ *Feeling desperate, I went to ask Grandpa for advice, but all he said was, "Cheer up. The first hundred years are the hardest."*

The first step is always the hardest. Starting a new endeavor is the hardest part of it. □ FRED: *I want to quit smoking, but I can't convince myself to sign up for the "stop smoking" program.* JILL: *The first step is always the hardest.* □ *If I can just start this project, I know the rest will be easy. The first step is always the hardest.*

The gods send nuts to those who have no teeth. People often get good fortune that is no use to them. □ *It's a pity that the novelist's work is getting critical recognition now, when she is so old and feebleminded that she can hardly remember her own name. The gods send nuts to those who have no teeth.* □ *Soon after Melissa lost her hearing, she won season tickets to the symphony. The gods send nuts to those who have no teeth.*

The good die young. Good people tend to die at an early age. □ *Marshall's twenty-year-old son died in a car crash; it did not comfort Marshall to think that the good die young.* □ JILL: *It doesn't seem fair that Laurie is dead. She was such a wonderful person.* JANE: *They always say that the good die young.*

The good is the enemy of the best. Instead of making things the best that they can, people often settle for making them merely good. □ MOTHER: *Aren't you going to rewrite your paper?* CHILD: *Why? It's good enough.* MOTHER: *The good is the enemy of the best.* □ PENELOPE: *I* *think I'll take a course in photography.* ALAN: *Why? You take perfectly good photographs already.* PENELOPE: *Maybe, but the good is the enemy of the best.*

The grass is always greener on the other side of the fence. People always think they would be happier in a different set of circumstances. (Usually implies that the other circumstances really are not any better.) □ JILL: *I wish I lived in Springfield. Everything seems so much nicer there.* MARK: *The grass is always greener on the other side of the fence.* □ JILL: *My job is so tedious. I wish I had my own business, like Beatrice does.* JANE: *Beatrice probably wishes she had the security of her old job. The grass is always greener on the other side of the fence.*

The greater the truth, the greater the libel It is more offensive to say something damaging and true about someone than it is to tell a damaging lie. □ JILL: *Fred's really upset. Someone's started a rumor that he's unfaithful to his wife.* JANE: *But it's true.* JILL: *Yeah, but the greater the truth, the greater the libel.* □ *It didn't bother the businessman when the newspapers printed unflattering things about him, as long as those things weren't true, but when one reporter found out about some of the bad things he really was doing, the businessman wanted to sue him. The greater the truth, the greater the libel.*

The hand that rocks the cradle rules the world. Mothers are the most powerful people, because they shape their children's personalities. □ *When Lena got pregnant, Lena's mother told her to take her responsibility seriously, because the hand that rocks the cradle rules the world.* □ MOTHER: *It's very sad to be a mother. Nobody pays any attention to you; you don't matter at all.* SON: *What do you mean you don't matter? The hand that rocks the cradle rules the world.*

The last straw See *The straw that broke the camel's back.*

The left hand doesn't know what the right hand is doing. One part of an organization does not know what another part is doing. (Biblical. Describes an organization in which people who should be communicating with one another are failing to do so.) □ *The left hand doesn't know what the right hand is doing at that car company. The sales force is taking orders for a car that the design department hasn't even designed yet.* □ *It was evident that the left hand did not know what the right hand was doing when we planned our potluck dinner party, since everyone brought dessert and no one brought a main dish.*

The less said (about something), the better. A way of indicating that you think something should not be talked about any further. □ SANDRA: *How are things going with your divorce proceedings?* ELLEN: *The less said, the better.* □ *The less said about my financial situation, the better.*

The lesser of two evils The least unpleasant of two unpleasant options. □ *Given the choice between marrying the old man and mortgaging her farm, Jenny decided that marriage was the lesser of two evils.* □ *I didn't want to dress too casually for the party, but I wasn't particularly eager to wear my stylish but uncomfortable shoes, either. In the end, looking too casual seemed the lesser of two evils.*

The long and the short of it The most important point; the summary of the matter. □ JILL: *Is there some reason that you've spent the last half hour complaining about Fred?* JANE: *The long and the short of it is, I hate working with him so much that I'm going to resign.* □ *Dad keeps saying that he can't spend the rest of his life in* *mourning for Mother. I finally asked him if he was thinking of getting married again. "That's the long and the short of it," he admitted.*

The longest way round is the nearest way home. See the following entry.

The longest way round is the shortest way home. AND **The longest way round is the nearest way home.** It may seem as if it will take too long to do something carefully and according to directions, but in fact it will take less time than doing something carelessly, because you will not have to fix it afterwards. □ JILL: *I don't have time to wash this fabric before I cut the pattern.* JANE: *If you don't take time to wash it now, you'll have to take time to make another shirt after you wash this one and it shrinks. The longest way round is the shortest way home.* □ *I would advise you to read the instructions before trying to use your new stereo. It takes some time, but the longest way round is the nearest way home.*

The love of money is the root of all evil. See *Money is the root of all evil.*

The mill cannot grind with water that is past. Do not waste the opportunities you now have; or, do not waste time wishing for what you had in the past. □ *If you want to go abroad, do it now, while you're young and have the money. The mill cannot grind with water that is past.* □ JILL: *I wish I hadn't sold my typewriter. I sure could use it now.* JANE: *Well, it's too late. The mill cannot grind with water that is past.*

The mills of God grind slowly, yet they grind exceeding small. It may take a long time, but evil will always be punished. □ JILL: *It really doesn't seem right that Fred can be so horrible and dishonest, but he always gets everything he wants.* JANE: *Be patient. The mills of God grind slowly, yet they grind exceeding small.* □ NANCY:

Every time I think of how cruelly Philip left me, and how happy he is with his new wife, I could just kill him. SANDRA: *He'll be punished eventually. The mills of God grind slowly, yet they grind exceeding small.*

The more the merrier   The more of something you have, the happier you will be. (Often used to invite more people to join you. Sometimes used ironically, as in the second example.) □ JILL: *Some of us are going to the movies after work.* JANE: *Can I come too?* JILL: *Sure! The more the merrier.* □ ALAN: *You don't mind washing the breakfast dishes along with the dinner dishes, do you?* SANDRA: *Of course not. The more the merrier.*

The more you get, the more you want. AND **The more you have, the more you want.**   People are never satisfied with what they have. □ *I've got one whole room full of books, but I can always think of more I wish I had. I guess it's true that the more you get, the more you want.* □ *You may think that you'll be content being department supervisor, but power is like anything else—the more you have, the more you want.*

The more you have, the more you want.   See the previous entry.

The mouse that has but one hole is quickly taken.   It is dangerous to always depend on just one thing, because if it fails you, you will not have any alternatives. □ *Don't put all your money in a single bank account. The mouse that has but one hole is quickly taken.* □ *My father advised me to learn more than one trade so if I couldn't get a job in one, I could rely on the others. "The mouse that has but one hole is quickly taken," he said.*

The nearer the church, the farther from God.   Church officials, or people who live near the church, are not truly pious. □ JILL: *I think our pastor is an evil man.* JANE: *I didn't think evil men could be pastors.* JILL: *Of* *course they can! The nearer the church, the farther from God.* □ *The Richardsons live just a block away from the church, and they're disgraceful enough to make me believe that the nearer the church, the farther from God.*

The only good Indian is a dead Indian. American Indians are inherently bad, and they will only stop being bad when they are dead. (Other nationalities or groups of people have been substituted for "Indian" in this saying. It is often quoted to demonstrate how frontier people felt about American Indians in the nineteenth century. Regarded as offensive.) □ *Even though Indians kept her family from starving during the winter of 1859, Irene had been taught that the only good Indian was a dead Indian, so that's what she believed.* □ *The American sergeant tried to convince his men that the only good German is a dead German, but since many of them were of German descent, he didn't succeed.*

The pen is mightier than the sword. Eloquent writing persuades people better than military force. □ *Believing that the pen is mightier than the sword, the rebels began publishing an underground newspaper.* □ ALAN: *Why do you want to become a journalist?* BILL: *The pen is mightier than the sword.*

The pot is calling the kettle black. AND **That's the pot calling the kettle black.** You should not criticize someone for a fault that you have too. (Not polite to say about the person you are addressing.) □ *Bill told Barbara she was sloppy, but Bill never cleans up after himself, either. That's the pot calling the kettle black.* □ *My sister says I dress funny, but if you've seen some of the clothes she wears, you know it's a case of the pot calling the kettle black.*

The proof is in the pudding. You cannot be sure that you have succeeded until you have examined the result of your efforts. □ JILL: *I think we've done a good job of fixing the lawn mower.* JANE: *Well, the proof is in the pudding. We haven't tried to mow the lawn with it yet.* □ *Andrea had studied hard all year, and the proof was in the pudding; she got the highest grades in her class.*

The road to hell is paved with good intentions. People often mean well but do bad things. (Can be a strong rebuke, implying that the person you are addressing did something bad and his or her good intentions do not matter.) □ SANDRA: *I'm sorry. I didn't mean to hurt your feelings; I only wanted to help you.* JANE: *Oh, yeah? The road to hell is paved with good intentions.* □ *Be careful. I know you mean well, but the road to hell is paved with good intentions.*

The rotten apple spoils the barrel. A bad person influences everyone he or she comes into contact with, making them bad too. (Also the cliché: **a rotten apple,** a person who is corrupting others.) □ *I teach the second grade, and there's one little girl in my class whom I really wish I could expel. She's disrespectful and won't obey me, and the other kids follow her example; the rotten apple spoils the barrel.* □ *Helen is the rotten apple that spoils the barrel in our office. Everyone sees her come in late to work and take long coffee breaks, and they think, "Why can't I do the same?"*

The spirit is willing, but the flesh is weak. People cannot always do what they know they ought to do; people are not always physically capable of doing what they are willing to do. (Biblical.) □ ALAN: *Have you started the diet your doctor recommended?* FRED: *The spirit is willing, but the flesh is weak.* □ SANDRA: *Help me carry some more of these crates down to the cellar.* JILL: *I've been carrying crates downstairs all morning, and my knees are starting to wobble. The spirit is willing, but the flesh is weak.*

The squeaking wheel gets the grease. AND **The squeaky wheel gets the grease.** People who complain the most will get what they want. □ *If you don't get good service at the hotel, make sure to tell the manager that you're dissatisfied. The squeaking wheel gets the grease.* □ *Leonard's always complaining. Nobody likes him, but we always give him what he wants. The squeaky wheel gets the grease.*

The squeaky wheel gets the grease. See the previous entry.

The straw that broke the camel's back AND **The last straw** The small problem that, when added to a lot of other previous problems, breaks someone's endurance. □ *Ellen's teenage son had done a lot of things that tried her patience: he stayed out late, he was rude to everyone, and he seemed determined to flunk out of school. But the straw that broke the camel's back was when she caught him putting out a cigarette on the arm of her antique chair.* □ *This is the last straw! I can't stand to work here anymore!*

The third time's the charm. The third time you try to do something, it will work. □ JILL: *I've called Miriam twice, but she doesn't answer her phone.* JANE: *Try again. The third time's the charm.* □ *After two unhappy love affairs, Kay was leery of going out with men, but her friends encouraged her, saying, "The third time's the charm."*

The time is ripe. It is the most favorable time to do something. □ *You ought to buy a house this year. Prices are so low, and you have enough money saved for a down payment. The time is ripe.* □ *Since Joe was in a good mood, I judged that the time was ripe to ask him for the favor I needed.*

The tree is known by its fruit. People judge your character by what you do. (Biblical.) □ *The politician may say she believes in more spending on child care, but the tree is known by its fruit; she hasn't voted for a single measure that would help.* □ *The tree is known by its fruit, and the fruit of this factory has been phenomenal air and water pollution, injured workers, and inferior products.*

The truth will out. The truth will always be discovered. (Can be used to remark that someone who had been concealing the truth is now revealing it, as in the second example.) □ *The embezzler may think that someone else will be blamed for his crime, but the truth will out.* □ EL-LEN: *Remember last week, when I told you I bought some shoes?* FRED: *Yes. . . .* ELLEN: *Well, before you look at the bill from the shoe store, I ought to tell you that I bought ten pairs.* FRED: *Aha. The truth will out.*

The unexpected always happens. The things you do not foresee will happen to you; when you plan, you cannot think of everything that might happen. □ *It took us an hour to drive to the restaurant, and when we got there, it was closed. I would never have expected a restaurant to be closed on a Friday night, but the unexpected always happens. Especially to me.* □ JILL: *I really wanted to impress my boyfriend's parents, so I invited them to dinner and cooked them a nice leg of lamb. When I set it down in front of them, they told me they are vegetarians.* JANE: *Poor Jill. The unexpected always happens.*

The way to a man's heart is through his stomach. If you want a man to love you, you should feed him good food. □ PENELOPE: *I want Keith to notice me, but he doesn't even know I'm alive.* MOTHER: *Invite him over and cook him a good meal. The way to a man's heart is through his stomach.* □ *If you want to attract men, learn* *to cook. The way to a man's heart is through his stomach, you know.*

The whole ball of wax   The whole thing. (Emphatic; casual.) □ *When Lena stays in a luxury hotel, she doesn't want just a pretty room. She wants excellent food, room service, courteous staff members, chocolates on her pillow every night—the whole ball of wax.* □ *The tycoon said, "I don't want to buy just one division of that company. I want to take over the whole ball of wax."*

The wish is father to the thought.   You believe something that you wish were true. □ *Adrienne hoped that her boss would resign, and the wish was father to the thought. Soon she had told everyone in the office that she was sure her boss was leaving.* □ JILL: *I think I heard that the city plans to build a park in that vacant lot.* JANE: *The wish is father to the thought, I'm afraid.*

The worth of a thing is what it will bring.   A thing is worth whatever someone will pay for it. □ ELLEN: *I'm thinking about selling my grandmother's silver tea set. What do you suppose it's worth?* FRED: *The worth of a thing is what it will bring.* □ JILL: *I can't believe the furniture store is asking $125 for that poorly made table. It isn't worth even half of that.* JANE: *Someone will probably pay that much for it anyhow. The worth of a thing is what it will bring.*

There ain't no such thing as a free lunch.   See *There's no such thing as a free lunch.*

There are other fish in the sea.   You will have other opportunities. (Usually used to console someone who has lost a girlfriend or boyfriend.) □ ANDREA: *I'll never love anyone else again; George is the only boy I could ever love.* ELLEN: *There are other fish in the sea, Andrea.* □ *Losing this one job isn't the end of the world. There are other fish in the sea.*

There are tricks in every trade. In every occupation, there are established ways of doing things. (Can imply that these established methods involve cheating other people. Also **the tricks of the trade,** the established ways of doing things in a certain kind of business.) □ *John thought that he wouldn't have to learn much in order to wait tables. But there are tricks in every trade, and the experienced waiters were able to teach him a lot.* □ *If you want to find out how to run a grocery store, go work for your Uncle Stanley. He's been running his store for thirty years, and he can show you the tricks of the trade.*

There are two sides to every question. There are valid reasons for holding opposing opinions. □ JIM: *I can't see why anyone would object to building a city park on the corner.* JOHN: *There are two sides to every question. Maybe the people who own the buildings on the corner don't want them knocked down.* □ FRED: *Only an idiot would want to go hang gliding. It's too dangerous.* ELLEN: *There are two sides to every question. Maybe some people think it's enjoyable enough to be worth the risk.*

There but for the grace of God (go I). I would likely have done the same thing if God had not been watching over me. (You can say this to refer to someone who has had bad luck; implies that the person is no less virtuous than you are, but is now miserable purely because of bad luck, which might happen to you as well.) □ JILL: *Ever since Julia's house burned down, she's been drinking heavily; she'll probably lose her job because of it.* JANE: *There but for the grace of God. . . .* □ *Whenever Sally saw a beggar, she thought, "There but for the grace of God go I."*

There is a remedy for everything except death. Everything but death can be cured; as long as you are alive, your problems can somehow be solved. □ BILL: *I'll never* recover from losing Nancy. FRED: *Nonsense. There is a remedy for everything except death.* □ *Whenever Linda despaired, she sternly reminded herself that there is a remedy for everything except death.*

There is a sin of omission as well as of commission. Failing to do something you ought to do can be as bad as doing something you ought not to do. (Also the cliché: **a sin of omission,** a failure to do something you ought to do.) □ JILL: *I didn't lie to Irene. I just didn't tell her that I was the one who dented her car in the parking lot.* JANE: *That sounds like a lie to me. There is a sin of omission as well as of commission, you know.* □ *Although Lisa didn't go out of her way to hurt her brother, neither did she tell him that the stairs were unsafe, which everyone agreed was a sin of omission.*

There is a tide in the affairs of men. If you have a favorable opportunity to do something, do it, or you will lose your chance. (From Shakespeare's play, *Julius Caesar.*) □ *I think that this is the best possible time to start our own business. We shouldn't hesitate. There is a tide in the affairs of men.* □ *Donna waited too long to carry out her plan, and so lost her best opportunity. There is a tide in the affairs of men.*

There is a time and a place for everything. Different things are appropriate on different occasions. □ *There is a time and a place for everything, but this formal dinner is not the time or the place to eat with your fingers.* □ ELLEN: *My husband bought me an evening gown covered with rhinestones. When will I ever wear it?* JANE: *There's a time and a place for everything.*

There is honor among thieves. Criminals do not commit crimes against each other. □ *The gangster was loyal to his associates and did not tell their names to the police, demonstrating that there is honor among thieves.* □ *Jasper* *and Clive defrauded their customers, their suppliers, and the government, but they always divided their profits fairly between the two of them. There is honor among thieves.*

There is no accounting for taste(s). You cannot blame different people because they like different things, even if you do not understand why they like what they like. □ BILL: *Why does Fred always go out with such silly women?* FRED: *There's no accounting for taste.* □ JILL: *I can't believe so many people are going to see that idiotic movie.* JANE: *There's no accounting for tastes.*

There is no pleasure without pain. For every pleasure you enjoy, you must suffer some pain. □ *We had a fabulous vacation, but it's going to take us years to pay for it. Oh, well, there's no pleasure without pain.* □ *Yesterday I basked in the warm sunshine all afternoon; today I'm badly sunburned. There is no pleasure without pain.*

There is no rest for the weary. Even people who are worn-out must continue to work. (Describes a situation in which a tired person has to do more work.) □ *By the time I finished doing the laundry, it was so late I had to begin cooking supper for the family. There is no rest for the weary.* □ ELLEN: *Thank you for mowing the lawn, honey. Now I need you to weed the garden.* FRED: *But I'm too tired!* ELLEN: *There is no rest for the weary. Come on.*

There is no royal road to learning. Learning things requires work. □ PENELOPE: *I don't see why we have to do homework every night. Why can't we just listen to the lectures?* NANCY: *There is no royal road to learning.* □ MIMI: *There must be some shortcut we can take for our English class—some way we can avoid having to read all those huge books.* BILL: *Don't be too sure. There is no royal road to learning.*

There is nothing new under the sun.   Everything that is happening now has happened before. (Biblical.) □ *Grandma said, "All this trouble with young people taking drugs—it's the same as when I was a youngster. There's nothing new under the sun."* □ JILL: *The newspaper today is shocking. Three prominent politicians have been convicted of fraud.* JANE: *That's not shocking. It only proves that there's nothing new under the sun.*

There is safety in numbers.   A group of people is less likely to be attacked than a single person. □ *Gail never went out after dark without at least three friends, since she knew that there is safety in numbers.* □ *We should gather together a group of people to make our complaint to the boss. There's safety in numbers.*

There's many a good tune played on an old fiddle.   Old people can be very capable. □ *Just because Nigel is old doesn't mean he's useless. There's many a good tune played on an old fiddle.* □ *Don't exclude me just because I'm old. There's many a good tune played on an old fiddle.*

There's many a slip 'twixt the cup and the lip.   Many things may happen to prevent you from carrying out what you intend to do. □ VINCENT: *Now that I have a contract with a publisher, nothing in the world can stop me from writing this book.* ALAN: *Don't be so sure. There's many a slip 'twixt the cup and the lip.* □ *I thought that once I bought my plane tickets, I was certain at last of making my trip to Japan. I forgot, however, that there's many a slip 'twixt the cup and the lip.*

There's many a true word spoken in jest.   See *Many a true word is spoken in jest.*

There's more than one way to skin a cat.   You can always find more than one way to do something. □ JILL: *How will we fix the sink without a wrench?* JANE: *There's* *more than one way to skin a cat.* □ *Our first approach didn't work, but we'll figure out some other way. There's more than one way to skin a cat.*

There's no fool like an old fool.   Old people are supposed to be wise, so if an old person behaves foolishly, it is worse than a young person behaving foolishly. □ *As old Mrs. Fleischman watched her husband try to dance the way their grandchildren danced, she muttered, "There's no fool like an old fool."* □ ALAN: *I try to reason with Grandpa, but he insists on sending money to all kinds of strange charities.* SANDRA: *There's no fool like an old fool.*

There's no place like home.   Home is the most satisfying place to be. □ *After his long trip, Bob came into his house, sat down in his favorite chair, and happily sighed, "There's no place like home."* □ SANDRA: *Are you glad to be home from school?* JENNY: *There's no place like home.*

There's no rose without a thorn.   To enjoy any beautiful or pleasant thing, you must endure something difficult or painful. □ ARTHUR: *My bride is lovely and gracious, but I'm discovering that she has a terrible temper.* BILL: *There's no rose without a thorn.* □ *The scenery by the lake is exquisite, but there are always crowds of obnoxious tourists whenever we go to see it. There's no rose without a thorn.*

(There's) no smoke without fire. AND **Where there's smoke there's fire.**   There is usually some truth behind every rumor. □ FRED: *We ought to fire Phil. Office gossip says he's lazy.* SANDRA: *You can't fire him just because of gossip!* FRED: *There's no smoke without fire.* □ *I'm going to withdraw all my money from that bank. I heard a rumor that the bank was in financial trouble, and where there's smoke there's fire.*

There's no such thing as a free lunch. AND **There ain't no such thing as a free lunch.** Everything costs something. (Casual. Can imply that you should be suspicious of anything that appears to be free.) □ FRED: *This advertisement says I can get an expensive camera for free!* SANDRA: *Don't be so gullible. There's no such thing as a free lunch.* □ *Anna gave me her sewing machine, but I had to give it $100 worth of repairs before I could even use it. There's no such thing as a free lunch.*

(There's) no time like the present. Do it now. (You can use this to suggest that something be done right away.) □ JILL: *When should we start cleaning up the house?* JANE: *No time like the present.* □ *Start studying for the big exam now, instead of waiting till the night before. There's no time like the present.*

There's none so blind as those who will not see. You cannot make someone pay attention to something that he or she does not want to notice. (You can use this to upbraid someone for being unwilling to notice what you are trying call attention to, as in the first example.) □ MOTHER: *This is the fifth time our daughter has been arrested for shoplifting. Don't you think we ought to seek some kind of help for her?* FATHER: *Don't be ridiculous. Our girl would never shoplift. I'm sure all those arrests were just some kind of mistake.* MOTHER: *There's none so blind as those who will not see.* □ *By October, it was obvious to everyone in the office that Richard was coming in drunk every morning. Obvious, that is, to everyone except his devoted secretary; there's none so blind as those who will not see.*

There's none so deaf as those who will not hear. If you tell someone something that he or she does not want to know, he or she will not pay attention to you. (You can use this to upbraid someone for being unwilling to listen to what you are trying to tell him or her.) □ *I tried* repeatedly to tell my supervisor about the low morale in our department, but there's none so deaf as those who will not hear. □ We all warned Joe about the dangers of smoking, but there's none so deaf as those who will not hear.

They also serve who only stand and wait.   Sometimes you must be patient and do nothing, even though you would like to be actively helping. (From John Milton's poem, "On His Blindness.") □ *During Melanie's illness, all her friends wanted to visit her in the hospital or help take care of her house, but her husband dissuaded them, saying, "They also serve who only stand and wait. All she needs right now are your good wishes."* □ JILL: *Can I help?* JANE: *No, we've got enough people helping.* JILL: *But I want to help.* JANE: *They also serve who only stand and wait.*

Things are seldom what they seem.   Things often appear different from what they really are. □ *Emily seems to be a fine young lady, but be careful. Things are seldom what they seem.* □ *To judge from his elegant clothing and luxurious car, William was a wealthy man. But things are seldom what they seem; in fact, he was in desperate need of money.*

Those who can, do; those who can't, teach.   People who are able to do something well can do that thing for a living, while people who are not able to do it that well make a living by teaching other people how to do it. (Used to disparage teachers. From George Bernard Shaw's *Man and Superman.*) □ VINCENT: *I'm so discouraged. My writing teacher told me my novel is hopeless.* JANE: *Don't listen to her, Vincent. Remember: those who can, do; those who can't, teach.* □ ARTIST: *For six months, I've been trying to make money by selling my paintings, and now I'm broke. What am I going to do?* FRIEND: *You could get a teaching job.* ARTIST: *But that would be* *admitting that I'm a failure. Those who can, do; those who can't, teach.*

Throw dirt enough, and some will stick.   If you persistently say bad things about someone, people will begin to believe your accusations, even if they are not true. (Sometimes *mud* is used instead of *dirt*.) □ *One of the candidates in the election kept accusing the other one of having cheated on his income tax, and eventually the voters believed it. As they say, throw dirt enough, and some will stick.* □ *Knowing that if she threw dirt enough, some would stick, Kathy continued to maintain that Louise had once been in prison.*

Tied to one's mother's apron strings   Always doing whatever one's mother says; dependent on one's mother. (Also the cliché: **cut the apron strings,** to stop depending on one's mother; to leave one's childhood home.) □ *Bert is thirty-two years old, but he's still tied to his mother's apron strings.* □ *Bert, it's time for you to cut the apron strings. Don't ask your mother for permission every time you want to do something.*

Time and tide wait for no man.   Things will not wait for you when you are late. □ *Hurry up or we'll miss the bus! Time and tide wait for no man.* □ ELLEN: *It's time to leave. Aren't you finished dressing yet?* FRED: *I can't decide which necktie looks best with this shirt.* ELLEN: *Time and tide wait for no man, dear.*

Time flies.   Time sometimes seems to pass very quickly. □ SANDRA: *Thanks for a lovely evening, but we have to leave now; it's almost midnight.* JILL: *Midnight? Really? Time flies!* □ *It seems like just yesterday that my niece celebrated her first birthday, and now she's starting high school. Time flies!*

Time is a great healer.   Emotional pain will grow less as time passes. □ *You may think your heart is broken and* *you can never possibly love again, but time is a great healer.* □ *Joanna had been miserable throughout high school, but time is a great healer, and she was eventually able to remember the happy times she had had then.*

Time is money. You should not waste time or dawdle, since you should use as much time as possible to make money. □ *I don't appreciate having to wait half the day to meet with you. Time is money.* □ *Don't sit at your desk and stare off into space; time is money!*

Time works wonders. The passing of time can resolve many problems. □ *I thought I would never forgive my ex-husband for leaving me, but now, ten years later, I feel pretty well disposed toward him. Time works wonders.* □ *You'll change your mind eventually. Time works wonders.*

Times change and we with time. As time passes, people and situations change. □ JILL: *Linda was such a conservative when we were in school; I don't understand how she can be so liberal now.* JANE: *Times change and we with time.* □ *When I was a child, I thought it was terribly rude for children to call adults by their first names, but now that I'm grown up, I encourage children to use my first name. Times change and we with time.*

Times change(, people change). As time passes, different things become acceptable. □ GRANDMOTHER: *In my day, no decent young woman would wear anything as immodest as what you've got on.* GRANDDAUGHTER: *Times change, Grandma.* □ ALAN: *When I was in business school, the practices you call good business were called dishonest.* FRED: *Yeah, well, times change, people change.*

'Tis better to have loved and lost than never to have loved at all. Love is such an important experience that even the pain of losing someone you love is better than not having loved that person. (A line from Alfred, Lord

Tennyson's poem, "In Memoriam A. H. H.") □ Tom: *I've been so miserable since Nancy and I broke up. I wish I'd never met her.* Fred: *Come on, now—'tis better to have loved and lost than never to have loved at all.* □ *Despite the grief that overwhelmed her after her husband died, Julia never doubted that 'tis better to have loved and lost than never to have loved at all.*

To err is human(, to forgive divine). You should not be too harsh with someone who makes a mistake, because all human beings make mistakes. (Often used as a roundabout way to ask someone to forgive you for making a mistake.) □ Jill: *How could you let my dog get out when I told you a hundred times that he should stay in the house!* Ellen: *To err is human, to forgive divine.* □ Mother: *Because you broke my vase, I am going to give you extra chores for two weeks.* Daughter: *But, Mom, to err is human . . . !*

To run with the hare and hunt with the hounds To support both sides of a dispute. □ *In our office politics, Sally always tries to run with the hare and hunt with the hounds, telling both the clerical workers and the management that she thinks they should prevail.* □ Bill: *Why do you spend so much time talking to that real-estate developer? He wants to knock our house down and build a shopping mall, you know!* Ellen: *I know. But if he thinks I'm on his side, maybe I can persuade him to leave our house alone.* Bill: *You can't run with the hare and hunt with the hounds, Ellen.*

Today here, tomorrow the world Successful in this location now, with later recognition in the rest of the world. (Describes something whose influence seems certain to spread. The name of an appropriate locality is usually substituted for *here.*) □ *I thought that silly fashion in clothes was unique to California, but it seems to be spreading. Today Los Angeles, tomorrow the world.* □

MAD SCIENTIST: *Release the mutant spores into the atmosphere!* ASSISTANT: *But if we do that, they'll take root all over the state!* MAD SCIENTIST: *Exactly! Today Nebraska, tomorrow the world!*

Tomorrow is another day.   Things may improve tomorrow; tomorrow you will have a chance to solve the problems that are upsetting you today. (Often used to encourage someone to relax and wait until tomorrow to do or worry about something. This saying was used by Scarlett O'Hara, the spoiled, headstrong heroine of Margaret Mitchell's novel *Gone With The Wind*; it may remind some people of Scarlett.) □ CHILD: *This math homework is horrible! I can't do it!* MOTHER: *Put it away for tonight and go to bed. You'll be able to think more clearly when you've had some sleep, and tomorrow is another day.* □ ALAN: *Everything went wrong for me today. I feel like crawling into a hole and never coming out again.* SANDRA: *I'm sorry today was so bad, but don't overreact. Tomorrow is another day.*

Tomorrow never comes.   When the day arrives that you are now calling "tomorrow," you will call that day "today" and a different day will be "tomorrow." Therefore, you should not resolve to do something "tomorrow," since that day will never arrive. □ JILL: *When are you going to go to lunch with me?* JANE: *Tomorrow.* JILL: *Tomorrow never comes.* □ SANDRA: *Don't bother me about fixing the plumbing today. I'll take care of it tomorrow.* ALAN: *Tomorrow never comes.*

Too little, too late   Not enough help to save the situation, and arriving too late. □ *After a lifetime of bad diet and no exercise, Lorna tried to save her health by improving her habits, but it was too little, too late.* □ FRED: *I know how to keep my business from going bankrupt. I'll invest all my savings in it.* BILL: *I'm sorry, Fred; even that much would be too little, too late.*

Too many chiefs and not enough Indians   Too many people want to be the leader, and not enough people are willing to follow. □ *Everyone on that committee wants to be in charge. Too many chiefs and not enough Indians.* □ *We'll never finish this project if everyone keeps trying to give orders. There are too many chiefs and not enough Indians.*

Too many cooks spoil the broth.   If too many people try to contribute to a project, the project will fail. □ *Everyone in the club wanted to help paint the sign. Joe finally chased them out, saying, "Too many cooks spoil the broth."* □ JILL: *Can Alicia and I help you get dinner ready?* JANE: *Just stay where you are. Too many cooks spoil the broth.*

Travel broadens the mind.   When you travel, you learn things about the people and places you see. □ MARIE: *I never realized how well off most Americans are until I visited Europe.* SANDRA: *So it's true that travel broadens the mind, huh?* □ *Everyone who gets the chance should go abroad. Travel broadens the mind.*

Truth is stranger than fiction.   See *Fact is stranger than fiction.*

Turn back the clock   To try to make things the way they were before; to reverse some change. (Usually used in the phrase, "You can't turn back the clock.") □ JILL: *I wish I was back in college. I had so much fun then.* JANE: *You can't turn back the clock. Even if you went back to school, it wouldn't be the same.* □ *The senator is trying to turn back the clock on all the important reforms that have taken place in the last fifteen years.*

Two heads are better than one.   Two people working together have a better chance of solving a problem than one person working alone. □ *Come over here and help me balance my checkbook. Two heads are better than* *one.* □ SANDRA: *Can you figure out what this insurance document means?* ALAN: *Why ask me? I don't know anything about insurance.* SANDRA: *Neither do I, but two heads are better than one.*

Two is company, (but) three's a crowd. A way of asking a third person to leave because you want to be alone with someone. (Usually implies that you want to be alone with the person because you are romantically interested in him or her.) □ *When Lucy followed Mark and Nora into the drawing room, Nora turned to her and said, "Two's company, but three's a crowd."* □ BILL: *Can I go to lunch with you and Warren?* JANE: *Two's company, three's a crowd, Bill.*

Two wrongs do not make a right. Someone else may do something bad and not be punished, but that does not mean you are allowed to do bad things; or, even if someone else hurts you, you should not hurt him or her in return. □ CHILD: *Bobby skipped school and didn't get a spanking. So how come you're spanking me for skipping school?* FATHER: *Two wrongs do not make a right.* □ JILL: *I'd really like to humiliate Fred, after he made fun of me in front of everyone at lunch.* JANE: *Now, now, Jill. Two wrongs don't make a right.*

U

Uneasy lies the head that wears a crown. A person who has a lot of power and prestige also has a lot of responsibilities, and therefore worries more than other people. (From Shakespeare's play, *Henry IV, Part II*.) □ *Susan began to have trouble sleeping shortly after she was promoted to head of her department. "Uneasy lies the head that wears a crown," her friends teased.* □ *The governor warned his successor that it was not always pleasant and satisfying to wield executive power. "Uneasy lies the head that wears a crown," he said.*

Union is strength. If people join together, they are more powerful than if they work by themselves. □ *The students decided to join together in order to present their grievances to the faculty, since union is strength.* □ *We cannot allow our opponents to divide us. Union is strength.*

United we stand, divided we fall. People who join together as a group are much harder to defeat than they would be separately. □ *The tenants of this building must band together if we are to make the landlord agree to our demands. United we stand, divided we fall!* □ *We had better all agree on what we are going to say to the boss before we go in there and say it. United we stand, divided we fall.*

V

Variety is the spice of life.   You should try many different kinds of experiences, because trying different things keeps life interesting.   □ *I know we usually spend our summer vacation camping out, but I think we should try something different this year. Variety is the spice of life.* □ *Lisa encouraged her friend Judy, a teacher, to go out and socialize with people in other professions. "Variety is the spice of life," she said.*

Velvety-soft   See *(As) soft as velvet.*

Virtue is its own reward.   You should not be virtuous in hopes of getting a reward, but because it makes you feel good to be virtuous.   □ BILL: *If I help you, will you pay me?* FRED: *Virtue is its own reward.* □ *Don't be kind to your older relatives because you want them to give you something. Virtue is its own reward.*

W

Walls have ears. Someone may be listening. (A warning that you think your conversation is being overheard.) □ JILL: *Did I tell you what I found out about Fred? He—* JANE: *Sshh! Walls have ears.* □ *Don't say anything about our business dealings in here. Walls have ears.*

Waste not, want not. If you do not waste anything, you will always have enough. □ *Always save the fabric scraps left over from your sewing projects; you can use them to make something else. Waste not, want not.* □ *Sam never let his leftovers spoil in the refrigerator, but made sure to eat them. "Waste not, want not," he said.*

Water over the dam AND **Water under the bridge** Events in the past that cannot be changed. □ *Your quarrel with Lena is water over the dam; now you ought to concentrate on getting along with her.* □ *George and I were friends once, but that's all water under the bridge now.*

Water under the bridge See the previous entry.

We must learn to walk before we can run. You must master a basic skill before you are able to learn more complex things. □ *Maria wanted to make a tailored jacket as her first sewing project, but her mother convinced her that she should make something much simpler; she would have to learn to walk before she could* *run.* □ *The piano teacher told his student, "Master the simpler pieces before you attempt complicated ones. You must learn to walk before you can run."*

Well begun is half done. Beginning a project well makes it easier to do the rest; once you have begun a project well, you do not need to put in much more effort to finish it. □ JILL: *I'm afraid I'll never be able to finish writing this report.* JANE: *You've already written a good introduction. Well begun is half done.* □ ALAN: *I thought that building this model airplane would be fun, but I've been working on it for a month and I've only finished the frame.* BILL: *Don't get discouraged. You did a good job on the frame, and well begun is half done.*

What can't be cured must be endured. If you cannot do anything about a problem, you will have to live with it. □ ALAN: *No matter what I do, I can't make the dog stop barking in the middle of the night.* SANDRA: *What can't be cured must be endured, then, I guess.* □ JILL: *It's been raining for five straight days now! I don't think I can stand it anymore.* JANE: *Well, you can't do anything about it. And what can't be cured must be endured.*

What goes up must come down. Anything that has risen or been raised up must eventually fall down. □ *Linda threw the ball so high we couldn't see it, and although we waited for several minutes we didn't see it fall. "What goes up must come down," Linda said, although our faith in that idea was now somewhat shaken.* □ *When it came time to move out of our second-floor apartment, we looked at our large, heavy sofa with dismay, not sure how we would get it down the stairs. "What goes up must come down," my husband said, "somehow."*

What in (the) Sam Hill What? (Emphatic and angry. Casual. A euphemism for "what in the hell.") □ *What in the Sam Hill do you think you are doing, throwing golf* *balls at my window?* □ *What in Sam Hill does Fred hope to accomplish by firing so many people?*

What must be, must be. AND **What will be, will be.** If something is fated to happen, you cannot stop it from happening; you cannot foretell the future. □ *Harry hoped for many months that he would regain the use of his legs after the accident, but it soon became apparent that he would not. "What must be, must be," he thought resignedly.* □ *I'd like to win the contest, but I can't be sure that I will. What will be, will be.*

What the eye doesn't see, the heart doesn't grieve over. You cannot be upset by something you do not know about. □ *When Robbie cracked his mother's favorite vase, he simply turned the cracked side toward the wall. "What the eye doesn't see, the heart doesn't grieve over," he theorized.* □ *Nancy figured that her affairs would not hurt her marriage as long as her husband knew nothing about them. "What the eye doesn't see, the heart doesn't grieve over," she assured herself.*

What will be, will be. See *What must be, must be.*

What you don't know can't hurt you. See the following entry.

What you don't know won't hurt you. AND **What you don't know can't hurt you.** If you do not know about a problem or a misdeed, you will not make yourself unhappy by worrying about it. (Often used to justify not telling someone about a problem or misdeed.) □ ELLEN: *What a beautiful diamond necklace! Thank you! But how on earth did you get the money to pay for it?* FRED: *What you don't know won't hurt you.* □ JILL: *Should we tell Arthur that we ate all the chocolates he was saving for the party?* JANE: *What Arthur doesn't know can't hurt him.*

What's done cannot be undone. You cannot change what has already happened. □ JILL: *I wish I hadn't insulted Maria.* JANE: *What's done cannot be undone.* □ *Daisy soon regretted telling Cliff that she loved him, but she knew that what's done cannot be undone.*

What's in a name? The name of a thing does not matter as much as the quality of the thing. (From Shakespeare's play, *Romeo and Juliet.*) □ PENELOPE: *I want to buy this pair of jeans.* MOTHER: *This other pair is much cheaper.* PENELOPE: *But it doesn't have the designer brand name.* MOTHER: *What's in a name?* □ JILL: *I went on a blind date last night. He had the ugliest name—Buford.* JANE: *What's in a name?*

What's sauce for the goose is sauce for the gander. What is good for one person is good for another; often, what is good for the woman in a couple is good for the man. □ SANDRA: *You're overweight; you should get more exercise.* ALAN: *But I don't really have time to exercise.* SANDRA: *When I was overweight, you told me to exercise; what's sauce for the goose is sauce for the gander.* □ *When I was feeling depressed last spring, Carla told me I should see a psychiatrist. So when she mentioned that she was feeling depressed, I gave her the same advice; what's sauce for the goose is sauce for the gander.*

What's yours is mine, and what's mine is mine. A humorous way of saying, "Everything belongs to me." (A jocular variant of "What's yours is mine, and what's mine is yours," an expression of generosity.) □ *I know you won't mind lending me your radio. After all, what's yours is mine, and what's mine is mine.* □ *The thief took his confederate's share of the money they had stolen, saying, "What's yours is mine, and what's mine is mine."*

When in Rome(, do as the Romans do). Behave however the people around you behave; adapt yourself to the customs of the places you visit. □ JILL: *Everyone in my new office dresses so casually. Should I dress that way, too?* JANE: *By all means. When in Rome, do as the Romans do.* □ *Everyone in this town seems to go to the fish fry on Friday nights, so I think we ought to as well. When in Rome. . . .*

When one door shuts, another opens. When you lose one opportunity, you often find a different one. □ JANE: *I just found out I'm failing two classes. I'll never get into college with grades like this.* JILL: *Well, maybe you'll find something better than college. When one door shuts, another opens.* □ *The skier lost the use of her legs in a terrible car accident. But in her new, sedentary life, she discovered that she enjoyed writing and did it well, and now she is a well-loved novelist. When one door shuts, another opens.*

When poverty comes in at the door, love flies out of the window. AND **When the wolf comes in at the door, love creeps out of the window.** If a couple gets married because they are in love, but they do not have enough money, they will stop loving each other when the money runs out. (Also **the wolf at the door,** starvation, poverty; **to keep the wolf from the door,** to ward off starvation.) □ *You young folks may think you can live on love alone, but when the wolf comes in at the door, love creeps out of the window.* □ *After Susan lost her job, she and her unemployed husband had a big argument. When the wolf comes in at the door, love creeps out of the window.*

When the cat's away, the mice will play. When no one in authority is present, the subordinates can do as they please. □ *When the teacher left for a few minutes, the children nearly wrecked the classroom. When the cat's away, the mice will play.* □ JILL: *You shouldn't be reading a* *novel at your desk.* JANE: *But the boss isn't here. And when the cat's away, the mice will play.*

When the going gets tough, the tough get going.   When things are difficult, strong people take action and do not despair. (Can be used to encourage someone to take action.) □ *The football team was losing the game, so at halftime the coach reminded them that when the going gets tough, the tough get going.* □ JILL: *I don't think I can walk all the way to the top of this hill; it's so steep!* JANE: *Don't give up. When the going gets tough, the tough get going.*

When the wolf comes in at the door, love creeps out of the window.   See *When poverty comes in at the door, love flies out of the window.*

Where ignorance is bliss, 'tis folly to be wise.   If knowing something makes you unhappy, it would be better not to know it. (Also the cliché: **ignorance is bliss**.) □ ELLEN: *The doctor didn't tell Dad that Mom probably won't recover from her illness. Do you think we should tell him?* BILL: *No. It would only make him unhappy and ruin their last months together. Where ignorance is bliss, 'tis folly to be wise.* □ *Because Alan knew enough about economics to tell that hard times were coming, he was gloomy while those around him, who did not foresee the trouble, were cheerful. Where ignorance is bliss, 'tis folly to be wise.*

Where there's a will, there's a way.   If you truly want to do something, you will find a way to do it, in spite of obstacles. □ *We'll get this piano up the stairs somehow. Where there's a will, there's a way.* □ *I have no doubt that Vincent will find a publisher for his novel. Where there's a will, there's a way.*

Where there's smoke there's fire.   See *(There's) no smoke without fire.*

While there's life there's hope. As long as you are alive, you should be hopeful, because it is possible that your situation will improve. □ NANCY: *What will we do, now that our house and everything we own has burned up?* BILL: *Where there's life there's hope.* □ ELLEN: *Ever since my divorce, it seems as if I have nothing to hope for.* JANE: *I know things seem bleak, but where there's life there's hope.*

Whom the gods love die young. Virtuous or gifted people die at an early age, because the gods want those people to be with them in the afterlife. □ *So many brilliant authors and artists died before the age of fifty that it's easy to believe that whom the gods love die young.* □ *Sarah was so virtuous throughout her short life; we could only make sense out of her death by thinking that whom the gods love die young.*

Why buy a cow when milk is so cheap? See the following entry.

Why buy a cow when you can get milk for free? AND **Why buy a cow when milk is so cheap?** Why pay for something that you can get for free otherwise. (Sometimes used to describe someone who will not marry because sex without any commitment is so easy to obtain. Jocular and crude.) □ *I don't have a car because someone always gives me a ride to work. Why buy a cow when you can get milk for free?* □ *Wanda told her daughter, "You may think that boy will marry you because you're willing to sleep with him, but why should he buy a cow if he can get milk for free?"*

Why keep a dog and bark yourself? You should not do something you have hired someone else to do. □ WIFE: *I'll just tuck the children in bed before we leave.* HUSBAND: *That's the baby-sitter's job, dear. Why keep a dog and bark yourself?* □ ELLEN: *The cleaning lady washes my* *floors every Tuesday, but I always wash them over again.* SANDRA: *Don't be silly, Ellen. Why keep a dog and bark yourself?*

Wild horses couldn't drag someone away from something. Someone is determined to remain with something. □ *Once Elaine starts playing a video game, wild horses can't drag her away from it.* □ *Jim was determined to remain fishing at the lake. Wild horses couldn't drag him away from it.*

Wonders never cease! What an amazing thing has happened! (You can say this when something very surprising happens. Somewhat ironic; this can imply that the surprising thing should have happened before, but did not.) □ FRED: *Hi, honey. I cleaned the kitchen for you.* ELLEN: *Wonders never cease!* □ JILL: *Did you hear? The company is allowing us to take a holiday tomorrow.* JANE: *Wonders never cease!* □ *Not only was my plane on time, the airline also delivered my luggage safely. Will wonders never cease?*

Y

You can catch more flies with honey than with vinegar.
It is easier to get what you want by flattering people and
being polite to them than by making demands. □ JILL:
*This meal is terrible. Let's get the restaurant manager
over here and make a scene unless he gives us our money
back.* JANE: *We might have more luck if we ask politely.
You can catch more flies with honey than with vinegar.*
□ *Frances tried to get permission to use her mother's car
by whining and threatening; she had never heard that
you can catch more flies with honey than with vinegar.*

**You can lead a horse to water, but you can't make it
drink.** You can present someone with an opportunity,
but you cannot force him or her to take advantage of it.
□ *I took my children to the library, but they were more
interested in running up and down the stairs than in
looking at the books. You can lead a horse to water, but
you can't make it drink.* □ JILL: *I told Katy about all the
jobs that are available at our company, but she hasn't
applied for any of them.* JANE: *You can lead a horse to
water, but you can't make it drink.*

You cannot get a quart into a pint pot. You cannot fit
too much of something into a space that is too small. □
*That dog is simply too big to get into this kennel. You
can't get a quart into a pint pot.* □ *Our refrigerator isn't*

big enough to fit that watermelon in. You can't get a quart into a pint pot.

You cannot get blood from a stone. AND **You cannot get blood from a turnip.** You cannot get help from an uncharitable person or money from someone who has none. □ *Jerry and James spent two hours trying to convince the old miser to contribute to the children's hospital; finally, James turned to Jerry and said in disgust, "This is hopeless. We can't get blood from a stone."* □ *The government can't increase taxes any further—nobody has the money! You can't get blood from a turnip.*

You cannot get blood from a turnip. See the previous entry.

You cannot have your cake and eat it (too). You cannot pursue two alternatives at the same time. □ JILL: *There's an apartment across the street from me, much bigger and prettier than mine, and it even costs less. I'd really like to rent it—but I don't want to go to the trouble of moving.* JANE: *You can't have your cake and eat it too.* □ FRED: *I want to lose weight, but I'm not willing to change the way I eat.* ALAN: *You can't have your cake and eat it.*

You cannot lose what you never had. You should not say you have lost something if you only wished that you had it to begin with. □ BILL: *I've lost Andrea. She's gotten engaged to Tom.* FRED: *But, Bill, Andrea was never your girlfriend. You can't lose what you never had.* □ JILL: *I lost my chance of getting promoted; they gave that job to Andrew.* JANE: *You can't lose what you never had.*

You cannot make a silk purse out of a sow's ear. You cannot make someone more refined than he or she is by nature. □ *I've given up trying to get my cousin to appreciate classical music. You can't make a silk purse out of a sow's ear.* □ SANDRA: *If I try hard enough, I can teach* *my student to be a decent writer.* ALAN: *I don't know, Sandra; you can't make a silk purse out of a sow's ear.*

You cannot make an omelet without breaking eggs. In order to get something, you must give up something else. □ JILL: *Why do they have to tear down that beautiful old building to build an office park?* JANE: *You can't make an omelet without breaking eggs.* □ ALAN: *We may make more money by raising our prices, but we'll also upset a lot of customers.* FRED: *You can't make an omelet without breaking eggs.*

You cannot make bricks without straw. You have to have all the necessary materials in order to make something. □ FRED: *Get that phone fixed by tomorrow.* SANDRA: *But I don't have the right parts. You can't make bricks without straw.* □ ELLEN: *I really wanted to give Fred a birthday party, but none of the people I invited were able to come.* JANE: *Don't blame yourself. You can't make bricks without straw.*

You cannot please everyone. No matter what you do, there will always be some people who do not like it. □ NANCY: *My mother wants me to have a big wedding in the church, but my fiancé's mother insists that we should have an informal ceremony. What am I going to do?* JANE: *Well, you can't please everyone. Just do what you and your fiancé want to do.* □ VINCENT: *I'd like you to read this draft of my novel. I've been asking all my friends to read it and tell me what they think, so I can rewrite it to please them all.* BILL: *But, Vincent, you can't please everyone.*

You cannot put new wine in old bottles. You should not try to combine incompatible things. □ *I think it is a mistake for the managers of that conservative gallery to exhibit modern paintings. You can't put new wine in old bottles.* □ *Doug's attempt to teach traditional Chinese* *medicine to doctors trained in Western medicine was not a success. "I guess I can't put new wine in old bottles," Doug thought ruefully.*

You cannot serve God and mammon. You cannot both be a good person and dedicate yourself to making money. (Biblical. *Mammon* means riches.) □ *The minister warned the businessman that he could not serve God and mammon, and encouraged him to donate some of his wealth to charity.* □ *The landlord was merciless, evicting several families just because they missed a single month's rent. He certainly demonstrated that you cannot serve God and mammon.*

You cannot teach an old dog new tricks. Someone who is used to doing things a certain way cannot change. (Usually not polite to say about the person you are talking to; you can say it about yourself or about a third person.) □ *I've been away from school for fifteen years; I can't go back to college now. You can't teach an old dog new tricks.* □ *Kevin's doctor told him not to eat starchy food anymore, but Kevin still has potatoes with every meal. I guess you can't teach an old dog new tricks.*

You can't win 'em all. You have to accept that you will not always succeed. □ JILL: *I didn't get that job I applied for.* JANE: *Well, you can't win 'em all.* □ *I was afraid that my father would berate me after our team lost the game, but instead he patted me on the shoulder and said, "You can't win 'em all."*

You do not get something for nothing. Everything costs something, and anything that appears to be free must be deceptive. □ JILL: *This newspaper ad says we can get a trip to Hawaii for free.* JANE: *There must be a catch to it somewhere. You don't get something for nothing.* □ *The guy at the door told me he'd give me a book for free, but it turned out to get the book I had to listen to him preach* *about his religion. Just as I suspected; you don't get something for nothing.*

You get what you pay for.   If you do not pay much money for something, it is probably of poor quality; if you pay well for something, it is more likely to be of good quality. □ ALAN: *I was so pleased to find shoes for such a low price, but look, they're falling apart already.* SANDRA: *You get what you pay for.* □ *This brand of soup is more expensive, but remember, you get what you pay for.*

You have to eat a peck of dirt before you die.   No one can escape eating a certain amount of dirt on his or her food; or, everyone must endure a number of unpleasant things in his or her lifetime. (Often said to console someone who has eaten some dirt or had to endure something unpleasant.) □ ELLEN: *Oh, no! I forgot to wash this apple before I took a bite out of it.* FRED: *You have to eat a peck of dirt before you die.* □ *When I told my father of my difficulties at school, he shrugged and said, "You have to eat a peck of dirt before you die."*

You must lose a fly to catch a trout.   You have to sacrifice something in order to get what you want. (Implies that what you sacrifice is minor compared to what you will get.) □ *Amy was willing to live cheaply for several years in order to save enough money to buy her own house. She knew that you must lose a fly to catch a trout.* □ ELLEN: *Let's go to the movies tonight.* FRED: *But we agreed we would give up going to the movies for six months and use the money we save for a big vacation.* ELLEN: *But it's so boring, not going to the movies.* FRED: *You have to lose a fly to catch a trout.*

You never know (what you can do) till you try.   Even if you think you are not able to do something, you should try to do it. □ JILL: *Want to go rock-climbing with me this weekend?* JANE: *Oh, I can't rock-climb.* JILL: *How do*

you know? Have you ever tried it? JANE: *No, not really.*
JILL: *You don't know what you can do till you try.* □
ALAN: *I'll never be able to learn to dance.* SANDRA: *You
don't know till you try.*

You never miss the water till the well runs dry.   People
are not grateful for what they have until they lose it. □
JILL: *I never realized what a good friend Jeanie was until
she moved away.* JANE: *You never miss the water till the
well runs dry.* □ *I never knew how wonderful it is to be
able to walk until I was confined to my wheelchair. I
guess you never miss the water till the well runs dry.*

You pays your money and you takes your chance(s).
You must resign yourself to taking risks; everything costs
something, but paying for something does not guarantee
that you will get it. (The grammatical errors are inten-
tional.) □ CUSTOMER: *Can you guarantee that this washing machine won't break?* SALESMAN: *No guarantees. You
pays your money and you takes your chances.* □ JILL:
Which color of yarn do I get? JANE: *You pays your money
and you takes your chances.*

You scratch my back, I'll scratch yours.   If you do what
I want you to do, I will do what you want me to do. (Implies that the deal you are making is somewhat dishonest
or covert.) □ POLITICIAN: *I need $300,000 for my cam-
paign.* BUSINESSMAN: *You'll get it—if you make sure that
the city does a lot of business with me once you get
elected. You scratch my back, I'll scratch yours.* □ PRO-
FESSOR: *I want you to encourage all your friends to nomi-
nate me for Teacher of the Year.* STUDENT: *OK. But you'll
have to give me an A in your class. You scratch my back,
I'll scratch yours.*

Your guess is as good as mine.   I do not know. (Casual.)
□ SANDRA: *Are there any good movies playing tonight?*
ALAN: *Your guess is as good as mine.* □ JILL: *How long*

should we bake this pie? JANE: *Your guess is as good as mine.*

You win a few, you lose a few. See the following entry.

You win some, you lose some. AND **You win a few, you lose a few.** You cannot always succeed. (You can say this when you have not succeeded, to show that you are not discouraged.) □ JILL: *I was sorry to hear that you didn't win your court case.* JANE: *Well, you win some, you lose some.* □ BILL: *I thought it was terrible that you didn't get a prize in the art contest.* VINCENT: *You win a few, you lose a few.*

Young men may die, but old men must die. Young people may be killed by accidents or disease, but old people cannot avoid dying for very long, simply because they are old. □ *When Grandfather was so sick, he told us, "Don't feel too bad if I pass on; it's my time. Young men may die, old men must die."* □ *I'm afraid old Mr. Ferris won't live much longer. Young men may die, but old men must die.*

Youth must be served. Young people should be allowed to have fun. □ *Don't lecture the young folks because they were out dancing all night. Youth must be served.* □ *I don't know where my daughter gets the energy to go to so many parties and date so many young men. Youth must be served, I suppose.*

PHRASE-FINDER INDEX

Use this index to find the form of an expression that you want to look up in the dictionary. First, pick out any major word in the phrase you are seeking. Second, look that word up in this index to find the form of the phrase used in the dictionary. Third, look up the phrase in the dictionary. See Using the Index below.

Some of the words occurring in the dictionary entries do not occur as entries in this index. Some words are omitted because they occur so frequently that their lists would cover many pages. In these instances, you should look up the phrase under some other word. Most of the grammar or function words are not indexed. In addition, the most numerous verbs, *be, get, go, have, make,* and *take,* are not indexed.

Using the Index

This index provides a convenient way to find the complete form of an entry from only a single major word in the entry phrase.

1. When you are trying to find an expression in this index, look up the noun first, if there is one.

2. When you are looking for a noun, try first to find the singular or simplest form of the noun.

3. When you are looking for a verb, try first to find the present tense or simplest form of the verb.

4. In most expressions where a noun or pronoun is a variable part of an expression, it will be represented by the words "someone" or "something" in the form of the expression used in the dictionary. If you do not find the

noun you want in the index, it may, in fact, be a variable word.

5. This is an index of forms, not meanings. The expressions in an index entry do not usually have any meanings in common.

ABANDON

Abandon hope, all ye who enter here. □ Like rats abandoning a sinking ship □ Rats abandon a sinking ship.

ABHOR

Nature abhors a vacuum.

ABSENCE

Absence makes the heart grow fonder. □ Conspicuous by one's absence

ABSOLUTE

Absolute power corrupts absolutely.

ACCIDENT

Accidents will happen.

ACCORD

According to Hoyle □ According to someone's lights

ACCOUNT

There is no accounting for taste(s).

ACCUSE

A guilty conscience needs no accuser. □ He who excuses himself accuses himself. □ Never ask pardon before you are accused.

ACE

Have an ace up one's sleeve

ACORN

Great oaks from little acorns grow.

ACTION

Actions speak louder than words.

ADAM

Not to know someone from Adam

ADD

Add insult to injury

ADO

Much ado about nothing

ADVICE

Nothing is given so freely as advice.

AFFAIR

There is a tide in the affairs of men.

AFRAID

He who rides a tiger is afraid to dismount.

AFT

The best-laid schemes of mice and men gang aft agley.

AGAIN

If at first you don't succeed, try, try again.

AGE

In this day and age □ The age of miracles is past.

AGLEY

The best-laid schemes of mice and men gang aft agley.

AGREE

Birds in their little nests agree.

AIR

(As) free as (the) air □ (As) light as air □ Build castles in the air

ALIKE

Great minds think alike. □ Share and share alike.

ALONE

He travels fastest who travels alone. □ Laugh and the world laughs with you; weep and you weep alone. □ Leave well enough alone. □ Man does not live by bread alone.

ALTER

Circumstances alter cases.

ALWAYS

A bad penny always turns up. □ A bully is always a coward. □ A rich man's joke is always funny. □ It's always darkest just before the dawn. □ Keep a thing seven years and you'll (always) find a use for it. □ Once a priest, always a priest □ Once a whore, always a whore □ The bread always falls on the buttered side. □ The customer is always right. □ The first step is always the hardest. □ The grass is always greener on the other side of the fence. □ The unexpected always happens.

ANGEL

Fools rush in where angels fear to tread.

ANGER

Do not let the sun go down on your anger.

ANOTHER

Another colony heard from □ Another country heard from □ He who fights and runs away, may live to fight another day. □ It's six of one, half a dozen of another. □ One good turn deserves another. □ One law for the rich and another for the poor □ One man's loss is another man's gain. □ One man's meat is another man's poison. □ Tomorrow is another day. □ When one door shuts, another opens.

ANSWER

A soft answer turneth away wrath.

ANY

A golden key can open any door. □ A rose by any other name would smell as sweet. □ A thing you don't want is dear at any price. □ Any port in a storm □ Eavesdroppers never hear any good of themselves. □ It's an ill wind that blows nobody (any) good. □ Listeners never hear any good of themselves.

APPEAR

Talk of the devil (and he is sure to appear).

APPEARANCE

Appearances can be deceiving.

APPLE

An apple a day keeps the doctor away. □ The rotten apple spoils the barrel.

APRIL

April showers bring May flowers.

APRON

Tied to one's mother's apron strings

ARCHITECT

Every man is the architect of his own fortune.

ARM

Governments have long arms. □ Kings have long arms. □ Stretch your arm no further than your sleeve will reach.

ARMY

An army marches on its stomach.

ARRIVE

It is better to travel hopefully than to arrive.

ARROW

(As) straight as an arrow □ (As) swift as an arrow

ASK

Ask me no questions, I'll tell you no lies. □ Ask no questions and hear no lies. □ It never hurts to ask. □ Never ask pardon before you are accused. □ Shoot first, ask questions later.

ASTRAY

The best-laid plans of mice and men oft go astray.

AWAY

A soft answer turneth away wrath. □ An apple a day keeps the doctor away. □ Burn not your house to fright the mouse away. □ Constant dripping wears away a stone.

□ Constant dropping wears away a stone. □ He who fights and runs away, may live to fight another day. □ When the cat's away, the mice will play. □ Wild horses couldn't drag someone away from something.

AXE

Have an axe to grind

BABE

Babe in the woods □ Out of the mouths of babes

BABY

(As) bald as a baby's backside □ (As) weak as a baby □ Don't throw the baby out with the bathwater.

BACK

Back to the salt mine. □ Give the shirt off one's back □ The straw that broke the camel's back □ Turn back the clock □ You scratch my back, I'll scratch yours.

BACKSIDE

(As) bald as a baby's backside

BACON

Bring home the bacon

BAD

A bad excuse is better than none. □ A bad penny always turns up. □ Bad money drives out good. □ Bad news travels fast. □ Fire is a good servant but a bad master. □ Go from bad to worse □ Good riddance to bad rubbish! □ Hope is a good breakfast but a bad supper. □ Make the best of a bad job □ Moving three times is as bad as a fire. □ Nothing so bad but (it) might have been worse.

BAG
Let the cat out of the bag

BALD
(As) bald as a baby's backside □ (As) bald as a coot

BALL
That's the way the ball bounces. □ The whole ball of wax

BANK
Cry all the way to the bank □ Laugh all the way to the bank

BARGAIN
It takes two to make a bargain.

BARK
A barking dog never bites. □ Bark up the wrong tree □ One's bark is worse than one's bite. □ Why keep a dog and bark yourself?

BARN
Cannot hit the broad side of a barn

BARREL
The rotten apple spoils the barrel.

BASKET
Don't put all your eggs in one basket.

BAT
(As) blind as a bat □ Have bats in the belfry □ Like a bat out of hell

BATHWATER
Don't throw the baby out with the bathwater.

BATTEN
Batten down the hatches

BEAN
Not worth a hill of beans

BEAR
(As) gruff as a bear □ Beware of Greeks bearing gifts.

BEARD
Beard someone in his den □ Beard the lion in his den

BEAT
Beat a dead horse □ If you can't beat them, join them.

BEAUTY
A thing of beauty is a joy forever. □ Beauty is in the eye of the beholder. □ Beauty is only skin-deep.

BEAVER
(As) busy as a beaver

BED
As you make your bed, so you must lie upon it. □ Between you and me and the bedpost □ Early to bed and early to rise, makes a man healthy, wealthy, and wise. □ Get up on the wrong side of the bed

BEDFELLOW
Politics makes strange bedfellows.

BEE
(As) busy as a bee □ Have a
bee in one's bonnet

BEER
Life isn't all beer and skittles.

BEGET
Love begets love.

BEGGAR
Beggars can't be choosers. □
If wishes were horses, then
beggars would ride. □ Set a
beggar on horseback, and
he'll ride to the devil.

BEGIN
Charity begins at home. □
He that would the daughter
win, must with the mother
first begin. □ He who begins
many things, finishes but
few. □ He who would climb
the ladder must begin at the
bottom. □ Life begins at
forty. □ Well begun is half
done.

BEHIND
Burn one's bridges (behind
one) □ If two ride on a horse,
one must ride behind.

BEHOLDER
Beauty is in the eye of the
beholder.

BELFRY
Have bats in the belfry

BELIEVE
A liar is not believed (even)
when he tells the truth. □

Believe nothing of what you
hear, and only half of what
you see. □ Seeing is believing.

BELLY
A growing youth has a wolf
in his belly.

BEND
As the twig is bent, so is the
tree inclined.

BENEFIT
Give someone the benefit of
the doubt

BEST
All's for the best in the best
of all possible worlds. □ An
old poacher makes the best
gamekeeper. □ East or west,
home is best. □ East, west,
home's best. □ (Even) the
best of friends must part. □
Experience is the best
teacher. □ God takes soonest
those he loveth best. □ He
who laughs last, laughs best.
□ Honesty is the best policy.
□ Hope for the best and prepare for the worst. □ Hunger
is the best sauce. □ Make the
best of a bad job □ Put one's
best foot forward □ Revenge
is a dish best served cold. □
The best defense is a good offense. □ The best is the enemy of the good. □ The
best-laid plans of mice and
men oft go astray. □ The
best-laid schemes of mice
and men gang aft agley. □
The best things come in small

packages. □ The best things in life are free. □ The good is the enemy of the best.

BETTER

A bad excuse is better than none. □ Better be an old man's darling than a young man's slave. □ Better (be) safe than sorry. □ Better be the head of a dog than the tail of a lion. □ Better late than never. □ Better left unsaid □ Better the devil you know than the devil you don't know. □ Discretion is the better part of valor. □ Example is better than precept. □ Half a loaf is better than none. □ Have better (or other) fish to fry □ It is better to be born lucky than rich. □ It is better to give than to receive. □ It is better to travel hopefully than to arrive. □ It is better to wear out than to rust out. □ Prevention is better than cure. □ Something is better than nothing. □ The less said (about something), the better. □ 'Tis better to have loved and lost than never to have loved at all. □ Two heads are better than one.

BEWARE

Beware of Greeks bearing gifts. □ Let the buyer beware.

BIG

Little pitchers have big ears. □ The bigger they are, the harder they fall. □ The biggest frog in the puddle □ The biggest toad in the puddle

BILL

(As) queer as a three-dollar bill

BIRD

A bird in the hand is worth two in the bush. □ A little bird told me. □ Birds in their little nests agree. □ Birds of a feather flock together. □ Fine feathers make fine birds. □ It's an ill bird that fouls its own nest. □ Kill two birds with one stone □ The early bird catches the worm.

BIT

Take the bit between one's teeth

BITE

A barking dog never bites. □ Bite the hand that feeds you □ Dead men don't bite. □ Don't bite off more than you can chew. □ Once bitten, twice shy □ One's bark is worse than one's bite.

BITTER

Take the bitter with the sweet

BLACK

(As) black as a sweep □ (As) black as coal □ (As) black as pitch □ That's the pot calling the kettle black. □ The devil is not so black as he is painted. □ The pot is calling the kettle black.

BLANKET
Born on the wrong side of the blanket

BLESS
A blessing in disguise □ Bless one's lucky star □ Bless one's stars □ Blessed is he who expects nothing, for he shall never be disappointed. □ It is more blessed to give than to receive.

BLIND
A nod's as good as a wink to a blind horse. □ (As) blind as a bat □ In the country of the blind, the one-eyed man is king. □ Love is blind. □ Men are blind in their own cause. □ The blind leading the blind □ There's none so blind as those who will not see.

BLISS
Where ignorance is bliss, 'tis folly to be wise.

BLOCK
A chip off the old block

BLOOD
(As) red as blood □ Blood is thicker than water. □ Blood-red □ Blood will have blood. □ Blood will tell. □ You cannot get blood from a stone. □ You cannot get blood from a turnip.

BLOW
It's an ill wind that blows nobody (any) good.

BLUE
A bolt from the blue □ Between the devil and the deep blue sea □ Once in a blue moon

BOARD
(As) flat as a board

BOAST
Nothing to boast about

BODY
Enough to keep body and soul together

BOIL
A watched pot never boils.

BOLD
(As) bold as brass □ Fortune favors the bold.

BOLT
A bolt from the blue □ Shut the stable door after the horse has bolted.

BONE
(As) dry as a bone □ Bone-dry □ Feel something in one's bones □ Hard words break no bones. □ Have a bone to pick (with someone) □ Sticks and stones may break my bones, but words will never hurt me.

BONNET
Have a bee in one's bonnet

BOOK
Don't judge a book by its cover. □ Read someone like a(n open) book.

BOOTSTRAP
Pull oneself up by the bootstraps

BORN

Born on the wrong side of the blanket □ Born with a silver spoon in one's mouth □ If you're born to be hanged then you'll never be drowned. □ It is better to be born lucky than rich.

BORROW

Neither a borrower nor a lender be.

BOTH

Burn the candle at both ends

BOTTLE

You cannot put new wine in old bottles.

BOTTOM

Every tub must stand on its own bottom. □ He who would climb the ladder must begin at the bottom. □ Let every tub stand on its own bottom.

BOUNCE

That's the way the ball bounces.

BOWL

Life is just a bowl of cherries.

BOY

All work and no play makes Jack a dull boy. □ Boys will be boys. □ Separate the men from the boys

BRAIN

An idle brain is the devil's workshop.

BRASS

(As) bold as brass □ Get down to brass tacks

BRAVE

Fortune favors the brave. □ None but the brave deserve the fair.

BREAD

Bread is the staff of life. □ Cast one's bread upon the waters □ Know which side one's bread is buttered on □ Man does not live by bread alone. □ The bread always falls on the buttered side.

BREADTH

Come within a hair's breadth of something.

BREAK

Hard words break no bones. □ Ignorance (of the law) is no excuse (for breaking it). □ Promises are like piecrust, made to be broken. □ Sticks and stones may break my bones, but words will never hurt me. □ The straw that broke the camel's back □ You cannot make an omelet without breaking eggs.

BREAKFAST

Hope is a good breakfast but a bad supper. □ Sing before breakfast, you'll cry before night. □ Sing before breakfast, you'll cry before supper.

BREAST

Hope springs eternal (in the human breast). □ Make a clean breast of it

BREED

Familiarity breeds contempt. □ Like breeds like.

BREVITY
Brevity is the soul of wit.

BRICK
You cannot make bricks without straw.

BRIDE
Happy is the bride that the sun shines on.

BRIDGE
Burn one's bridges (behind one) □ Cross that bridge when one comes to it □ Water under the bridge

BRIGHT
(As) bright as a button □ (As) bright as a new pin □ Bright-eyed and bushy-tailed

BRING
April showers bring May flowers. □ Bring home the bacon □ The worth of a thing is what it will bring.

BROAD
Cannot hit the broad side of a barn

BROADEN
Travel broadens the mind.

BROOM
A new broom sweeps clean. □ New brooms sweep clean.

BROTH
Too many cooks spoil the broth.

BROTHER
Am I my brother's keeper? □ I am not my brother's keeper.

BROW
By the sweat of one's brow

BRUSH
Tar someone with the same brush

BUCKET
A drop in the bucket

BUG
(As) snug as a bug in a rug

BUILD
Build castles in the air □ It is easier to tear down than to build up. □ Rome was not built in a day.

BULL
Like a bull in a china shop □ Seize the bull by the horns. □ Take the bull by the horns.

BULLY
A bully is always a coward.

BUMP
Like a bump on a log

BURN
A burnt child dreads the fire. □ Burn not your house to fright the mouse away. □ Burn one's bridges (behind one) □ Burn the candle at both ends □ Burn the midnight oil □ Fiddle while Rome burns □ If you play with fire you get burned. □ Money burns a hole in someone's pocket.

BURY
Bury the hatchet □ Let the dead bury the dead.

BUSH
A bird in the hand is worth two in the bush.

BUSHEL
Hide one's light under a bushel

BUSHY
Bright-eyed and bushy-tailed

BUSINESS
Business before pleasure □ Mind your own business! □ Punctuality is the soul of business.

BUSY
(As) busy as a beaver □ (As) busy as a bee □ (As) busy as a cat on a hot tin roof □ Busiest men find the most time. □ The busiest men have the most leisure.

BUTTER
Butter wouldn't melt (in someone's mouth). □ Fine words butter no parsnips. □ Know which side one's bread is buttered on □ The bread always falls on the buttered side.

BUTTERFLY
(As) gaudy as a butterfly

BUTTON
(As) bright as a button

BUY
Buy a pig in a poke □ Let the buyer beware. □ Why buy a cow when milk is so cheap? □ Why buy a cow when you can get milk for free?

BYGONES
Let bygones be bygones.

CACKLE
He that would have eggs must endure the cackling of hens.

CAESAR
Caesar's wife must be above suspicion.

CAKE
Let them eat cake. □ You cannot have your cake and eat it (too).

CALL
Call a spade a spade □ Call no man happy till he dies. □ Cannot call one's soul one's own □ He who pays the piper calls the tune. □ Many are called but few are chosen. □ That's the pot calling the kettle black. □ The pot is calling the kettle black.

CALM
After a storm comes a calm. □ Cool, calm, and collected □ The calm before the storm

CAMEL
Strain at gnats and swallow camels □ The straw that broke the camel's back

CANDLE
Burn the candle at both ends □ Can't hold a candle to someone

CANOE
Paddle one's own canoe

CAPACITY
Genius is an infinite capacity for taking pains.

CARD
Lucky at cards, unlucky in love

CAREFUL
If you can't be good, be careful.

CARRY
Carry coals to Newcastle □ Never make a threat you cannot carry out.

CART
Don't put the cart before the horse.

CASE
Circumstances alter cases.

CAST
Cast one's bread upon the waters □ Cast pearls before swine □ Cast the first stone □ Coming events cast their shadows before.

CASTLE
A castle in Spain □ A man's home is his castle. □ Build castles in the air

CAT
A cat can look at a king. □ A cat has nine lives. □ A cat in gloves catches no mice. □ All cats are gray in the dark. □ (As) busy as a cat on a hot tin roof □ Curiosity killed the cat. □ (Has the) cat got your tongue? □ Keep no more cats than will catch mice. □ Let the cat out of the bag □ Not enough room to swing a cat □ Rain cats and dogs □ There's more than one way to skin a cat. □ When the cat's away, the mice will play.

CATCH
A cat in gloves catches no mice. □ Catch as catch can □ First catch your hare. □ If you run after two hares you will catch neither. □ Keep no more cats than will catch mice. □ Set a thief to catch a thief. □ The early bird catches the worm. □ You can catch more flies with honey than with vinegar. □ You must lose a fly to catch a trout.

CAUSE
Men are blind in their own cause.

CEASE
Wonders never cease!

CERTAIN
Nothing is certain but death and taxes. □ Nothing is certain but the unforeseen.

CHAFF
Separate the wheat from the chaff

CHAIN
A chain is no stronger than its weakest link.

CHANCE
You pays your money and you takes your chance(s). □ A leopard cannot change his spots.

CHANGE
Don't change horses in midstream. □ Times change and we with time. □ Times change(, people change).

CHARITY
Charity begins at home.

CHARM
The third time's the charm.

CHEAP
Talk is cheap. ☐ Why buy a cow when milk is so cheap?

CHEAT
Cheats never prosper.

CHERRY
(As) red as a cherry ☐ Life is just a bowl of cherries.

CHEW
Don't bite off more than you can chew.

CHICKEN
Don't count your chickens before they are hatched. ☐ The chickens come home to roost

CHIEF
Too many chiefs and not enough Indians

CHILD
A burnt child dreads the fire. ☐ Children and fools tell the truth. ☐ Children should be seen and not heard. ☐ Heaven protects children, sailors, and drunken men. ☐ It is a wise child that knows its own father. ☐ Monday's child is fair of face. ☐ Spare the rod and spoil the child. ☐ The child is father of the man. ☐ The devil's children have the devil's luck.

CHINA
Like a bull in a china shop

CHIP
A chip off the old block ☐ Have a chip on one's shoulder ☐ Let the chips fall where they may.

CHOOSE
Beggars can't be choosers. ☐ Many are called but few are chosen.

CHRISTMAS
Christmas comes but once a year.

CHURCH
The nearer the church, the farther from God.

CHURCHMOUSE
(As) poor as a churchmouse

CIGAR
Close, but no cigar.

CIRCUMSTANCE
Circumstances alter cases.

CITE
The devil can cite Scripture for his own purpose.

CIVILITY
Civility costs nothing.

CLAM
(As) happy as a clam

CLEAN
A new broom sweeps clean. ☐ (As) clean as a hound's tooth ☐ (As) clean as a whistle ☐ Make a clean breast of it ☐ New brooms sweep clean.

CLEANLINESS
Cleanliness is next to godliness.

CLIMB
He who would climb the ladder must begin at the bottom.

CLOCK
Turn back the clock

CLOCKWORK
(As) regular as clockwork

CLOSE
Close, but no cigar. ☐ Close enough for government work

CLOSET
Every family has a skeleton in the closet.

CLOTHES
A wolf in sheep's clothing ☐ Clothes make the man.

CLOUD
Every cloud has a silver lining.

CLUTCH
A drowning man will clutch at a straw.

COAL
(As) black as coal ☐ Carry coals to Newcastle ☐ Haul someone over the coals. ☐ Rake someone over the coals

COBBLER
Let the cobbler stick to his last.

COLD
(As) cold as a witch's tit ☐ (As) cold as marble ☐ Cold hands, warm heart ☐ Feed a cold and starve a fever. ☐ Revenge is a dish best served cold.

COLLECT
Cool, calm, and collected

COLONY
Another colony heard from

COMB
Go over something with a fine-tooth comb. ☐ Go through something with a fine-tooth comb.

COME
After a storm comes a calm. ☐ All good things must (come to an) end. ☐ Christmas comes but once a year. ☐ Come easy, go easy. ☐ Come on like gangbusters ☐ Come out smelling like a rose ☐ Come up roses ☐ Come within a hair's breadth of something. ☐ Come within an inch of something. ☐ Coming events cast their shadows before. ☐ Cross that bridge when one comes to it ☐ Easy come, easy go. ☐ Everything comes to him who waits. ☐ First come, first served. ☐ Good things come in small packages. ☐ Good things come to him who waits. ☐ If the mountain will not come to Mahomet, Mahomet must go to the mountain. ☐ If (the) worst comes to (the) worst ☐ March comes in like a lion, and goes out like a lamb. ☐ Misfortunes never come singly. ☐ Morning dreams come true. ☐ Nothing comes of nothing. ☐ The best things

come in small packages. ☐
The chickens come home to
roost ☐ Tomorrow never
comes. ☐ What goes up must
come down. ☐ When pov-
erty comes in at the door,
love flies out of the window.
☐ When the wolf comes in at
the door, love creeps out of
the window.

COMMAND
He that cannot obey cannot
command.

COMMISSION
There is a sin of omission as
well as of commission.

COMMON
An ounce of common sense is
worth a pound of theory. ☐
(As) common as dirt

COMPANY
A man is known by the company he keeps. ☐ Desert and
reward seldom keep com-
pany. ☐ Misery loves com-
pany. ☐ Two is company,
(but) three's a crowd.

CONFESSION
(Open) confession is good for
the soul.

CONQUER
Divide and conquer.

CONSCIENCE
A guilty conscience needs no
accuser. ☐ Conscience does
make cowards of us all.

CONSENT
Silence gives consent.

CONSPICUOUS
Conspicuous by one's ab-
sence

CONSTANT
Constant dripping wears
away a stone. ☐ Constant
dropping wears away a stone.

CONTEMPT
Familiarity breeds contempt.

CONTENT
A contented mind is a perpetual feast.

CONVICTION
Have the courage of one's
convictions

COOK
Too many cooks spoil the
broth.

COOKIE
That's the way the cookie
crumbles.

COOL
(As) cool as a cucumber ☐
Cool, calm, and collected

COOT
(As) bald as a coot

CORRUPT
Absolute power corrupts absolutely.

COST
Civility costs nothing. ☐
Cost a pretty penny ☐ Cour-
tesy costs nothing.

COUNCIL
Councils of war never fight.

COUNT
Don't count your chickens
before they are hatched.

COUNTRY

Another country heard from □ A prophet is not without honor save in his own country. □ Happy is the country which has no history. □ In the country of the blind, the one-eyed man is king. □ So many countries, so many customs

COURAGE

Have the courage of one's convictions

COURSE

The course of true love never did run smooth.

COURTESY

Courtesy costs nothing.

COVER

Don't judge a book by its cover.

COW

Why buy a cow when milk is so cheap? □ Why buy a cow when you can get milk for free?

COWARD

A bully is always a coward. □ Conscience does make cowards of us all. □ Cowards die many times before their death(s).

CRACK

He that would eat the kernel must crack the nut.

CRADLE

The hand that rocks the cradle rules the world.

CRAZY

(As) crazy as a loon □ Crazy like a fox

CREAK

A creaking door hangs longest. □ A creaking gate hangs longest.

CREDIT

Give credit where credit is due.

CREEP

When the wolf comes in at the door, love creeps out of the window.

CRICKET

(As) merry as a cricket

CRIME

Poverty is not a crime.

CROP

Good seed makes a good crop.

CROSS

Cross that bridge when one comes to it □ Cross the stream where it is shallowest. □ Crosses are ladders that lead to heaven.

CROW

(As) hoarse as a crow

CROWD

Far from the madding crowd □ Two is company, (but) three's a crowd.

CROWN

Uneasy lies the head that wears a crown.

CRUMBLE
That's the way the cookie crumbles.

CRUST
Promises are like piecrust, made to be broken.

CRY
Cry all the way to the bank □ Don't cry before you are hurt. □ Don't cry over spilled milk. □ It's no use crying over spilled milk. □ Sing before breakfast, you'll cry before night. □ Sing before breakfast, you'll cry before supper.

CUCUMBER
(As) cool as a cucumber

CUP
My cup runneth over. □ Not one's cup of tea □ There's many a slip 'twixt the cup and the lip.

CURE
An ounce of prevention is worth a pound of cure. □ Prevention is better than cure. □ What can't be cured must be endured.

CURIOSITY
Curiosity killed the cat.

CURTAIN
Ring down the curtain

CUSTOM
So many countries, so many customs

CUSTOMER
The customer is always right.

CUT
Cut off one's nose to spite one's face

DAM
Water over the dam

DAMN
Damn someone with faint praise □ Damned if you do, damned if you don't.

DANGEROUS
A little knowledge is a dangerous thing. □ A little learning is a dangerous thing.

DARK
All cats are gray in the dark. □ It's always darkest just before the dawn. □ The darkest hour is just before the dawn.

DARLING
Better be an old man's darling than a young man's slave.

DAUGHTER
He that would the daughter win, must with the mother first begin. □ Like mother, like daughter

DAWN
It's always darkest just before the dawn. □ The darkest hour is just before the dawn.

DAY
An apple a day keeps the doctor away. □ Every dog has his day. □ First see the light of day □ He who fights and runs away, may live to

fight another day. ☐ In this day and age ☐ One of these days is none of these days. ☐ Rome was not built in a day. ☐ Save for a rainy day ☐ Sufficient unto the day is the evil thereof. ☐ Tomorrow is another day.

DEAD

(As) dead as a doornail ☐ (As) dead as the dodo ☐ (As) silent as the dead ☐ Beat a dead horse ☐ Dead men don't bite. ☐ Dead men tell no tales. ☐ Deader than a doornail ☐ Flog a dead horse ☐ It's ill waiting for dead men's shoes. ☐ Let the dead bury the dead. ☐ Never speak ill of the dead. ☐ The female of the species is more deadly than the male. ☐ The only good Indian is a dead Indian.

DEAF

(As) deaf as a post ☐ There's none so deaf as those who will not hear.

DEAR

A thing you don't want is dear at any price.

DEATH

(As) pale as death ☐ (As) still as death ☐ (As) sure as death ☐ Cowards die many times before their death(s). ☐ Death is the great leveler. ☐ Like death warmed over ☐ Nothing is certain but death and taxes. ☐ There is a rem-

edy for everything except death.

DECEIVE

Appearances can be deceiving.

DEEP

Beauty is only skin-deep. ☐ Between the devil and the deep blue sea ☐ Still waters run deep.

DEFENSE

The best defense is a good offense.

DEFER

Hope deferred makes the heart sick. ☐ Hope deferred maketh the heart sick.

DELAY

Desires are nourished by delays.

DEN

Beard someone in his den ☐ Beard the lion in his den

DENMARK

Something is rotten in (the state of) Denmark.

DESERT

Desert and reward seldom keep company.

DESERVE

None but the brave deserve the fair. ☐ One good turn deserves another.

DESIRE

Desires are nourished by delays.

DESPERATE
Desperate diseases must have desperate remedies.

DEVIL
An idle brain is the devil's workshop. □ Better the devil you know than the devil you don't know. □ Between the devil and the deep blue sea □ Devil take the hindmost □ Every man for himself (and the devil take the hindmost). □ Give the devil his due □ He who sups with the devil should have a long spoon. □ Needs must when the devil drives. □ Set a beggar on horseback, and he'll ride to the devil. □ Speak of the devil (and in he walks). □ Talk of the devil (and he is sure to appear). □ Tell the truth and shame the devil. □ The devil can cite Scripture for his own purpose. □ The devil can quote Scripture for his own purpose. □ The devil finds work for idle hands to do. □ The devil is not so black as he is painted. □ The devil looks after his own. □ The devil to pay □ The devil's children have the devil's luck.

DIE
Call no man happy till he dies. □ Cowards die many times before their death(s). □ Eat, drink, and be merry, for tomorrow we die. □ Live by the sword, die by the sword. □ Never say die. □ Old habits die hard. □ The good die young. □ Whom the gods love die young. □ You have to eat a peck of dirt before you die. □ Young men may die, but old men must die.

DIFFER
Tastes differ.

DIFFERENT
Different strokes for different folks

DIFFICULT
The difficult is done at once; the impossible takes a little longer.

DILIGENCE
Diligence is the mother of good luck.

DIRT
(As) common as dirt □ Throw dirt enough, and some will stick. □ You have to eat a peck of dirt before you die.

DIRTY
Do not wash your dirty linen in public.

DISAPPOINT
Blessed is he who expects nothing, for he shall never be disappointed.

DISCRETION
An ounce of discretion is worth a pound of wit. □ Discretion is the better part of valor.

DISEASE
Desperate diseases must have desperate remedies.

DISGUISE
A blessing in disguise

DISH
Revenge is a dish best served cold.

DISHWATER
(As) dull as dishwater

DISMOUNT
He who rides a tiger is afraid to dismount.

DISPOSE
Man proposes, God disposes.

DISTANCE
Distance lends enchantment (to the view).

DITCHWATER
(As) dull as ditchwater

DIVIDE
A house divided against itself cannot stand. □ Divide and conquer. □ United we stand, divided we fall.

DIVINE
To err is human(, to forgive divine).

DOCTOR
An apple a day keeps the doctor away.

DODO
(As) dead as the dodo

DOG
A barking dog never bites. □ Better be the head of a dog than the tail of a lion. □ Dog does not eat dog. □ Every dog has his day. □ If you lie down with dogs, you will get up with fleas. □ Let sleeping dogs lie. □ Love me, love my dog. □ Rain cats and dogs □ Why keep a dog and bark yourself? □ You cannot teach an old dog new tricks.

DOLLAR
(As) queer as a three-dollar bill □ (As) sound as a dollar

DOOR
A creaking door hangs longest. □ A door must be either shut or open. □ A golden key can open any door. □ Lock the stable door after the horse is stolen □ Shut the stable door after the horse has bolted. □ When one door shuts, another opens. □ When poverty comes in at the door, love flies out of the window. □ When the wolf comes in at the door, love creeps out of the window.

DOORNAIL
(As) dead as a doornail □ Deader than a doornail

DOSE
Give someone a dose of his own medicine

DOUBT
Beyond a shadow of a doubt □ Give someone the benefit of the doubt

DOZEN
It's six of one, half a dozen of another. □ Nineteen to the dozen

DRAG
Wild horses couldn't drag someone away from something.

DRAW
One has to draw the line somewhere.

DREAD
A burnt child dreads the fire.

DREAM
Dream of a funeral and you hear of a marriage. □ Morning dreams come true.

DRINK
Drink like a fish □ Eat, drink, and be merry, for tomorrow we die. □ You can lead a horse to water, but you can't make it drink.

DRIP
Constant dripping wears away a stone.

DRIVE
(As) pure as the driven snow □ Bad money drives out good. □ Needs must when the devil drives.

DROP
A drop in the bucket □ A drop in the ocean □ At the drop of a hat □ Constant dripping wears away a stone.

DROWN
A drowning man will clutch at a straw. □ If you're born to be hanged then you'll never be drowned.

DRUM
(As) tight as a drum

DRUNK
(As) drunk as a lord □ (As) drunk as a skunk □ Heaven protects children, sailors, and drunken men.

DRY
(As) dry as a bone □ Bone-dry □ Dry as dust □ Put your trust in God, and keep your powder dry. □ You never miss the water till the well runs dry.

DUCK
Duck soup

DUE
Give credit where credit is due. □ Give the devil his due

DULL
All work and no play makes Jack a dull boy. □ (As) dull as dishwater □ (As) dull as ditchwater □ Never a dull moment

DUST
Dry as dust

EAR
Fields have eyes, and woods have ears. □ In (at) one ear and out (of) the other □ Little pitchers have big ears. □ Walls have ears. □ You cannot make a silk purse out of a sow's ear.

EARLY
Early ripe, early rotten. □ Early to bed and early to rise, makes a man healthy, wealthy, and wise. □ The early bird catches the worm.

EARN

A penny saved is a penny earned.

EAST

East is East and West is West (and never the twain shall meet). □ East or west, home is best. □ East, west, home's best.

EASY

(As) easy as A, B, C □ Come easy, go easy. □ Easier said than done. □ Easy come, easy go. □ It is easier to tear down than to build up. □ It is easy to be wise after the event.

EAT

Dog does not eat dog. □ Eat, drink, and be merry, for tomorrow we die. □ Eat someone out of house and home □ Eat to live, not live to eat. □ He that would eat the kernel must crack the nut. □ Let them eat cake. □ You cannot have your cake and eat it (too). □ You have to eat a peck of dirt before you die.

EAVESDROPPERS

Eavesdroppers never hear any good of themselves.

EEL

(As) slippery as an eel

EGG

Don't put all your eggs in one basket. □ Don't teach your grandmother to suck eggs. □ He that would have eggs must endure the cackling of

hens. □ Kill the goose that lays the golden egg(s). □ You cannot make an omelet without breaking eggs.

EITHER

A door must be either shut or open.

EMPTY

An empty sack cannot stand upright. □ Empty vessels make the most sound.

ENCHANTMENT

Distance lends enchantment (to the view).

END

All good things must (come to an) end. □ Burn the candle at both ends □ Someone cannot see beyond the end of his nose. □ The end justifies the means.

ENDURE

He that would have eggs must endure the cackling of hens. □ What can't be cured must be endured.

ENEMY

Be one's own worst enemy □ The best is the enemy of the good. □ The good is the enemy of the best.

ENOUGH

A word to the wise (is enough). □ Close enough for government work □ Enough is as good as a feast. □ Enough to keep body and soul together □ Give someone enough rope and he'll hang himself. □ Leave well enough alone. □ Not enough room to swing a cat □ Throw dirt enough, and some will stick. □ Too many chiefs and not enough Indians

ENTER
Abandon hope, all ye who enter here.

EQUAL
(All) other things being equal

ERR
To err is human(, to forgive divine).

ESCAPE
Escape by the skin of one's teeth □ Little thieves are hanged, but great ones escape.

ETERNAL
Hope springs eternal (in the human breast).

EVEN
A liar is not believed (even) when he tells the truth. □ Even a worm will turn. □ (Even) the best of friends must part.

EVENT
Coming events cast their shadows before. □ It is easy to be wise after the event. □ Every cloud has a silver lining. □ Every dog has his day. □ Every family has a skeleton in the closet. □ Every horse thinks its own pack heaviest. □ Every Jack has his Jill. □ Every man for

himself (and the devil take the hindmost). □ Every man has his price. □ Every man is the architect of his own fortune. □ Every man to his taste. □ Every tub must stand on its own bottom. □ Have a finger in every pie □ Let every tub stand on its own bottom. □ There are tricks in every trade. □ There are two sides to every question.

EVIL
Evil be to him who evil thinks. □ Idleness is the root of all evil. □ Money is the root of all evil. □ See no evil, hear no evil, speak no evil. □ Sufficient unto the day is the evil thereof. □ The lesser of two evils □ The love of money is the root of all evil.

EXAMPLE
Example is better than precept.

EXCEED
The mills of God grind slowly, yet they grind exceeding small.

EXCEPT
There is a remedy for everything except death.

EXCEPTION
The exception proves the rule.

EXCUSE
A bad excuse is better than none. □ He who excuses himself accuses himself. □

Ignorance (of the law) is no excuse (for breaking it).

EXIST

If God did not exist, it would be necessary to invent Him.

EXPECT

Blessed is he who expects nothing, for he shall never be disappointed.

EXPERIENCE

Experience is the best teacher. ☐ Experience is the father of wisdom. ☐ Experience is the mother of wisdom. ☐ Experience is the teacher of fools.

EYE

An eye for an eye (and a tooth for a tooth). ☐ Beauty is in the eye of the beholder. ☐ Bright-eyed and bushy-tailed ☐ Fields have eyes, and woods have ears. ☐ Here's mud in your eye! ☐ In the country of the blind, the one-eyed man is king. ☐ Pull the wool over someone's eyes ☐ What the eye doesn't see, the heart doesn't grieve over.

FACE

(As) plain as the nose on one's face ☐ Cut off one's nose to spite one's face ☐ Monday's child is fair of face.

FACT

Fact is stranger than fiction.

FAINT

Damn someone with faint praise ☐ Faint heart never won fair lady.

FAIR

All's fair in love and war. ☐ Faint heart never won fair lady. ☐ Hoist your sail when the wind is fair. ☐ Monday's child is fair of face. ☐ None but the brave deserve the fair.

FAITH

Faith will move mountains.

FALL

A reed before the wind lives on, while mighty oaks do fall. ☐ Fall between two stools ☐ He that is down need fear no fall. ☐ How the mighty have fallen. ☐ Let the chips fall where they may. ☐ Pride goes before a fall. ☐ Pride goeth before a fall. ☐ The bigger they are, the harder they fall. ☐ The bread always falls on the buttered side. ☐ United we stand, divided we fall.

FAMILIARITY

Familiarity breeds contempt.

FAMILY

Every family has a skeleton in the closet. ☐ The family that prays together stays together.

FAR

Far from the madding crowd

FARTHER

The nearer the church, the farther from God.

FAST

Bad news travels fast. □ He travels fastest who travels alone.

FAT

(As) fat as a pig □ The fat is in the fire.

FATHER

Experience is the father of wisdom. □ It is a wise child that knows its own father. □ Like father, like son □ The child is father of the man. □ The wish is father to the thought.

FAVOR

Fortune favors the bold. □ Fortune favors the brave.

FEAR

Fools rush in where angels fear to tread. □ He that is down need fear no fall.

FEAST

A contented mind is a perpetual feast. □ Enough is as good as a feast.

FEATHER

(As) light as a feather □ Birds of a feather flock together. □ Fine feathers make fine birds.

FEED

Bite the hand that feeds you □ Feed a cold and starve a fever.

FEEL

Feel something in one's bones

FELL

Little strokes fell great oaks.

FEMALE

The female of the species is more deadly than the male.

FENCE

Good fences make good neighbors. □ The grass is always greener on the other side of the fence.

FEVER

Feed a cold and starve a fever.

FEW

He who begins many things, finishes but few. □ Many are called but few are chosen. □ You win a few, you lose a few.

FICTION

Fact is stranger than fiction. □ Truth is stranger than fiction.

FIDDLE

(As) fit as a fiddle □ Fiddle while Rome burns □ There's many a good tune played on an old fiddle.

FIELD

Fields have eyes, and woods have ears.

FIGHT

Councils of war never fight. □ Fight fire with fire □ Fight tooth and nail □ He who fights and runs away, may live to fight another day.

FILL

Little and often fills the purse.

FIND

A good man is hard to find. □ Busiest men find the most time. □ Finders keepers(, losers weepers). □ Keep a thing seven years and you'll (always) find a use for it. □ Love will find a way. □ Seek and ye shall find. □ The devil finds work for idle hands to do.

FINE

A fine kettle of fish □ Fine feathers make fine birds. □ Fine words butter no parsnips. □ Go over something with a fine-tooth comb. □ Go through something with a fine-tooth comb.

FINGER

Fingers were made before forks. □ Have a finger in every pie

FINISH

Give us the tools, and we will finish the job. □ He who begins many things, finishes but few. □ Nice guys finish last.

FIRE

A burnt child dreads the fire. □ (As) hot as fire □ Fight fire with fire □ Fire is a good servant but a bad master. □ Have too many irons in the fire □ If you play with fire you get burned. □ Moving three times is as bad as a fire. □ Out of the frying pan into the fire. □ The fat is in the fire. □ (There's) no smoke without fire. □ Where there's smoke there's fire.

FIRST

Cast the first stone □ First catch your hare. □ First come, first served. □ First impressions are the most lasting. □ First see the light of day □ First things first □ He that would the daughter win, must with the mother first begin. □ If at first you don't succeed, try, try again. □ Self-preservation is the first law of nature. □ Shoot first, ask questions later. □ The first hundred years are the hardest. □ The first step is always the hardest.

FISH

A fine kettle of fish □ A fish out of water □ Drink like a fish □ Have better (or other) fish to fry □ There are other fish in the sea.

FIT

(As) fit as a fiddle □ If the shoe fits(, wear it).

FLAT

(As) flat as a board □ (As) flat as a pancake

FLATTERY

Imitation is the sincerest form of flattery.

FLEA

If you lie down with dogs, you will get up with fleas.

FLESH
The spirit is willing, but the flesh is weak.

FLOCK
Birds of a feather flock together.

FLOG
Flog a dead horse

FLOOR
Get in on the ground floor

FLOWER
April showers bring May flowers.

FLY
Time flies. □ When poverty comes in at the door, love flies out of the window. □ You can catch more flies with honey than with vinegar. □ You must lose a fly to catch a trout.

FOLK
Different strokes for different folks □ Idle folk have the least leisure.

FOLLY
Where ignorance is bliss, 'tis folly to be wise.

FOND
Absence makes the heart grow fonder.

FOOL
A fool and his money are soon parted. □ A fool's paradise □ Children and fools tell the truth. □ Experience is the teacher of fools. □ Fool me once, shame on you; fool me twice, shame on me. □

Fools rush in where angels fear to tread. □ There's no fool like an old fool.

FOOLISH
Penny wise and pound foolish

FOOT
Have one foot in the grave □ I would not touch it with a ten-foot pole. □ Not to let the grass grow under one's feet □ Put one's best foot forward □ Put one's foot down □ Put one's foot in it

FOREARMED
Forewarned is forearmed.

FOREVER
A thing of beauty is a joy forever.

FOREWARN
Forewarned is forearmed.

FORGET
Forgive and forget. □ Gone (before) but not forgotten

FORGIVE
Forgive and forget. □ To err is human(, to forgive divine).

FORK
Fingers were made before forks.

FORM
Imitation is the sincerest form of flattery.

FORTUNE
Every man is the architect of his own fortune. □ Fortune favors the bold. □ Fortune favors the brave.

FORTY

Life begins at forty.

FORWARD

Put one's best foot forward

FOUL

It's an ill bird that fouls its own nest.

FOUR

Between you and me and these four walls

FOX

Crazy like a fox

FREE

(As) free as (the) air □ Nothing is given so freely as advice. □ The best things in life are free. □ There ain't no such thing as a free lunch. □ There's no such thing as a free lunch. □ Why buy a cow when you can get milk for free?

FRIEND

A friend in need is a friend indeed. □ (Even) the best of friends must part. □ He that hath a full purse never wanted a friend. □ Lend your money and lose your friend. □ Short reckonings make long friends.

FRIENDSHIP

A hedge between keeps friendship green.

FRIGHT

Burn not your house to fright the mouse away.

FROG

The biggest frog in the puddle

FRUIT

Stolen fruit is sweetest. □ The tree is known by its fruit.

FRUITCAKE

(As) nutty as a fruitcake □ Nuttier than a fruitcake

FRY

Have better (or other) fish to fry □ Out of the frying pan into the fire.

FULL

He that hath a full purse never wanted a friend.

FUNERAL

Dream of a funeral and you hear of a marriage.

FUNNY

A rich man's joke is always funny.

FURTHER

Stretch your arm no further than your sleeve will reach.

FURY

Hell hath no fury like a woman scorned.

GAIN

No pain, no gain □ Nothing ventured, nothing gained. □ One man's loss is another man's gain.

GAMEKEEPER

An old poacher makes the best gamekeeper.

GANDER

What's sauce for the goose is sauce for the gander.

GANG

The best-laid schemes of mice and men gang aft agley.

GANGBUSTERS

Come on like gangbusters

GARBAGE

Garbage in, garbage out.

GATE

A creaking gate hangs longest.

GATHER

A rolling stone gathers no moss. □ Gather ye rosebuds while ye may.

GAUDY

(As) gaudy as a butterfly

GENEROUS

Be just before you're generous.

GENIUS

Genius is an infinite capacity for taking pains. □ Genius is ten percent inspiration and ninety percent perspiration.

GENTLE

(As) gentle as a lamb

GHOST

(As) pale as a ghost

GIFT

Beware of Greeks bearing gifts. □ Don't look a gift horse in the mouth.

GIVE

Give credit where credit is due. □ Give someone a dose of his own medicine □ Give someone an inch and he'll take a mile. □ Give someone an inch and he'll take a yard. □ Give someone enough rope and he'll hang himself. □ Give someone the benefit of the doubt □ Give the devil his due □ Give the shirt off one's back □ Give us the tools, and we will finish the job. □ He gives twice who gives quickly. □ It is better to give than to receive. □ It is more blessed to give than to receive. □ Nothing is given so freely as advice. □ Silence gives consent.

GLASS

(As) smooth as glass □ People who live in glass houses shouldn't throw stones.

GLITTER

All that glitters is not gold.

GLOVE

A cat in gloves catches no mice.

GNAT

Strain at gnats and swallow camels

GOAT

Separate the sheep from the goats

GOD

Doesn't have the sense God gave geese □ God helps them that help themselves. □ God takes soonest those he loveth best. □ God's in his heaven; all's right with the world. □

If God did not exist, it would be necessary to invent Him. □ Man proposes, God disposes. □ Put your trust in God, and keep your powder dry. □ Take the goods the gods provide. □ The gods send nuts to those who have no teeth. □ The mills of God grind slowly, yet they grind exceeding small. □ The nearer the church, the farther from God. □ There but for the grace of God (go I). □ Whom the gods love die young. □ You cannot serve God and Mammon.

GODLINESS

Cleanliness is next to godliness.

GOLD

A golden key can open any door. □ All that glitters is not gold. □ (As) good as gold □ Kill the goose that lays the golden egg(s). □ Silence is golden.

GOOD

A good husband makes a good wife. □ A good Jack makes a good Jill. □ A good man is hard to find. □ A good time was had by all. □ A miss is as good as a mile. □ A nod's as good as a wink to a blind horse. □ All good things must (come to an) end. □ (As) good as gold □ Bad money drives out good. □ Diligence is the mother of good luck. □ Eavesdroppers never hear any good of themselves. □ Enough is as good as a feast. □ Fire is a good servant but a bad master. □ Good fences make good neighbors. □ Good men are scarce. □ Good riddance to bad rubbish! □ Good seed makes a good crop. □ Good things come in small packages. □ Good things come to him who waits. □ Have too much of a good thing □ Hope is a good breakfast but a bad supper. □ If you can't be good, be careful. □ It's an ill wind that blows nobody (any) good. □ Listeners never hear any good of themselves. □ No news is good news. □ One good turn deserves another. □ (Open) confession is good for the soul. □ Take the goods the gods provide. □ The best defense is a good offense. □ The best is the enemy of the good. □ The good die young. □ The good is the enemy of the best. □ The only good Indian is a dead Indian. □ The road to hell is paved with good intentions. □ There's many a good tune played on an old fiddle. □ (As) silly as a goose □ Doesn't have the sense God gave geese □ Kill the goose that lays the golden egg(s). □ What's sauce for the goose is sauce for the gander.

GOVERNMENT

Close enough for government work □ Governments have long arms.

GRACE

There but for the grace of God (go I).

GRACEFUL

(As) graceful as a swan

GRANDMOTHER

Don't teach your grandmother to suck eggs.

GRASS

Not to let the grass grow under one's feet □ The grass is always greener on the other side of the fence.

GRAVE

(As) grave as a judge □ (As) silent as the grave □ Have one foot in the grave □ Make one turn (over) in one's grave

GRAY

All cats are gray in the dark.

GREASE

Like greased lightning □ The squeaking wheel gets the grease. □ The squeaky wheel gets the grease.

GREAT

Death is the great leveler. □ Great minds think alike. □ Great oaks from little acorns grow. □ Little strokes fell great oaks. □ Little thieves are hanged, but great ones escape. □ The greater the truth, the greater the libel □ Time is a great healer.

GREEK

Beware of Greeks bearing gifts. □ It's (all) Greek to me.

GREEN

A hedge between keeps friendship green. □ The grass is always greener on the other side of the fence.

GRIEVE

What the eye doesn't see, the heart doesn't grieve over.

GRIND

Have an axe to grind □ The mill cannot grind with water that is past. □ The mills of God grind slowly, yet they grind exceeding small.

GRINDSTONE

Keep one's nose to the grindstone.

GRIST

Grist for someone's mill □ Grist for the mill

GROUND

Get in on the ground floor

GROW

A growing youth has a wolf in his belly. □ Absence makes the heart grow fonder. □ Great oaks from little acorns grow. □ Money does not grow on trees. □ Not to let the grass grow under one's feet

GRUFF

(As) gruff as a bear

GUILTY

A guilty conscience needs no accuser.

GUY

Nice guys finish last.

HABIT

Old habits die hard.

HAIR

Come within a hair's breadth of something.

HALF

A trouble shared is a trouble halved. ☐ Believe nothing of what you hear, and only half of what you see. ☐ Half a loaf is better than none. ☐ Half the truth is often a whole lie. ☐ Half the world knows not how the other half lives. ☐ It's six of one, half a dozen of another. ☐ Well begun is half done.

HALLOO

Never halloo till you are out of the woods.

HAND

A bird in the hand is worth two in the bush. ☐ Bite the hand that feeds you ☐ Cold hands, warm heart ☐ If "ifs" and "ands" were pots and pans (there'd be no work for tinkers' hands). ☐ Many hands make light work. ☐ One hand for oneself and one for the ship. ☐ The devil finds work for idle hands to do. ☐ The hand that rocks the cradle rules the world. ☐ The left hand doesn't know what the right hand is doing.

HANDBASKET

Going to hell in a handbasket

HANDSOME

Handsome is as handsome does.

HANG

A creaking door hangs longest. ☐ A creaking gate hangs longest. ☐ Give someone enough rope and he'll hang himself. ☐ If you're born to be hanged then you'll never be drowned. ☐ Little thieves are hanged, but great ones escape. ☐ One might as well be hanged for a sheep as for a lamb.

HAPPEN

Accidents will happen. ☐ The unexpected always happens.

HAPPY

(As) happy as a clam ☐ (As) happy as a lark ☐ Call no man happy till he dies. ☐ Happy is the bride that the sun shines on. ☐ Happy is the country which has no history.

HARD

A good man is hard to find. ☐ (As) hard as nails ☐ Between a rock and a hard place ☐ Hard words break no bones. ☐ Old habits die hard. ☐ The bigger they are, the harder they fall. ☐ The first hundred years are the hardest. ☐ The first step is always the hardest.

HARE

(As) mad as a March hare ☐

First catch your hare. ☐ If you run after two hares you will catch neither. ☐ To run with the hare and hunt with the hounds

HASTE
Haste makes waste. ☐ Make haste slowly. ☐ Marry in haste, (and) repent at leisure. ☐ More haste, less speed

HAT
At the drop of a hat

HATCH
Batten down the hatches ☐ Don't count your chickens before they are hatched.

HATCHET
Bury the hatchet

HATTER
(As) mad as a hatter

HAUL
Haul someone over the coals.

HAY
Make hay while the sun shines.

HAYSTACK
Look for a needle in a haystack

HEAD
A still tongue makes a wise head. ☐ Better be the head of a dog than the tail of a lion. ☐ Hit the nail on the head ☐ Not able to make head or tail of something ☐ Two heads are better than one. ☐ Uneasy lies the head that wears a crown.

HEAL
Physician, heal thyself. ☐ Time is a great healer.

HEALTHY
Early to bed and early to rise, makes a man healthy, wealthy, and wise.

HEAR
Another colony heard from ☐ Another country heard from ☐ Ask no questions and hear no lies. ☐ Believe nothing of what you hear, and only half of what you see. ☐ Children should be seen and not heard. ☐ Dream of a funeral and you hear of a marriage. ☐ Eavesdroppers never hear any good of themselves. ☐ Listeners never hear any good of themselves. ☐ See no evil, hear no evil, speak no evil. ☐ There's none so deaf as those who will not hear.

HEART
A heavy purse makes a light heart. ☐ A light purse makes a heavy heart. ☐ Absence makes the heart grow fonder. ☐ Cold hands, warm heart ☐ Faint heart never won fair lady. ☐ Home is where the heart is. ☐ Hope deferred makes the heart sick. ☐ It is a poor heart that never rejoices. ☐ It is a sad heart that never rejoices. ☐ One's heart is in one's mouth ☐ The way to a man's heart is through his stomach. ☐ What the eye

doesn't see, the heart doesn't grieve over.

HEAT

If you can't stand the heat, get out of the kitchen. □ It's not the heat, it's the humidity.

HEAVEN

Crosses are ladders that lead to heaven. □ God's in his heaven; all's right with the world. □ Heaven protects children, sailors, and drunken men. □ Marriages are made in heaven.

HEAVY

A heavy purse makes a light heart. □ A light purse makes a heavy heart. □ Every horse thinks its own pack heaviest.

HEDGE

A hedge between keeps friendship green.

HELL

Going to hell in a handbasket □ He that would go to sea for pleasure, would go to hell for a pastime. □ Hell hath no fury like a woman scorned. □ Like a bat out of hell □ The road to hell is paved with good intentions.

HELP

God helps them that help themselves.

HEN

(As) scarce as hen's teeth □ He that would have eggs must endure the cackling of hens. □ Scarcer than hen's teeth

HER

Someone will get his (or hers).

HERE

Abandon hope, all ye who enter here. □ Here today, (and) gone tomorrow. □ Here's mud in your eye! □ Today here, tomorrow the world

HESITATE

He who hesitates is lost.

HIDE

Hide one's light under a bushel

HILL

(As) old as the hills □ Make a mountain out of a molehill □ Not worth a hill of beans □ What in (the) Sam Hill

HINDMOST

Devil take the hindmost □ Every man for himself (and the devil take the hindmost).

HISTORY

Happy is the country which has no history. □ History repeats itself.

HIT

Cannot hit the broad side of a barn □ Hit the nail on the head

HITCH

Hitch your wagon to a star.

HOARSE
(As) hoarse as a crow

HOIST
Hoist with one's own petard □ Hoist your sail when the wind is fair.

HOLD
Can't hold a candle to someone

HOLE
A square peg in a round hole □ Money burns a hole in someone's pocket. □ The mouse that has but one hole is quickly taken.

HOME
A man's home is his castle. □ A woman's place is in the home. □ Bring home the bacon □ Charity begins at home. □ East or west, home is best. □ East, west, home's best. □ Eat someone out of house and home □ Home is where the heart is. □ Men make houses, women make homes. □ Nothing to write home about □ The chickens come home to roost □ The longest way round is the nearest way home. □ The longest way round is the shortest way home. □ There's no place like home.

HONEST
Honesty is the best policy.

HONEY
(As) sweet as honey □ Sweeter than honey □ You can catch more flies with honey than with vinegar.

HONOR
A prophet is not without honor save in his own country. □ There is honor among thieves.

HOPE
Abandon hope, all ye who enter here. □ Hope deferred makes the heart sick. □ Hope deferred maketh the heart sick. □ Hope for the best and prepare for the worst. □ Hope is a good breakfast but a bad supper. □ Hope springs eternal (in the human breast). □ While there's life there's hope.

HOPEFUL
It is better to travel hopefully than to arrive.

HORN
Seize the bull by the horns. □ Take the bull by the horns.

HORSE
A nod's as good as a wink to a blind horse. □ (As) strong as a horse □ Beat a dead horse □ Don't change horses in mid-stream. □ Don't look a gift horse in the mouth. □ Don't put the cart before the horse. □ Every horse thinks its own pack heaviest. □ Flog a dead horse □ For want of a nail the shoe was lost; for want of a shoe the horse was lost; and for want of a horse the man was lost.

☐ Get it straight from the horse's mouth ☐ If two ride on a horse, one must ride behind. ☐ If wishes were horses, then beggars would ride. ☐ Lock the stable door after the horse is stolen ☐ Shut the stable door after the horse has bolted. ☐ Wild horses couldn't drag someone away from something. ☐ You can lead a horse to water, but you can't make it drink.

HORSEBACK

Set a beggar on horseback, and he'll ride to the devil.

HOT

(As) busy as a cat on a hot tin roof ☐ (As) hot as fire ☐ Strike while the iron is hot.

HOUND

(As) clean as a hound's tooth ☐ To run with the hare and hunt with the hounds

HOUR

The darkest hour is just before the dawn.

HOUSE

A house divided against itself cannot stand. ☐ Burn not your house to fright the mouse away. ☐ Eat someone out of house and home ☐ Men make houses, women make homes. ☐ People who live in glass houses shouldn't throw stones.

HOW

Half the world knows not how the other half lives. ☐ How the mighty have fallen.

HOYLE

According to Hoyle

HUMAN

Hope springs eternal (in the human breast). ☐ To err is human(, to forgive divine).

HUMIDITY

It's not the heat, it's the humidity.

HUNDRED

The first hundred years are the hardest.

HUNGER

Hunger is the best sauce.

HUNGRY

(As) hungry as a hunter

HUNT

(As) hungry as a hunter ☐ To run with the hare and hunt with the hounds

HURT

Don't cry before you are hurt. ☐ It never hurts to ask. ☐ Sticks and stones may break my bones, but words will never hurt me. ☐ What you don't know can't hurt you. ☐ What you don't know won't hurt you.

HUSBAND

A good husband makes a good wife.

IDLE

An idle brain is the devil's workshop. ☐ Idle folk have the least leisure. ☐ Idle

people have the least leisure.
□ The devil finds work for
idle hands to do.

IDLENESS
Idleness is the root of all evil.

IGNORANCE
Ignorance (of the law) is no
excuse (for breaking it). □
Where ignorance is bliss, 'tis
folly to be wise.

ILL
It's an ill bird that fouls its
own nest. □ It's an ill wind
that blows nobody (any)
good. □ It's ill waiting for
dead men's shoes. □ Never
speak ill of the dead.

IMITATION
Imitation is the sincerest
form of flattery.

IMPOSSIBLE
The difficult is done at once;
the impossible takes a little
longer.

IMPRESSION
First impressions are the
most lasting.

INCH
Come within an inch of
something. □ Give someone
an inch and he'll take a mile.
□ Give someone an inch and
he'll take a yard.

INCLINE
As the twig is bent, so is the
tree inclined.

INDEED
A friend in need is a friend
indeed.

INDIAN
The only good Indian is a
dead Indian. □ Too many
chiefs and not enough Indians

INDISPENSABLE
No one is indispensable.

INFALLIBLE
No one is infallible.

INFINITE
Genius is an infinite capacity
for taking pains.

INJURY
Add insult to injury

INSPIRATION
Genius is ten percent inspiration and ninety percent perspiration.

INSULT
Add insult to injury

INTENTION
The road to hell is paved with
good intentions.

INVENT
If God did not exist, it would
be necessary to invent Him.

INVENTION
Necessity is the mother of invention.

IRON
Have too many irons in the
fire □ Strike while the iron is
hot.

JACK
A good Jack makes a good
Jill. □ A jack of all trades is a
master of none. □ All work
and no play makes Jack a

dull boy. □ Before you can say Jack Robinson □ Every Jack has his Jill.

JANUARY

(As) slow as molasses in January □ Slower than molasses in January

JAYBIRD

(As) naked as a jaybird

JEST

Many a true word is spoken in jest. □ There's many a true word spoken in jest.

JILL

A good Jack makes a good Jill. □ Every Jack has his Jill.

JOB

(As) patient as Job □ Give us the tools, and we will finish the job. □ Make the best of a bad job

JOIN

If you can't beat them, join them. □ If you can't lick 'em, join 'em.

JOKE

A rich man's joke is always funny.

JONES

Keep up with the Joneses

JOY

A thing of beauty is a joy forever.

JUDGE

(As) grave as a judge □ (As) sober as a judge □ Don't judge a book by its cover. □

Judge not, lest ye be judged. □ Judge not, that ye be not judged.

JUST

Be just before you're generous. □ It's always darkest just before the dawn. □ Life is just a bowl of cherries. □ The darkest hour is just before the dawn.

JUSTIFY

The end justifies the means.

KEEN

(As) keen as mustard

KEEP

A hedge between keeps friendship green. □ A man is known by the company he keeps. □ Am I my brother's keeper? □ An apple a day keeps the doctor away. □ Desert and reward seldom keep company. □ Enough to keep body and soul together □ Finders keepers(, losers weepers). □ I am not my brother's keeper. □ Keep a stiff upper lip. □ Keep a thing seven years and you'll (always) find a use for it. □ Keep no more cats than will catch mice. □ Keep one's nose to the grindstone. □ Keep up with the Joneses □ Keep your shop and your shop will keep you. □ Put your trust in God, and keep your powder dry. □ Why keep a dog and bark yourself?

KERNEL
He that would eat the kernel must crack the nut.

KETTLE
A fine kettle of fish □ That's the pot calling the kettle black. □ The pot is calling the kettle black.

KEY
A golden key can open any door.

KILL
Curiosity killed the cat. □ It is not work that kills, but worry. □ It is the pace that kills. □ Kill the goose that lays the golden egg(s). □ Kill two birds with one stone

KIND
It takes all kinds (to make a world).

KING
A cat can look at a king. □ In the country of the blind, the one-eyed man is king. □ Kings have long arms.

KITCHEN
If you can't stand the heat, get out of the kitchen.

KNOCK
Opportunity knocks but once.

KNOW
A man is known by the company he keeps. □ Better the devil you know than the devil you don't know. □ Half the world knows not how the other half lives. □ If the truth were known □ It is a wise child that knows its own father. □ Know thyself. □ Know which side one's bread is buttered on □ Necessity knows no law. □ Not to know someone from Adam □ The left hand doesn't know what the right hand is doing. □ The tree is known by its fruit. □ What you don't know can't hurt you. □ What you don't know won't hurt you. □ You never know (what you can do) till you try.

KNOWLEDGE
A little knowledge is a dangerous thing. □ Knowledge is power.

LADDER
Crosses are ladders that lead to heaven. □ He who would climb the ladder must begin at the bottom.

LADY
Faint heart never won fair lady.

LAMB
(As) gentle as a lamb □ (As) meek as a lamb □ In like a lion, out like a lamb. □ March comes in like a lion, and goes out like a lamb. □ One might as well be hanged for a sheep as for a lamb.

LANE
It is a long lane that has no turning.

LARK
(As) happy as a lark

LAST

First impressions are the most lasting. □ He who laughs last, laughs best. □ He who laughs last, laughs longest. □ Let the cobbler stick to his last. □ Nice guys finish last. □ The last straw

LATE

Better late than never. □ It is never too late to learn. □ It is never too late to mend. □ Shoot first, ask questions later. □ Too little, too late

LAUGH

He who laughs last, laughs best. □ He who laughs last, laughs longest. □ Laugh all the way to the bank □ Laugh and the world laughs with you; weep and you weep alone. □ Laugh out of the other side of one's mouth

LAW

Ignorance (of the law) is no excuse (for breaking it). □ Necessity knows no law. □ One law for the rich and another for the poor □ Possession is nine-tenths of the law. □ Self-preservation is the first law of nature.

LAY

Kill the goose that lays the golden egg(s). □ The best-laid plans of mice and men oft go astray. □ The best-laid schemes of mice and men gang aft agley.

LEAD

Crosses are ladders that lead to heaven. □ The blind leading the blind □ You can lead a horse to water, but you can't make it drink.

LEAP

Look before you leap.

LEARN

A little learning is a dangerous thing. □ It is never too late to learn. □ There is no royal road to learning. □ We must learn to walk before we can run.

LEAST

Idle folk have the least leisure. □ Idle people have the least leisure.

LEATHER

(As) tough as (shoe) leather

LEAVE

Better left unsaid □ Leave no stone unturned □ Leave well enough alone. □ The left hand doesn't know what the right hand is doing.

LEG

Someone puts his pants on one leg at a time

LEISURE

Idle folk have the least leisure. □ Idle people have the least leisure. □ Marry in haste, (and) repent at leisure. □ The busiest men have the most leisure.

LEND

Distance lends enchantment

(to the view). □ Lend your money and lose your friend.

LENDER

Neither a borrower nor a lender be.

LEOPARD

A leopard cannot change his spots.

LESS

More haste, less speed □ The less said (about something), the better. □ The lesser of two evils

LEST

Judge not, lest ye be judged.

LET

Do not let the sun go down on your anger. □ Do not let the sun go down on your wrath. □ Let bygones be by-gones. □ Let every tub stand on its own bottom. □ Let sleeping dogs lie. □ Let the buyer beware. □ Let the cat out of the bag □ Let the chips fall where they may. □ Let the cobbler stick to his last. □ Let the dead bury the dead. □ Let them eat cake. □ Not to let the grass grow under one's feet

LEVELER

Death is the great leveler.

LIAR

A liar is not believed (even) when he tells the truth.

LIBEL

The greater the truth, the greater the libel

LICK

If you can't lick 'em, join 'em.

LIE

As you make your bed, so you must lie upon it. □ Ask me no questions, I'll tell you no lies. □ Ask no questions and hear no lies. □ Half the truth is often a whole lie. □ If you lie down with dogs, you will get up with fleas. □ Let sleeping dogs lie. □ Un-easy lies the head that wears a crown.

LIFE

Art is long and life is short. □ Bread is the staff of life. □ Life begins at forty. □ Life is just a bowl of cherries. □ Life is short and time is swift. □ Life isn't all beer and skittles. □ The best things in life are free. □ Vari-ety is the spice of life. □ While there's life there's hope.

LIGHT

A heavy purse makes a light heart. □ A light purse makes a heavy heart. □ According to someone's lights □ (As) light as a feather □ (As) light as air □ First see the light of day □ Hide one's light under a bushel □ Many hands make light work.

LIGHTNING

(As) quick as lightning □ (As) swift as lightning □ Lightning never strikes (the same place) twice. ☐ Like greased lightning

LINE
Every cloud has a silver lining. ☐ One has to draw the line somewhere. ☐ Put something on the line ☐ Read between the lines.

LINEN
Do not wash your dirty linen in public.

LINK
A chain is no stronger than its weakest link.

LION
(As) strong as a lion ☐ Beard the lion in his den ☐ Better be the head of a dog than the tail of a lion. ☐ In like a lion, out like a lamb. ☐ March comes in like a lion, and goes out like a lamb.

LIP
Keep a stiff upper lip. ☐ There's many a slip 'twixt the cup and the lip.

LISTENER
Listeners never hear any good of themselves.

LITTLE
A little bird told me. ☐ A little knowledge is a dangerous thing. ☐ A little learning is a dangerous thing. ☐ Birds in their little nests agree. ☐ Great oaks from little acorns grow. ☐ Little and often fills the purse. ☐ Little pitchers have big ears. ☐ Little

strokes fell great oaks. ☐ Little thieves are hanged, but great ones escape. ☐ Little things please little minds. ☐ The difficult is done at once; the impossible takes a little longer. ☐ Too little, too late

LIVE
A cat has nine lives. ☐ A reed before the wind lives on, while mighty oaks do fall. ☐ Eat to live, not live to eat. ☐ Half the world knows not how the other half lives. ☐ He lives long who lives well. ☐ He who fights and runs away, may live to fight another day. ☐ Live by the sword, die by the sword. ☐ Man does not live by bread alone. ☐ People who live in glass houses shouldn't throw stones.

LOAF
Half a loaf is better than none.

LOCK
Lock the stable door after the horse is stolen

LOG
Like a bump on a log ☐ Sleep like a log

LONG
A creaking door hangs longest. ☐ A creaking gate hangs longest. ☐ Art is long and life is short. ☐ Governments have long arms. ☐ He lives long who lives well. ☐ He who laughs last, laughs

longest. □ He who sups with the devil should have a long spoon. □ It is a long lane that has no turning. □ Kings have long arms. □ Make a long story short □ Short reckonings make long friends. □ The difficult is done at once; the impossible takes a little longer. □ The long and the short of it □ The longest way round is the nearest way home. □ The longest way round is the shortest way home.

LOOK

A cat can look at a king. □ Don't look a gift horse in the mouth. □ Look before you leap. □ Look for a needle in a haystack □ The devil looks after his own.

LOON

(As) crazy as a loon

LORD

(As) drunk as a lord □ Everybody loves a lord.

LOSE

A tale never loses in the telling. □ Finders keepers(, losers weepers). □ For want of a nail the shoe was lost; for want of a shoe the horse was lost; and for want of a horse the man was lost. □ He who hesitates is lost. □ Lend your money and lose your friend. □ 'Tis better to have loved and lost than never to have loved at all. □ You can-

not lose what you never had. □ You must lose a fly to catch a trout. □ You win a few, you lose a few. □ You win some, you lose some.

LOSS

One man's loss is another man's gain.

LOUD

Actions speak louder than words.

LOVE

All's fair in love and war. □ Everybody loves a lord. □ God takes soonest those he loveth best. □ Love begets love. □ Love is blind. □ Love makes the world go round. □ Love me, love my dog. □ Love will find a way. □ Lucky at cards, unlucky in love □ Misery loves company. □ Not able to get something for love or money □ One cannot love and be wise. □ The course of true love never did run smooth. □ The love of money is the root of all evil. □ 'Tis better to have loved and lost than never to have loved at all. □ When poverty comes in at the door, love flies out of the window. □ When the wolf comes in at the door, love creeps out of the window. □ Whom the gods love die young.

LUCK

□ As luck would have it □

Bless one's lucky star □ Diligence is the mother of good luck. □ It is better to be born lucky than rich. □ Lucky at cards, unlucky in love □ The devil's children have the devil's luck.

LUMP

If you don't like it, (you can) lump it.

LUNCH

There ain't no such thing as a free lunch. □ There's no such thing as a free lunch.

MAD

(As) mad as a hatter □ (As) mad as a March hare □ Far from the madding crowd

MAHOMET

If the mountain will not come to Mahomet, Mahomet must go to the mountain.

MALE

The female of the species is more deadly than the male.

MAMMON

You cannot serve God and Mammon.

MAN

A drowning man will clutch at a straw. □ A good man is hard to find. □ A man is known by the company he keeps. □ A man's home is his castle. □ A rich man's joke is always funny. □ As a man sows, so shall he reap. □ Be one's own man □ Better be an old man's darling than a young man's slave. □ Busiest men find the most time. □ Call no man happy till he dies. □ Clothes make the man. □ Dead men don't bite. □ Dead men tell no tales. □ Early to bed and early to rise, makes a man healthy, wealthy, and wise. □ Every man for himself (and the devil take the hindmost). □ Every man has his price. □ Every man is the architect of his own fortune. □ Every man to his taste. □ For want of a nail the shoe was lost; for want of a shoe the horse was lost; and for want of a horse the man was lost. □ Good men are scarce. □ Heaven protects children, sailors, and drunken men. □ In the country of the blind, the one-eyed man is king. □ It's ill waiting for dead men's shoes. □ Man does not live by bread alone. □ Man proposes, God disposes. □ Men are blind in their own cause. □ Men make houses, women make homes. □ No man can serve two masters. □ One man's loss is another man's gain. □ One man's meat is another man's poison. □ Separate the men from the boys □ The best-laid plans of mice and men oft go astray. □ The best-laid schemes of mice and men gang aft agley. □ The busiest men have the most leisure. □ The child is father of the man. □ The way to a man's heart is through his stomach. □ There is a tide in the affairs of men. □ Time and tide wait for no man. □ Young men may die, but old men must die.

MANNER
Other times, other manners

MANY
Cowards die many times before their death(s). □ Have too many irons in the fire □ He who begins many things, finishes but few. □ Many a true word is spoken in jest. □ Many are called but few are chosen. □ Many hands make light work. □ So many countries, so many customs □ There's many a good tune played on an old fiddle. □ There's many a slip 'twixt the cup and the lip. □ There's many a true word spoken in jest. □ Too many chiefs and not enough Indians □ Too many cooks spoil the broth.

MARBLE
(As) cold as marble

MARCH
An army marches on its stomach. □ (As) mad as a March hare □ March comes in like a lion, and goes out like a lamb.

MARRIAGE
Dream of a funeral and you hear of a marriage. □ Marriages are made in heaven.

MARRY
Marry in haste, (and) repent at leisure.

MASTER
A jack of all trades is a master of none. □ Be one's own master □ Fire is a good servant but a bad master. □ No man can serve two masters.

MAY
April showers bring May flowers. □ Gather ye rosebuds while ye may. □ He who fights and runs away, may live to fight another day. □ Let the chips fall where they may. □ Sticks and stones may break my bones, but words will never hurt me. □ Young men may die, but old men must die.

MEAN
The end justifies the means.

MEAT
One man's meat is another man's poison.

MEDICINE
Give someone a dose of his own medicine

MEEK
(As) meek as a lamb

MEET
East is East and West is West (and never the twain shall meet).

MELT
Butter wouldn't melt (in someone's mouth).

MEND
It is never too late to mend.

MERRY
(As) merry as a cricket □ Eat, drink, and be merry, for tomorrow we die. □ The more the merrier

MID
Don't change horses in midstream.

MIDNIGHT
Burn the midnight oil

MIGHT
A reed before the wind lives on, while mighty oaks do fall. □ How the mighty have fallen. □ Might makes right. □ Nothing so bad but (it) might have been worse. □ One might as well be hanged for a sheep as for a lamb. □ The pen is mightier than the sword.

MILE
A miss is as good as a mile. □ Give someone an inch and he'll take a mile.

MILK
Don't cry over spilled milk. □ It's no use crying over spilled milk. □ Why buy a cow when milk is so cheap? □ Why buy a cow when you can get milk for free?

MILL
Grist for someone's mill □ Grist for the mill □ The mill cannot grind with water that is past. □ The mills of God grind slowly, yet they grind exceeding small.

MIND
A contented mind is a perpetual feast. □ Great minds think alike. □ Little things please little minds. □ Mind one's p's and q's. □ Mind your own business! □ Out of sight, out of mind. □ Small things please small minds. □ Travel broadens the mind.

MINE
Back to the salt mine. □ What's yours is mine, and what's mine is mine.

MIRACLE
The age of miracles is past.

MISERY
Misery loves company.

MISFORTUNE
Misfortunes never come singly.

MISS
A miss is as good as a mile. □ You never miss the water till the well runs dry.

MISTAKE
If you don't make mistakes you don't make anything.

MODERATION
Moderation in all things.

MOLASSES
(As) slow as molasses in January □ Slower than molasses in January

MOLE
Make a mountain out of a molehill

MOMENT
Never a dull moment

MONDAY
Monday's child is fair of face.

MONEY
A fool and his money are soon parted. □ Bad money drives out good. □ It takes money to make money. □ Lend your money and lose your friend. □ Money burns a hole in someone's pocket. □ Money does not grow on trees. □ Money is power. □ Money is the root of all evil. □ Not able to get something for love or money □ Put your money where your mouth is. □ The love of money is the root of all evil. □ Time is money. □ You pays your money and you takes your chance(s).

MONKEY
Monkey see, monkey do.

MOON
Once in a blue moon

MORE
Don't bite off more than you can chew. □ It is more blessed to give than to receive. □ Keep no more cats than will catch mice. □ More haste, less speed □ The female of the species is more deadly than the male. □ The more the merrier □ The more you get, the more you want. □ The more you have, the more you want. □ There's more than one way to skin a cat. □ You can catch more flies with honey than with vinegar.

MORNING
Morning dreams come true.

MOSS
A rolling stone gathers no moss.

MOST
Busiest men find the most time. □ Empty vessels make the most sound. □ First impressions are the most lasting. □ The busiest men have the most leisure.

MOTHER
Diligence is the mother of good luck. □ Experience is the mother of wisdom. □ He that would the daughter win, must with the mother first begin. □ Like mother, like daughter □ Necessity is the mother of invention. □ Tied to one's mother's apron strings

MOUNTAIN
Faith will move mountains. □ If the mountain will not come to Mahomet, Mahomet must go to the mountain. □ Make a mountain out of a molehill

MOUSE
A cat in gloves catches no mice. □ (As) quiet as a

mouse □ Burn not your house to fright the mouse away. □ Keep no more cats than will catch mice. □ The best-laid plans of mice and men oft go astray. □ The best-laid schemes of mice and men gang aft agley. □ The mouse that has but one hole is quickly taken. □ When the cat's away, the mice will play.

MOUTH

Born with a silver spoon in one's mouth □ Butter wouldn't melt (in someone's mouth). □ By word of mouth □ Don't look a gift horse in the mouth. □ Get it straight from the horse's mouth □ Laugh out of the other side of one's mouth □ One's heart is in one's mouth □ Out of the mouths of babes □ Put your money where your mouth is.

MOVE

Faith will move mountains. □ Moving three times is as bad as a fire.

MUCH

Have too much of a good thing □ Much ado about nothing

MUD

Here's mud in your eye!

MULE

(As) obstinate as a mule □ (As) stubborn as a mule

MURDER

Murder will out.

MUSTARD

(As) keen as mustard

NAIL

(As) hard as nails □ Fight tooth and nail □ For want of a nail the shoe was lost; for want of a shoe the horse was lost; and for want of a horse the man was lost. □ Hit the nail on the head

NAKED

(As) naked as a jaybird

NAME

A rose by any other name would smell as sweet. □ What's in a name?

NATURE

Nature abhors a vacuum. □ Self-preservation is the first law of nature.

NEAT

(As) neat as a pin

NECESSARY

If God did not exist, it would be necessary to invent Him. □ Make a virtue of necessity □ Necessity is the mother of invention. □ Necessity knows no law.

NEED

A friend in need is a friend indeed. □ A guilty conscience needs no accuser. □ He that is down need fear no fall. □ Needs must when the devil drives.

NEEDLE
Look for a needle in a haystack

NEIGHBOR
Good fences make good neighbors.

NEST
Birds in their little nests agree. □ It's an ill bird that fouls its own nest.

NEW
A new broom sweeps clean. □ (As) bright as a new pin □ Bad news travels fast. □ New brooms sweep clean. □ No news is good news. □ There is nothing new under the sun. □ You cannot put new wine in old bottles. □ You cannot teach an old dog new tricks.

NEWCASTLE
Carry coals to Newcastle

NEXT
Cleanliness is next to godliness.

NICE
Nice guys finish last.

NIGHT
Ships that pass in the night □ Sing before breakfast, you'll cry before night.

NINE
A cat has nine lives. □ A stitch in time saves nine. □ Possession is nine-tenths of the law.

NINETEEN
Nineteen to the dozen

NINETY
Genius is ten percent inspiration and ninety percent perspiration.

NOD
A nod's as good as a wink to a blind horse.

NOURISH
Desires are nourished by delays.

NUMBER
There is safety in numbers.

NUT
He that would eat the kernel must crack the nut. □ The gods send nuts to those who have no teeth.

NUTTY
(As) nutty as a fruitcake □ Nuttier than a fruitcake

OAK
A reed before the wind lives on, while mighty oaks do fall. □ Great oaks from little acorns grow. □ Little strokes fell great oaks.

OBEY
He that cannot obey cannot command.

OBSTINATE
(As) obstinate as a mule

OCEAN
A drop in the ocean

OFFENSE
The best defense is a good offense.

OFT

The best-laid plans of mice and men oft go astray.

OIL

Burn the midnight oil □ Pour oil on troubled waters

OLD

A chip off the old block □ An old poacher makes the best gamekeeper. □ (As) old as the hills □ Better be an old man's darling than a young man's slave. □ Old habits die hard. □ There's many a good tune played on an old fiddle. □ There's no fool like an old fool. □ You cannot put new wine in old bottles. □ You cannot teach an old dog new tricks. □ Young men may die, but old men must die.

OMELET

You cannot make an omelet without breaking eggs.

OMISSION

There is a sin of omission as well as of commission.

ONCE

A word (once) spoken is past recalling. □ Christmas comes but once a year. □ Fool me once, shame on you; fool me twice, shame on me. □ Once a priest, always a priest □ Once a whore, always a whore □ Once bitten, twice shy □ Once in a blue moon □ One cannot be in two places at once. □ Opportu-

nity knocks but once. □ The difficult is done at once; the impossible takes a little longer.

ONLY

Beauty is only skin-deep. □ Believe nothing of what you hear, and only half of what you see. □ From the sublime to the ridiculous is only a step. □ (Only) time will tell. □ The only good Indian is a dead Indian. □ They also serve who only stand and wait.

OPEN

A door must be either shut or open. □ A golden key can open any door. □ (Open) confession is good for the soul. □ Read someone like a(n open) book. □ When one door shuts, another opens.

OPPORTUNITY

Opportunity knocks but once. □ Opportunity makes a thief.

OTHER

A rose by any other name would smell as sweet. □ (All) other things being equal □ Do unto others as you would have them do unto you. □ Half the world knows not how the other half lives. □ Have better (or other) fish to fry □ In (at) one ear and out (of) the other □ Laugh out of the other side of one's mouth □ Other times, other manners □ The grass is always greener on the other side of the fence. □ There are other fish in the sea.

OUNCE

An ounce of common sense is worth a pound of theory. □ An ounce of discretion is worth a pound of wit. □ An ounce of prevention is worth a pound of cure.

OWN

A prophet is not without honor save in his own country. □ Be one's own man □ Be one's own master □ Be one's own worst enemy □ Cannot call one's soul one's own □ Every horse thinks its own pack heaviest. □ Every man is the architect of his own fortune. □ Every tub must stand on its own bottom. □ Give someone a dose of his own medicine □ Hoist with one's own petard □ It is a wise child that knows its own father. □ It's an ill bird that fouls its own nest. □ Let every tub stand on its own bottom. □ Men are blind in their own cause. □ Mind your own business! □ Paddle one's own canoe □ The devil can cite Scripture for his own purpose. □ The devil can quote Scripture for his own purpose. □ The devil looks after his own. □ Virtue is its own reward.

OX

(As) strong as an ox

PACE

It is the pace that kills.

PACK

Every horse thinks its own pack heaviest.

PACKAGE

Good things come in small packages. □ The best things come in small packages.

PADDLE

Paddle one's own canoe

PAIN

Genius is an infinite capacity for taking pains. □ No pain, no gain □ There is no pleasure without pain.

PAINT

The devil is not so black as he is painted.

PALE

(As) pale as a ghost □ (As) pale as death

PAN

If "ifs" and "ands" were pots and pans (there'd be no work for tinkers' hands). □ Out of the frying pan into the fire.

PANCAKE

(As) flat as a pancake

PANT

Someone puts his pants on one leg at a time.

PAPER

Not worth the paper it's written on

PARADISE
A fool's paradise

PARDON
Never ask pardon before you are accused.

PARSNIP
Fine words butter no parsnips.

PART
A fool and his money are soon parted. □ Discretion is the better part of valor. □ (Even) the best of friends must part.

PASS
Ships that pass in the night

PAST
A word (once) spoken is past recalling. □ The age of miracles is past. □ The mill cannot grind with water that is past.

PASTIME
He that would go to sea for pleasure, would go to hell for a pastime.

PATIENCE
Patience is a virtue.

PATIENT
(As) patient as Job

PAUL
Rob Peter to pay Paul

PAVE
The road to hell is paved with good intentions.

PAY
He who pays the piper calls the tune. □ Pay the piper □

Pay through the nose □ Rob Peter to pay Paul □ The devil to pay □ You get what you pay for. □ You pays your money and you takes your chance(s).

PEA
Like two peas in a pod

PEACE
If you want peace, (you must) prepare for war.

PEACOCK
(As) proud as a peacock □ (As) vain as a peacock

PEARL
Cast pearls before swine

PECK
You have to eat a peck of dirt before you die.

PEG
A square peg in a round hole

PEN
The pen is mightier than the sword.

PENNY
A bad penny always turns up. □ A penny for your thoughts! □ A penny saved is a penny earned. □ Cost a pretty penny □ Penny wise and pound foolish

PEOPLE
Idle people have the least leisure. □ People who live in glass houses shouldn't throw stones. □ Times change(, people change).

PERCENT
Genius is ten percent inspiration and ninety percent perspiration.

PERFECT
Practice makes perfect.

PERPETUAL
A contented mind is a perpetual feast.

PERSPIRATION
Genius is ten percent inspiration and ninety percent perspiration.

PETARD
Hoist with one's own petard

PETER
Rob Peter to pay Paul

PHYSICIAN
Physician, heal thyself.

PICK
Have a bone to pick (with someone)

PICTURE
A picture is worth a thousand words.

PIE
Have a finger in every pie □ Promises are like piecrust, made to be broken.

PIG
(As) fat as a pig □ Buy a pig in a poke

PIKESTAFF
(As) plain as a pikestaff

PIN
(As) bright as a new pin □ (As) neat as a pin

PINT
You cannot get a quart into a pint pot.

PIPE
Put that in your pipe and smoke it!

PIPER
He who pays the piper calls the tune. □ Pay the piper

PITCH
(As) black as pitch

PITCHER
Little pitchers have big ears.

PLACE
A place for everything, and everything in its place. □ A woman's place is in the home. □ Between a rock and a hard place □ Lightning never strikes (the same place) twice. □ One cannot be in two places at once. □ There is a time and a place for everything. □ There's no place like home.

PLAIN
(As) plain as a pikestaff □ (As) plain as the nose on one's face

PLAN
The best-laid plans of mice and men oft go astray.

PLAY
All work and no play makes Jack a dull boy. □ If you play with fire you get burned. □ There's many a good tune played on an old fiddle. □

When the cat's away, the mice will play.

PLEASE
(As) pleased as Punch □ Little things please little minds. □ Small things please small minds. □ You cannot please everyone.

PLEASURE
Business before pleasure □ He that would go to sea for pleasure, would go to hell for a pastime. □ Stolen pleasures are sweetest. □ There is no pleasure without pain.

POACHER
An old poacher makes the best gamekeeper.

POCKET
Money burns a hole in someone's pocket. □ Shrouds have no pockets.

POD
Like two peas in a pod

POINT
At this point in time

POISON
One man's meat is another man's poison.

POKE
(As) stiff as a poker □ Buy a pig in a poke

POLE
I would not touch it with a ten-foot pole.

POLICY
Honesty is the best policy.

POLITIC
Politics makes strange bedfellows.

POOR
(As) poor as a churchmouse □ It is a poor heart that never rejoices. □ One law for the rich and another for the poor

POPPY
(As) red as a poppy

PORT
Any port in a storm

POSSESSION
Possession is nine-tenths of the law.

POSSIBLE
All's for the best in the best of all possible worlds.

POST
(As) deaf as a post □ Between you and me and the bedpost

POT
A watched pot never boils. □ If "ifs" and "ands" were pots and pans (there'd be no work for tinkers' hands). □ That's the pot calling the kettle black. □ The pot is calling the kettle black. □ You cannot get a quart into a pint pot.

POUND
An ounce of common sense is worth a pound of theory. □ An ounce of discretion is worth a pound of wit. □ An ounce of prevention is worth

a pound of cure. ☐ Penny wise and pound foolish

POUR

It never rains but it pours. ☐ Pour oil on troubled waters

POVERTY

Poverty is no sin. ☐ Poverty is not a crime. ☐ When poverty comes in at the door, love flies out of the window.

POWDER

Put your trust in God, and keep your powder dry.

POWER

Absolute power corrupts absolutely. ☐ Knowledge is power. ☐ Money is power.

PRACTICE

Practice makes perfect. ☐ Practice what you preach.

PRAISE

Damn someone with faint praise ☐ Self-praise is no recommendation.

PRAY

The family that prays together stays together.

PREACH

Practice what you preach.

PRECEPT

Example is better than precept.

PREPARE

Hope for the best and prepare for the worst. ☐ If you want peace, (you must) prepare for war.

PRESENT

(There's) no time like the present.

PRESERVATION

Self-preservation is the first law of nature.

PRETTY

Cost a pretty penny ☐ Pretty is as pretty does.

PREVENTION

An ounce of prevention is worth a pound of cure. ☐ Prevention is better than cure.

PRICE

A thing you don't want is dear at any price. ☐ Every man has his price.

PRIDE

Pride goes before a fall. ☐ Pride goeth before a fall.

PRIEST

Once a priest, always a priest

PROCRASTINATION

Procrastination is the thief of time.

PROMISE

Promises are like piecrust, made to be broken.

PROOF

The proof is in the pudding.

PROPHET

A prophet is not without honor save in his own country.

PROPOSE

Man proposes, God disposes.

PROSPER

Cheats never prosper.

PROTECT

Heaven protects children, sailors, and drunken men.

PROUD

(As) proud as a peacock

PROVE

The exception proves the rule.

PROVIDE

Take the goods the gods provide.

PUBLIC

Do not wash your dirty linen in public.

PUDDING

The proof is in the pudding.

PUDDLE

The biggest frog in the puddle □ The biggest toad in the puddle

PULL

Pull oneself up by the bootstraps □ Pull the wool over someone's eyes

PUNCH

(As) pleased as Punch

PUNCTUALITY

Punctuality is the soul of business.

PURE

(As) pure as the driven snow

PURPOSE

The devil can cite Scripture for his own purpose. □ The devil can quote Scripture for his own purpose.

PURSE

A heavy purse makes a light heart. □ A light purse makes a heavy heart. □ He that hath a full purse never wanted a friend. □ Little and often fills the purse. □ You cannot make a silk purse out of a sow's ear.

PUT

Don't put all your eggs in one basket. □ Don't put off for tomorrow what you can do today. □ Don't put the cart before the horse. □ Put one's best foot forward □ Put one's foot down □ Put one's foot in it □ Put one's shoulder to the wheel □ Put something on the line □ Put that in your pipe and smoke it! □ Put your money where your mouth is. □ Put your trust in God, and keep your powder dry. □ Someone puts his pants on one leg at a time □ You cannot put new wine in old bottles.

QUARREL

It takes two to make a quarrel.

QUART

You cannot get a quart into a pint pot.

QUEER

(As) queer as a three-dollar bill

QUESTION

Ask me no questions, I'll tell you no lies. □ Ask no questions and hear no lies. □ Shoot first, ask questions later. □ There are two sides to every question.

QUICK

(As) quick as lightning □ He gives twice who gives quickly. □ The mouse that has but one hole is quickly taken.

QUIET

(As) quiet as a mouse

QUOTE

The devil can quote Scripture for his own purpose.

RACE

Slow and steady wins the race.

RAIN

(As) right as rain □ It never rains but it pours. □ Rain cats and dogs □ Save for a rainy day

RAKE

Rake someone over the coals

RAT

Like rats abandoning a sinking ship. □ Rats abandon a sinking ship.

RAZOR

(As) sharp as a razor □ Razor-sharp

REACH

Stretch your arm no further than your sleeve will reach.

READ

Read between the lines. □ Read someone like a(n open) book.

REAP

As a man sows, so shall he reap. □ As you sow, so shall you reap. □ Sow the wind and reap the whirlwind

REASON

Neither rhyme nor reason

RECALL

A word (once) spoken is past recalling.

RECEIVE

It is better to give than to receive. □ It is more blessed to give than to receive.

RECKON

Short reckonings make long friends.

RECOMMENDATION

Self-praise is no recommendation.

RED

(As) red as a cherry □ (As) red as a poppy □ (As) red as a rose □ (As) red as a ruby □ (As) red as blood □ Blood-red □ Rose-red □ Ruby-red

REED

A reed before the wind lives on, while mighty oaks do fall.

REGULAR

(As) regular as clockwork

REJOICE

It is a poor heart that never rejoices. □ It is a sad heart that never rejoices.

REMEDY

Desperate diseases must have desperate remedies. □ There is a remedy for everything except death.

REPEAT

History repeats itself.

REPENT

Marry in haste, (and) repent at leisure.

REST

There is no rest for the weary.

REVENGE

Revenge is a dish best served cold. □ Revenge is sweet.

REWARD

Desert and reward seldom keep company. □ Virtue is its own reward.

RHYME

Neither rhyme nor reason

RICH

A rich man's joke is always funny. □ It is better to be born lucky than rich. □ One law for the rich and another for the poor

RIDDANCE

Good riddance to bad rubbish!

RIDE

He who rides a tiger is afraid to dismount. □ If two ride on a horse, one must ride behind. □ If wishes were horses, then beggars would ride. □ Set a beggar on horseback, and he'll ride to the devil.

RIDICULOUS

From the sublime to the ridiculous is only a step.

RIGHT

(As) right as a trivet □ (As) right as rain □ God's in his heaven; all's right with the world. □ Might makes right. □ The customer is always right. □ The left hand doesn't know what the right hand is doing. □ Two wrongs do not make a right.

RING

Ring down the curtain

RIPE

Early ripe, early rotten. □ Soon ripe, soon rotten. □ The time is ripe.

RISE

Early to bed and early to rise, makes a man healthy, wealthy, and wise.

ROAD

The road to hell is paved with good intentions. □ There is no royal road to learning.

ROB

Rob Peter to pay Paul

ROBINSON

Before you can say Jack Robinson

ROCK

(As) solid as a rock □ (As) steady as a rock □ Between a rock and a hard place □ Rock-solid □ Rock-steady □

The hand that rocks the cradle rules the world.

ROD

Spare the rod and spoil the child.

ROLL

A rolling stone gathers no moss.

ROMAN

When in Rome(, do as the Romans do).

ROME

Fiddle while Rome burns □ Rome was not built in a day. □ When in Rome(, do as the Romans do).

ROOF

(As) busy as a cat on a hot tin roof

ROOM

Not enough room to swing a cat

ROOST

The chickens come home to roost

ROOT

Idleness is the root of all evil. □ Money is the root of all evil. □ The love of money is the root of all evil.

ROPE

Give someone enough rope and he'll hang himself.

ROSE

A rose by any other name would smell as sweet. □ (As) red as a rose □ Come out smelling like a rose □ Come up roses □ Rose-red □ There's no rose without a thorn.

ROSEBUD

Gather ye rosebuds while ye may.

ROT

Early ripe, early rotten. □ Something is rotten in (the state of) Denmark. □ Soon ripe, soon rotten. □ The rotten apple spoils the barrel.

ROUGH

Take the rough with the smooth

ROUND

A square peg in a round hole □ Love makes the world go round. □ The longest way round is the nearest way home. □ The longest way round is the shortest way home.

ROYAL

There is no royal road to learning.

RUBBISH

Good riddance to bad rubbish!

RUBY

(As) red as a ruby □ Ruby-red

RUG

(As) snug as a bug in a rug

RULE

The exception proves the rule. □ The hand that rocks the cradle rules the world.

RUN

He who fights and runs away, may live to fight another day. □ If you run after two hares you will catch neither. □ My cup runneth over. □ Still waters run deep. □ The course of true love never did run smooth. □ To run with the hare and hunt with the hounds □ We must learn to walk before we can run. □ You never miss the water till the well runs dry.

RUSH

Fools rush in where angels fear to tread.

RUST

It is better to wear out than to rust out.

SACK

An empty sack cannot stand upright.

SAD

It is a sad heart that never rejoices.

SAFE

Better (be) safe than sorry.

SAFETY

There is safety in numbers.

SAIL

Hoist your sail when the wind is fair. □ Take the wind out of someone's sails

SAILOR

Heaven protects children, sailors, and drunken men.

SALT

Back to the salt mine.

SAM

What in (the) Sam Hill

SAME

Lightning never strikes (the same place) twice. □ Tar someone with the same brush

SAUCE

Hunger is the best sauce. □ What's sauce for the goose is sauce for the gander.

SAVE

A penny saved is a penny earned. □ A prophet is not without honor save in his own country. □ A stitch in time saves nine. □ Save for a rainy day

SAY

Before you can say Jack Robinson □ Do as I say, not as I do. □ Easier said than done. □ Never say die. □ No sooner said than done □ The less said (about something), the better.

SCARCE

(As) scarce as hen's teeth □ Good men are scarce. □ Scarcer than hen's teeth

SCHEME

The best-laid schemes of mice and men gang aft agley.

SCHOOL

Never tell tales out of school.

SCORN

Hell hath no fury like a woman scorned.

SCRATCH
You scratch my back, I'll scratch yours.

SCRIPTURE
The devil can cite Scripture for his own purpose. □ The devil can quote Scripture for his own purpose.

SEA
Between the devil and the deep blue sea □ He that would go to sea for pleasure, would go to hell for a pastime. □ There are other fish in the sea.

SECOND
Have second thoughts

SEE
Believe nothing of what you hear, and only half of what you see. □ Cannot see the wood for the trees □ Children should be seen and not heard. □ First see the light of day □ Monkey see, monkey do. □ See no evil, hear no evil, speak no evil. □ Seeing is believing. □ Someone cannot see beyond the end of his nose. □ There's none so blind as those who will not see. □ What the eye doesn't see, the heart doesn't grieve over.

SEED
Good seed makes a good crop.

SEEK
Seek and ye shall find.

SEEM
Things are seldom what they seem.

SEIZE
Seize the bull by the horns.

SELDOM
Desert and reward seldom keep company. □ Things are seldom what they seem.

SELF
Self-praise is no recommendation. □ Self-preservation is the first law of nature.

SEND
The gods send nuts to those who have no teeth.

SENSE
An ounce of common sense is worth a pound of theory. □ Doesn't have the sense God gave geese

SEPARATE
Separate the men from the boys □ Separate the sheep from the goats □ Separate the wheat from the chaff

SERVANT
Fire is a good servant but a bad master.

SERVE
First come, first served. □ If you would be well served, serve yourself. □ No man can serve two masters. □ Revenge is a dish best served cold. □ They also serve who only stand and wait. □ You cannot serve God and

Mammon. □ Youth must be served.

SET
Set a beggar on horseback, and he'll ride to the devil. □ Set a thief to catch a thief.

SEVEN
At sixes and sevens □ Keep a thing seven years and you'll (always) find a use for it.

SHADOW
Beyond a shadow of a doubt □ Coming events cast their shadows before.

SHALLOW
Cross the stream where it is shallowest.

SHAME
Fool me once, shame on you; fool me twice, shame on me. □ Tell the truth and shame the devil.

SHARE
A trouble shared is a trouble halved. □ Share and share alike.

SHARP
(As) sharp as a razor □ (As) sharp as a tack □ Razor-sharp

SHEEP
A wolf in sheep's clothing □ One might as well be hanged for a sheep as for a lamb. □ Separate the sheep from the goats

SHEET
(As) white as a sheet

SHINE
Happy is the bride that the sun shines on. □ Make hay while the sun shines.

SHIP
Like rats abandoning a sinking ship □ One hand for oneself and one for the ship. □ Rats abandon a sinking ship. □ Ships that pass in the night

SHIRT
Give the shirt off one's back

SHOE
(As) tough as (shoe) leather □ For want of a nail the shoe was lost; for want of a shoe the horse was lost; and for want of a horse the man was lost. □ If the shoe fits(, wear it). □ It's ill waiting for dead men's shoes.

SHOOT
Shoot first, ask questions later.

SHOP
Keep your shop and your shop will keep you. □ Like a bull in a china shop

SHORT
Art is long and life is short. □ Life is short and time is swift. □ Make a long story short □ Short reckonings make long friends. □ The long and the short of it □ The longest way round is the shortest way home.

SHOULDER
Have a chip on one's shoulder □ Put one's shoulder to the wheel

SHOWER
April showers bring May flowers.

SHROUD
Shrouds have no pockets.

SHUT
A door must be either shut or open. □ Shut the stable door after the horse has bolted. □ When one door shuts, another opens.

SHY
Once bitten, twice shy

SICK
Hope deferred makes the heart sick. □ Hope deferred maketh the heart sick.

SIDE
Born on the wrong side of the blanket □ Cannot hit the broad side of a barn □ Get up on the wrong side of the bed □ Know which side one's bread is buttered on □ Laugh out of the other side of one's mouth □ The bread always falls on the buttered side. □ The grass is always greener on the other side of the fence. □ There are two sides to every question.

SIGHT
Out of sight, out of mind.

SILENCE
Silence gives consent. □ Silence is golden.

SILENT
(As) silent as the dead □ (As) silent as the grave

SILK
You cannot make a silk purse out of a sow's ear.

SILLY
(As) silly as a goose

SILVER
Born with a silver spoon in one's mouth □ Every cloud has a silver lining.

SIN
(As) ugly as sin □ Poverty is no sin. □ There is a sin of omission as well as of commission.

SINCEREST
Imitation is the sincerest form of flattery.

SING
Sing before breakfast, you'll cry before night. □ Sing before breakfast, you'll cry before supper.

SINGLE
Misfortunes never come singly.

SINK
Like rats abandoning a sinking ship □ Rats abandon a sinking ship.

SIX
At sixes and sevens □ It's six

of one, half a dozen of another.

SKELETON
Every family has a skeleton in the closet.

SKIN
Beauty is only skin-deep. □ Escape by the skin of one's teeth □ There's more than one way to skin a cat.

SKITTLE
Life isn't all beer and skittles.

SKUNK
(As) drunk as a skunk

SLAVE
Better be an old man's darling than a young man's slave.

SLEEP
Let sleeping dogs lie. □ Sleep like a log □ Sleep like a top

SLEEVE
Have an ace up one's sleeve □ Stretch your arm no further than your sleeve will reach.

SLIP
There's many a slip 'twixt the cup and the lip.

SLIPPERY
(As) slippery as an eel

SLOW
(As) slow as molasses in January □ Make haste slowly. □ Slow and steady wins the race. □ Slow but sure □ Slower than molasses in January □ The mills of God

grind slowly, yet they grind exceeding small.

SMALL
Good things come in small packages. □ Small things please small minds. □ The best things come in small packages. □ The mills of God grind slowly, yet they grind exceeding small.

SMELL
A rose by any other name would smell as sweet. □ Come out smelling like a rose

SMOKE
Put that in your pipe and smoke it! □ (There's) no smoke without fire. □ Where there's smoke there's fire.

SMOOTH
(As) smooth as glass □ Take the rough with the smooth □ The course of true love never did run smooth.

SNOW
(As) pure as the driven snow □ (As) white as snow □ Snow-white

SNUG
(As) snug as a bug in a rug

SOBER
(As) sober as a judge

SOFT
A soft answer turneth away wrath. □ (As) soft as down □ (As) soft as velvet □ Velvety-soft

SOLID
(As) solid as a rock □ Rock-solid

SOLOMON
(As) wise as Solomon

SOME
Throw dirt enough, and some will stick. □ You win some, you lose some.

SON
Like father, like son

SOON
A fool and his money are soon parted. □ God takes soonest those he loveth best. □ No sooner said than done □ Soon ripe, soon rotten.

SORRY
Better (be) safe than sorry.

SOUL
Brevity is the soul of wit. □ Cannot call one's soul one's own □ Enough to keep body and soul together □ (Open) confession is good for the soul. □ Punctuality is the soul of business.

SOUND
(As) sound as a dollar □ Empty vessels make the most sound.

SOUP
Duck soup

SOUR
(As) sour as vinegar

SOW
As a man sows, so shall he reap. □ As you sow, so shall you reap. □ Sow the wind and reap the whirlwind □ You cannot make a silk purse out of a sow's ear.

SPADE
Call a spade a spade

SPAIN
A castle in Spain

SPARE
Spare the rod and spoil the child.

SPEAK
A word (once) spoken is past recalling. □ Actions speak louder than words. □ Many a true word is spoken in jest. □ Never speak ill of the dead. □ See no evil, hear no evil, speak no evil. □ Speak of the devil (and in he walks). □ There's many a true word spoken in jest.

SPECIES
The female of the species is more deadly than the male.

SPEED
More haste, less speed

SPICE
Variety is the spice of life.

SPILL
Don't cry over spilled milk. □ It's no use crying over spilled milk.

SPIRIT
The spirit is willing, but the flesh is weak.

SPITE

Cut off one's nose to spite one's face

SPOIL

Spare the rod and spoil the child. □ The rotten apple spoils the barrel. □ Too many cooks spoil the broth.

SPOON

Born with a silver spoon in one's mouth □ He who sups with the devil should have a long spoon.

SPOT

A leopard cannot change his spots.

SPRING

Hope springs eternal (in the human breast).

SQUARE

A square peg in a round hole

SQUEAK

The squeaking wheel gets the grease. □ The squeaky wheel gets the grease.

STABLE

Lock the stable door after the horse is stolen □ Shut the stable door after the horse has bolted.

STAFF

Bread is the staff of life.

STAND

A house divided against itself cannot stand. □ An empty sack cannot stand upright. □ Every tub must stand on its own bottom. □ If you can't stand the heat, get out of the kitchen. □ Let every tub stand on its own bottom. □ Stand the test of time □ They also serve who only stand and wait. □ United we stand, divided we fall.

STAR

Bless one's lucky star □ Bless one's stars □ Hitch your wagon to a star.

STARVE

Feed a cold and starve a fever.

STATE

Something is rotten in (the state of) Denmark.

STAY

The family that prays together stays together.

STEADY

(As) steady as a rock □ Rock-steady □ Slow and steady wins the race.

STEAL

Lock the stable door after the horse is stolen □ Stolen fruit is sweetest. □ Stolen pleasures are sweetest.

STEEL

(As) true as steel

STEP

From the sublime to the ridiculous is only a step. □ The first step is always the hardest.

STICK

Let the cobbler stick to his last. □ Sticks and stones may

break my bones, but words will never hurt me. □ Throw dirt enough, and some will stick.

STIFF

(As) stiff as a poker □ Keep a stiff upper lip.

STILL

A still tongue makes a wise head. □ (As) still as death □ Still waters run deep.

STITCH

A stitch in time saves nine.

STOMACH

An army marches on its stomach. □ The way to a man's heart is through his stomach.

STONE

A rolling stone gathers no moss. □ Cast the first stone □ Constant dripping wears away a stone. □ Constant dropping wears away a stone. □ Kill two birds with one stone □ Leave no stone unturned □ People who live in glass houses shouldn't throw stones. □ Sticks and stones may break my bones, but words will never hurt me. □ You cannot get blood from a stone.

STOOL

Fall between two stools

STORM

After a storm comes a calm. □ Any port in a storm □ The calm before the storm

STORY

Make a long story short

STRAIGHT

(As) straight as an arrow □ Get it straight from the horse's mouth

STRAIN

Strain at gnats and swallow camels

STRANGE

Fact is stranger than fiction. □ Politics makes strange bedfellows. □ Truth is stranger than fiction.

STRAW

A drowning man will clutch at a straw. □ The last straw □ The straw that broke the camel's back □ You cannot make bricks without straw.

STREAM

Cross the stream where it is shallowest. □ Don't change horses in mid-stream.

STRENGTH

Union is strength.

STRETCH

Stretch your arm no further than your sleeve will reach.

STRIKE

Lightning never strikes (the same place) twice. □ Strike while the iron is hot.

STRING

Tied to one's mother's apron strings

STROKE

Different   strokes   for

different folks □ Little
strokes fell great oaks.

STRONG

A chain is no stronger than
its weakest link. □ (As)
strong as a horse □ (As)
strong as a lion □ (As) strong
as an ox

STUBBORN

(As) stubborn as a mule

SUBLIME

From the sublime to the ridiculous is only a step.

SUCCEED

If at first you don't succeed,
try, try again. □ Nothing
succeeds like success.

SUCCESS

Nothing succeeds like success.

SUCK

Don't teach your grand-
mother to suck eggs.

SUFFICIENT

A word to the wise is sufficient. □ Sufficient unto the
day is the evil thereof.

SUGAR

(As) sweet as sugar

SUMMER

One swallow does not a summer make. □ One swallow
does not make a summer.

SUN

Do not let the sun go down
on your anger. □ Do not let
the sun go down on your
wrath. □ Happy is the bride

that the sun shines on. □
Make hay while the sun
shines. □ There is nothing
new under the sun.

SUP

He who sups with the devil
should have a long spoon.

SUPPER

Hope is a good breakfast but
a bad supper. □ Sing before
breakfast, you'll cry before
supper.

SURE

(As) sure as death □ Slow
but sure □ Talk of the devil
(and he is sure to appear).

SUSPICION

Caesar's wife must be above
suspicion.

SWALLOW

One swallow does not a summer make. □ One swallow
does not make a summer. □
Strain at gnats and swallow
camels

SWAN

(As) graceful as a swan

SWEAT

By the sweat of one's brow

SWEEP

A new broom sweeps clean.
□ (As) black as a sweep □
New brooms sweep clean.

SWEET

A rose by any other name
would smell as sweet. □ (As)
sweet as honey □ (As) sweet
as sugar □ Revenge is sweet.
□ Stolen fruit is sweetest. □

Stolen pleasures are sweetest. □ Sweeter than honey □ Take the bitter with the sweet

SWIFT

(As) swift as an arrow □ (As) swift as lightning □ (As) swift as the wind □ (As) swift as thought □ Life is short and time is swift.

SWINE

Cast pearls before swine

SWING

Not enough room to swing a cat

SWORD

Live by the sword, die by the sword. □ The pen is mightier than the sword.

TACK

(As) sharp as a tack □ Get down to brass tacks

TAIL

Better be the head of a dog than the tail of a lion. □ Bright-eyed and bushy-tailed □ Not able to make head or tail of something

TALE

A tale never loses in the telling. □ Dead men tell no tales. □ Never tell tales out of school. □ Talk is cheap. □ Talk of the devil (and he is sure to appear).

TANGO

It takes two to tango.

TAR

Tar someone with the same brush

TASTE

Every man to his taste. □ Tastes differ. □ There is no accounting for taste(s).

TAX

Nothing is certain but death and taxes.

TEA

Not one's cup of tea

TEACH

Don't teach your grandmother to suck eggs. □ Experience is the best teacher. □ Experience is the teacher of fools. □ Those who can, do; those who can't, teach. □ You cannot teach an old dog new tricks.

TEAR

It is easier to tear down than to build up.

TELL

A liar is not believed (even) when he tells the truth. □ A little bird told me. □ A tale never loses in the telling. □ Ask me no questions, I'll tell you no lies. □ Blood will tell. □ Children and fools tell the truth. □ Dead men tell no tales. □ Never tell tales out of school. □ (Only) time will tell. □ Tell the truth and shame the devil.

TEN

Genius is ten percent inspiration and ninety percent perspiration. □ I would not touch it with a ten-foot pole. □ Possession is nine-tenths of the law.

TEST
Stand the test of time

THEORY
An ounce of common sense is worth a pound of theory.

THICK
(As) thick as thieves □ Blood is thicker than water.

THIEF
(As) thick as thieves □ Little thieves are hanged, but great ones escape. □ Opportunity makes a thief. □ Procrastination is the thief of time. □ Set a thief to catch a thief. □ There is honor among thieves.

THING
A little knowledge is a dangerous thing. □ A little learning is a dangerous thing. □ A thing of beauty is a joy forever. □ A thing you don't want is dear at any price. □ All good things must (come to an) end. □ (All) other things being equal □ First things first □ Good things come in small packages. □ Good things come to him who waits. □ Have too much of a good thing □ He who begins many things, finishes but few. □ If a thing is worth doing, it's worth doing well.

□ If you want a thing done well, do it yourself. □ Keep a thing seven years and you'll (always) find a use for it. □ Little things please little minds. □ Moderation in all things. □ Small things please small minds. □ The best things come in small packages. □ The best things in life are free. □ The worth of a thing is what it will bring. □ There ain't no such thing as a free lunch. □ There's no such thing as a free lunch. □ Things are seldom what they seem.

THINK
Every horse thinks its own pack heaviest. □ Evil be to him who evil thinks. □ Great minds think alike.

THIRD
The third time's the charm.

THORN
There's no rose without a thorn.

THOUGHT
A penny for your thoughts! □ (As) swift as thought □ Have second thoughts □ The wish is father to the thought.

THOUSAND
A picture is worth a thousand words.

THREAT
Never make a threat you cannot carry out.

THREE
(As) queer as a three-dollar bill □ Moving three times is as bad as a fire. □ Two is company, (but) three's a crowd.

THROUGH
Go through something with a fine-tooth comb. □ Pay through the nose □ The way to a man's heart is through his stomach.

THROW
Don't throw the baby out with the bathwater. □ People who live in glass houses shouldn't throw stones. □ Throw dirt enough, and some will stick.

TICK
(As) tight as a tick

TIDE
There is a tide in the affairs of men. □ Time and tide wait for no man.

TIE
Tied to one's mother's apron strings

TIGER
He who rides a tiger is afraid to dismount.

TIGHT
(As) tight as a drum □ (As) tight as a tick

TILL
Call no man happy till he dies.

TIME
A good time was had by all.

□ A stitch in time saves nine. □ At this point in time □ Busiest men find the most time. □ Cowards die many times before their death(s). □ Life is short and time is swift. □ Moving three times is as bad as a fire. □ (Only) time will tell. □ Other times, other manners □ Procrastination is the thief of time. □ Someone puts his pants on one leg at a time □ Stand the test of time □ The third time's the charm. □ The time is ripe. □ There is a time and a place for everything. □ (There's) no time like the present. □ Time and tide wait for no man. □ Time flies. □ Time is a great healer. □ Time is money. □ Time works wonders. □ Times change and we with time. □ Times change(, people change).

TIN
(As) busy as a cat on a hot tin roof

TINKER
If "ifs" and "ands" were pots and pans (there'd be no work for tinkers' hands).

TIT
(As) cold as a witch's tit

TOAD
(As) ugly as a toad □ The biggest toad in the puddle

TOAST
(As) warm as toast

TODAY

Don't put off for tomorrow what you can do today. □ Here today, (and) gone tomorrow. □ Today here, tomorrow the world

TOGETHER

Birds of a feather flock together. □ Enough to keep body and soul together □ The family that prays together stays together.

TOMORROW

Don't put off for tomorrow what you can do today. □ Eat, drink, and be merry, for tomorrow we die. □ Here today, (and) gone tomorrow. □ Today here, tomorrow the world □ Tomorrow is another day. □ Tomorrow never comes.

TONGUE

A still tongue makes a wise head. □ (Has the) cat got your tongue?

TOO

Have too many irons in the fire □ Have too much of a good thing □ It is never too late to learn. □ It is never too late to mend. □ Too little, too late □ Too many chiefs and not enough Indians □ Too many cooks spoil the broth. □ You cannot have your cake and eat it (too).

TOOL

Give us the tools, and we will finish the job.

TOOTH

An eye for an eye (and a tooth for a tooth). □ (As) clean as a hound's tooth □ (As) scarce as hen's teeth □ Escape by the skin of one's teeth □ Fight tooth and nail □ Go over something with a fine-tooth comb. □ Go through something with a fine-tooth comb. □ Scarcer than hen's teeth □ Take the bit between one's teeth □ The gods send nuts to those who have no teeth.

TOP

Sleep like a top

TOUCH

I would not touch it with a ten-foot pole.

TOUGH

(As) tough as (shoe) leather □ When the going gets tough, the tough get going.

TRADE

A jack of all trades is a master of none. □ There are tricks in every trade.

TRAVEL

Bad news travels fast. □ He travels fastest who travels alone. □ It is better to travel hopefully than to arrive. □ Travel broadens the mind.

TREAD

Fools rush in where angels fear to tread.

TREE

As the twig is bent, so is the tree inclined. □ Bark up the wrong tree □ Cannot see the wood for the trees □ Money does not grow on trees. □ The tree is known by its fruit.

TRICK

There are tricks in every trade. □ You cannot teach an old dog new tricks.

TRIVET

(As) right as a trivet

TROUBLE

A trouble shared is a trouble halved. □ Never trouble trouble till trouble troubles you. □ Pour oil on troubled waters

TROUT

You must lose a fly to catch a trout.

TRUE

(As) true as steel □ Many a true word is spoken in jest. □ Morning dreams come true. □ The course of true love never did run smooth. □ There's many a true word spoken in jest.

TRUST

Put your trust in God, and keep your powder dry.

TRUTH

A liar is not believed (even) when he tells the truth. □ Children and fools tell the truth. □ Half the truth is often a whole lie. □ If the truth were known □ Tell the truth and shame the devil. □ The greater the truth, the greater the libel □ The truth will out. □ Truth is stranger than fiction.

TRY

If at first you don't succeed, try, try again. □ You never know (what you can do) till you try.

TUB

Every tub must stand on its own bottom. □ Let every tub stand on its own bottom.

TUNE

He who pays the piper calls the tune. □ There's many a good tune played on an old fiddle.

TURN

A bad penny always turns up. □ A soft answer turneth away wrath. □ Even a worm will turn. □ It is a long lane that has no turning. □ Make one turn (over) in one's grave □ One good turn deserves another. □ Turn back the clock

TURNIP

You cannot get blood from a turnip.

TWAIN

East is East and West is West

(and never the twain shall meet).

TWICE
Fool me once, shame on you; fool me twice, shame on me. □ He gives twice who gives quickly. □ Lightning never strikes (the same place) twice. □ Once bitten, twice shy

TWIG
As the twig is bent, so is the tree inclined.

TWO
A bird in the hand is worth two in the bush. □ Fall between two stools □ If two ride on a horse, one must ride behind. □ If you run after two hares you will catch neither. □ It takes two to make a bargain. □ It takes two to make a quarrel. □ It takes two to tango. □ Kill two birds with one stone □ Like two peas in a pod □ No man can serve two masters. □ One cannot be in two places at once. □ The lesser of two evils □ There are two sides to every question. □ Two heads are better than one. □ Two is company, (but) three's a crowd. □ Two wrongs do not make a right.

UGLY
(As) ugly as a toad □ (As) ugly as sin

UNDONE
What's done cannot be undone.

UNEASY
Uneasy lies the head that wears a crown.

UNEXPECTED
The unexpected always happens.

UNFORESEEN
Nothing is certain but the unforeseen.

UNION
Union is strength.

UNITE
United we stand, divided we fall.

UNLUCKY
Lucky at cards, unlucky in love

UNSAID
Better left unsaid

UNTURNED
Leave no stone unturned

UPPER
Keep a stiff upper lip.

UPRIGHT
An empty sack cannot stand upright.

USE
It's no use crying over spilled milk. □ Keep a thing seven years and you'll (always) find a use for it.

VACUUM
Nature abhors a vacuum.

VAIN
(As) vain as a peacock

VALOR
Discretion is the better part of valor.

VARIETY
Variety is the spice of life.

VELVET
(As) soft as velvet □ Velvety-soft

VENTURE
Nothing ventured, nothing gained.

VESSEL
Empty vessels make the most sound.

VIEW
Distance lends enchantment (to the view).

VINEGAR
(As) sour as vinegar □ You can catch more flies with honey than with vinegar.

VIRTUE
Make a virtue of necessity □ Patience is a virtue. □ Virtue is its own reward.

WAGON
Hitch your wagon to a star.

WAIT
Everything comes to him who waits. □ Good things come to him who waits. □ It's ill waiting for dead men's shoes. □ They also serve who only stand and wait. □ Time and tide wait for no man.

WALK
Speak of the devil (and in he walks). □ We must learn to walk before we can run.

WALL
Between you and me and these four walls □ Walls have ears.

WANT
A thing you don't want is dear at any price. □ For want of a nail the shoe was lost; for want of a shoe the horse was lost; and for want of a horse the man was lost. □ He that hath a full purse never wanted a friend. □ If you want a thing done well, do it yourself. □ If you want peace, (you must) prepare for war. □ The more you get, the more you want. □ The more you have, the more you want. □ Waste not, want not.

WAR
All's fair in love and war. □ Councils of war never fight. □ If you want peace, (you must) prepare for war.

WARM
(As) warm as toast □ Cold hands, warm heart □ Like death warmed over

WASH
Do not wash your dirty linen in public.

WASTE
Haste makes waste. □ Waste not, want not.

WATCH

A watched pot never boils.

WATER

A fish out of water □ Blood is thicker than water. □ Cast one's bread upon the waters □ Pour oil on troubled waters □ Still waters run deep. □ The mill cannot grind with water that is past. □ Water over the dam □ Water under the bridge □ You can lead a horse to water, but you can't make it drink. □ You never miss the water till the well runs dry.

WAX

The whole ball of wax

WAY

Cry all the way to the bank □ Laugh all the way to the bank □ Love will find a way. □ That's the way the ball bounces. □ That's the way the cookie crumbles. □ The longest way round is the nearest way home. □ The longest way round is the shortest way home. □ The way to a man's heart is through his stomach. □ There's more than one way to skin a cat. □ Where there's a will, there's a way.

WEAK

A chain is no stronger than its weakest link. □ (As) weak as a baby □ The spirit is willing, but the flesh is weak.

WEALTHY

Early to bed and early to rise, makes a man healthy, wealthy, and wise.

WEAR

Constant dripping wears away a stone. □ Constant dropping wears away a stone. □ If the shoe fits(, wear it). □ It is better to wear out than to rust out. □ Uneasy lies the head that wears a crown.

WEARY

There is no rest for the weary.

WEEP

Finders keepers(, losers weepers). □ Laugh and the world laughs with you; weep and you weep alone.

WELL

He lives long who lives well. □ If a thing is worth doing, it's worth doing well. □ If you want a thing done well, do it yourself. □ If you would be well served, serve yourself. □ Leave well enough alone. □ One might as well be hanged for a sheep as for a lamb. □ There is a sin of omission as well as of commission. □ Well begun is half done. □ You never miss the water till the well runs dry.

WEST

East is East and West is West (and never the twain shall meet). □ East or west, home

317

is best. □ East, west, home's best.

WHEAT
Separate the wheat from the chaff

WHEEL
Put one's shoulder to the wheel □ The squeaking wheel gets the grease. □ The squeaky wheel gets the grease.

WHIRLWIND
Sow the wind and reap the whirlwind

WHISTLE
(As) clean as a whistle

WHITE
(As) white as a sheet □ (As) white as snow □ Snow-white

WHOLE
Half the truth is often a whole lie. □ The whole ball of wax

WHORE
Once a whore, always a whore

WIFE
A good husband makes a good wife. □ Caesar's wife must be above suspicion.

WILD
Wild horses couldn't drag someone away from something.

WIN
He that would the daughter win, must with the mother first begin. □ Slow and

steady wins the race. □ You can't win 'em all. □ You win a few, you lose a few. □ You win some, you lose some.

WIND
A reed before the wind lives on, while mighty oaks do fall. □ (As) swift as the wind □ Go like the wind □ Hoist your sail when the wind is fair. □ It's an ill wind that blows nobody (any) good. □ Like the wind □ Sow the wind and reap the whirlwind □ Take the wind out of someone's sails

WINDOW
When poverty comes in at the door, love flies out of the window. □ When the wolf comes in at the door, love creeps out of the window.

WINE
You cannot put new wine in old bottles.

WINK
A nod's as good as a wink to a blind horse.

WISDOM
Experience is the father of wisdom. □ Experience is the mother of wisdom.

WISE
A still tongue makes a wise head. □ A word to the wise (is enough). □ A word to the wise is sufficient. □ (As) wise as Solomon □ Early to bed and early to rise, makes a man healthy, wealthy, and

wise. □ It is a wise child that knows its own father. □ It is easy to be wise after the event. □ One cannot love and be wise. □ Penny wise and pound foolish □ Where ignorance is bliss, 'tis folly to be wise.

WISH

If wishes were horses, then beggars would ride. □ The wish is father to the thought.

WIT

An ounce of discretion is worth a pound of wit. □ Brevity is the soul of wit.

WITCH

(As) cold as a witch's tit

WOLF

A growing youth has a wolf in his belly. □ A wolf in sheep's clothing □ When the wolf comes in at the door, love creeps out of the window.

WOMAN

A woman's place is in the home. □ A woman's work is never done. □ Hell hath no fury like a woman scorned. □ Men make houses, women make homes.

WON

Faint heart never won fair lady.

WONDER

Time works wonders. □ Wonders never cease!

WOOD

Babe in the woods □ Cannot see the wood for the trees □ Fields have eyes, and woods have ears. □ Never halloo till you are out of the woods. □ Someone is not out of the woods yet.

WOOL

Pull the wool over someone's eyes

WORD

A picture is worth a thousand words. □ A word (once) spoken is past recalling. □ A word to the wise (is enough). □ A word to the wise is sufficient. □ Actions speak louder than words. □ By word of mouth □ Fine words butter no parsnips. □ Hard words break no bones. □ Many a true word is spoken in jest. □ Sticks and stones may break my bones, but words will never hurt me. □ There's many a true word spoken in jest.

WORK

A woman's work is never done. □ All work and no play makes Jack a dull boy. □ Close enough for government work □ If "ifs" and "ands" were pots and pans (there'd be no work for tinkers' hands). □ It is not work that kills, but worry. □ Many hands make light work. □ The devil finds work for idle hands to do. □ Time works wonders.

WORKSHOP
An idle brain is the devil's workshop.

WORLD
All's for the best in the best of all possible worlds. □ God's in his heaven; all's right with the world. □ Half the world knows not how the other half lives. □ It takes all kinds (to make a world). □ Laugh and the world laughs with you; weep and you weep alone. □ Love makes the world go round. □ The hand that rocks the cradle rules the world. □ Today here, tomorrow the world

WORM
Even a worm will turn. □ The early bird catches the worm.

WORRY
It is not work that kills, but worry.

WORSE
Go from bad to worse □ Nothing so bad but (it) might have been worse. □ One's bark is worse than one's bite.

WORST
Be one's own worst enemy □ Hope for the best and prepare for the worst. □ If (the) worst comes to (the) worst

WORTH
A bird in the hand is worth two in the bush. □ A picture is worth a thousand words. □ An ounce of common sense is worth a pound of theory. □ An ounce of discretion is worth a pound of wit. □ An ounce of prevention is worth a pound of cure. □ If a thing is worth doing, it's worth doing well. □ Not worth a hill of beans □ Not worth the paper it's written on □ The worth of a thing is what it will bring.

WRATH
A soft answer turneth away wrath. □ Do not let the sun go down on your wrath.

WRITE
Not worth the paper it's written on □ Nothing to write home about

WRONG
Bark up the wrong tree □ Born on the wrong side of the blanket □ Get up on the wrong side of the bed □ If anything can go wrong, it will. □ Two wrongs do not make a right.

YARD
Give someone an inch and he'll take a yard.

YEAR
Christmas comes but once a year. □ Keep a thing seven years and you'll (always) find a use for it. □ The first hundred years are the hardest.

YET

Someone is not out of the woods yet. □ The mills of God grind slowly, yet they grind exceeding small.

YOUNG

Better be an old man's darling than a young man's slave. □ The good die young. □ Whom the gods love die young. □ Young men may die, but old men must die.

YOUTH

A growing youth has a wolf in his belly. □ Youth must be served.

Life is Just a Bowl of Cherries